EAST LND

BORN & BLED

EAST END
BORN & BLED

THE REMARKABLE STORY OF LONDON BOXING

JEFF JONES

AMBERLEY

I will never hear the last of it if I don't make one specific acknowledgement first. I would like to thank my wife, Brenda, for putting up with my many hours of typing away for almost two years of writing and my frequent days out doing field work on the subject.

One big general thanks to all those many cockney characters I met along the way who helped put this book together.

First published 2020

Amberley Publishing
The Hill, Stroud
Gloucestershire, GL5 4EP

www.amberley-books.com

Copyright © Jeff Jones, 2020

The right of Jeff Jones to be identified as the Author of this work has been asserted in accordance with the Copyrights, Designs and Patents Act 1988.

ISBN 978 1 4456 9497 9 (paperback)
ISBN 978 1 4456 9498 6 (ebook)

British Library Cataloguing in Publication Data.
A catalogue record for this book is available from the British Library.

Typesetting by Aura Technology and Software Services, India. Printed in the UK.

CONTENTS

PREFACE

I was born in Leyton, East London, in 1949, one of the so called 'Baby Boomers' who arrived shortly after the war. Like most babies of the time, I was delivered at home. My three elder sisters were probably waiting outside the bedroom door to have a look at the new household addition. The midwife had called.

The East End of London was slowly recovering from the war as I was growing up. It had taken the brunt of the German bombing raids. Life in the area was still tough for many; in reality, for me, it never felt that way. In fact, I suspect that in many respects mine was an idyllic childhood compared to many.

The vast majority of East London terracing was your standard two-up-two-down. Our house was a touch larger, being three up and three down – no indoor toilet though. That meant a trip out the back door, and it could be quite 'parky' in the winter months.

Summer months were spent playing in the streets or on nearby bombsites that were still evident in the area. I was cricket and football mad. Leyton County Cricket Ground was just a short walk away and Leyton Orient FC's Brisbane Road stadium was opposite the end of our road.

My early footballing and cricketing skills were developed on the streets of Leyton, but at the age of thirteen I joined the Eton Manor Boys Club. They had their club house at Hackney Wick and their playing fields were just a ten-minute walk from my house near to Hackney Marshes, where they had some decent facilities.

I spent almost five years at this super club, where dozens of different sports could be played. This included boxing. Kids were encouraged to try their hand at everything. I did try boxing, and got punched quite hard on the nose within a few minutes. The result: a nose bleed and a resolve never to step through the ropes again. Boxing was one sport I was not going to take up. However, I did love watching some of the sparring matches between the older boys there.

In those days, professional boxing was everywhere. A twenty-minute walk from my house were the Leyton Baths. Here, in the winter months, they would board over the baths and hold both wrestling and boxing events. Some very decent fights took place at the baths. I was just thirteen years old when they stopped holding fights there.

I remember reading some of the exotic names of the fighters who appeared on the posters and billboards advertising the fights. Alien names like Boswell St Louis, Con Mount Bassie and Harry Dodo. I think the latter might be extinct now!

Apart from boxing and wrestling, they also ran pop concerts at Leyton Baths. I managed to see some really top bands of the day including The Rolling Stones, The Kinks, Animals and the Yardbirds. The pouting Jagger, all up front and in ya' face fronting the Stones, and the shy and retiring genius that was Clapton, quietly producing magic at the back of the stage for the Yardbirds and John Mayall & the Bluesbreakers. The Beatles played one gig there in 1963.

A neighbour of mine, Harry Cox, a council carpenter, used to be responsible for boarding over the baths for these events. I don't think he had a particularly good reputation as a craftsman, so I stood with some trepidation on the boards as hundreds of people jumped up and down on them during the concerts. I often thought, 'Harry, I bloody well hope you done a good job here mate, otherwise I'm in the deep end!'

All sports, including boxing at Eton Manor, were purely amateur. Their amateur 'stars' boxed against other amateur club boxers. These were good nights. Sadly, I can remember coming home from there one Friday evening in November 1963 to be told the news of the assassination of President John F. Kennedy. They often say if you were around at that time you would always remember exactly where you were when Kennedy was shot. I was at the Manor.

Fast forward fifty-three years. I had retired from work and was enjoying doing some work on local history and family history. It included doing a bit of research on my old club, Eton Manor, around the time of their centenary in 2015/16. I also love reading biographies, and it was during my research that, by pure coincidence, I found myself reading actor Ray Winstone's biography. Like me, Ray is a West Ham Football Club supporter and fellow season ticket holder. Unlike me, he was an excellent boxer in his youth.

The research I was doing, the book that I was reading and my memories of boxing events made me realise just how huge boxing was at both amateur and professional level in this part of our capital. The following year I started seriously researching the subject of boxing in the East End. It soon became evident how great a part the sport played in the history of London's East End.

I hope that this book, although filled with boxing facts and figures, succeeds in painting a picture of what life was like in East London, where boxing and life were inextricably linked for almost three centuries.

FOREWORD

I love reading books like this. Being an East Ender myself made it all the more interesting. I was born in Poplar, so I grew up bang in the middle of the East End. I suppose at the time I never realised what a unique and interesting place it was. I was just another East End kid growing up. Like the author, I was one of the baby-boomers playing on the streets and bomb-sites just after the war.

I was sports mad but never boxed. Lots of kids did though. Those were the ones you wanted to have as mates back in those days.

It was a tough place to live, and reading through the pages of this book emphasises the point. I earned a living from football. A few from the area in my time, and several before me, did so as well. We were the lucky ones compared to those that pulled on a pair of boxing gloves to earn a wage.

It doesn't come as too much of a surprise that boxing was such a popular sport in the East End. It sort of goes with the territory. Brain or brawn can get you on in life. I went to the Sir Humphrey Gilbert School in Stepney. It sounded quite posh; it was anything but. I don't think anyone from my school went on to university when I was there, so most made a living the hard way. Loads of them found work in and around the docks.

This book tells the story of boxing in the East End and the community in which it flourished, and it brings back many memories. I remember a lot of the places mentioned in the book, particularly the pubs. One of them, The Two Puddings in Stratford, is where I first met my wife, Sandra. I drank in a few others as well!

I found it fascinating. I hope others do too.

Harry Redknapp

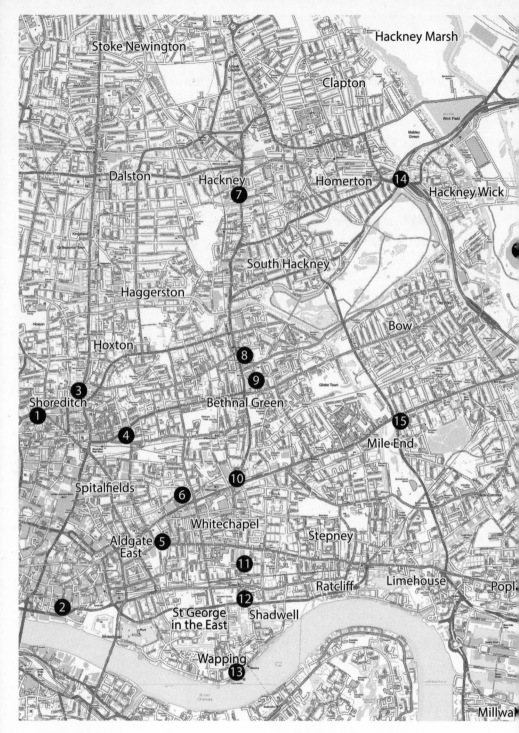

1. Harris Lebus
2. Billingsgate Market (old)
3. Shoreditch Town Hall & Blue Anchor
4. Repton Boxing Club
5. Premierland
6. Wonderland Arena
7. Devonshire Club
8. York Hall
9. Bethnall Green Tube station & Excelsior Hall and Baths
10. The Blind Beggar
11. Judeans Athletic Club & St George's Boxing Club
12. Broads Street Boxing Club
13. Prospect of Whitby & Town of Ramsgate
14. Eton Manor Boys' Club

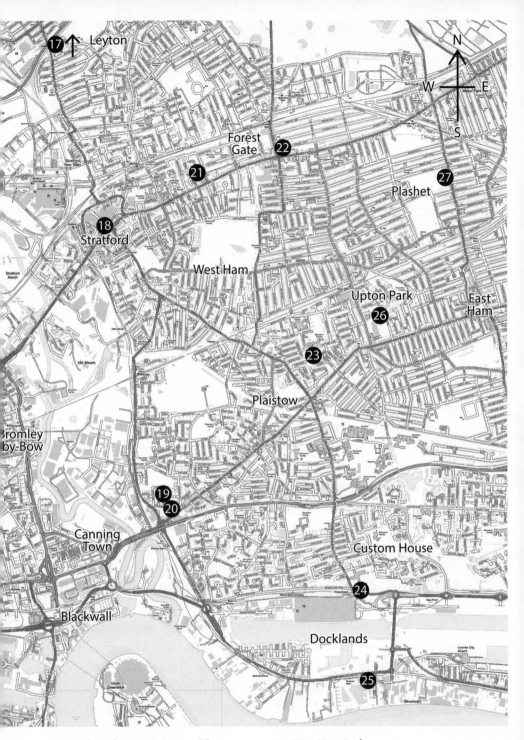

15. Mile End Arena & Paragon Theatre
16. West Ham Football Club (London
    Stadium), Olympic Park
17. Leyton Baths
18. Two Puddings
19. Bridge House
20. Royal Oak Gym

21. West Ham Baths
22. Upper Cut Club
23. West Ham Boxing Club (old)
24. Port of London Authority (PLA)
25. Tate & Lyle
26. Boleyn Ground (Upton Park)
27. Ruskin Arms

INTRODUCTION

Why has boxing got such a strong connection with London's East End? What makes it so special to the area that it has woven itself deep into the fabric of the East End, becoming part of Cockney culture?

Many places in the world have produced a world-class sportsman over the years, and a few places have developed a reputation for producing a number of very good sportsmen in one particular field. Mumbai, or Bombay as it was previously known, has produced several world-class cricketers: Ravi Shastri, Vijay Merchant, Sunil Gavaskar, Sachin Tendulkar and Dilip Vengsarkar all learnt their craft in this cricket-mad city.

The Tyne and Wear area in the north-east of England was considered a hotbed of soccer not so very long ago, producing among others Bobby and Jackie Charlton, Jackie Milburn, Paul Gascoigne, Alan Ball, Brian Robson and Alan Shearer.

Even more impressive is the number of rugby union players who came out of the Rhondda Valley area of South Wales. For years it has housed the conveyor belt that rolled off some of rugby's greatest players: Gareth Edwards, Barry John, John Bevan, J. P. R. Williams,

Cliff Jones, John Dawes and Cliff Morgan all played their rugby in the shadows of the Pitheads.

Boxing also had places that proved a catalyst for young boxers. The Bronx and Brooklyn areas of New York are still famous today for great boxing gyms like Gleason's and Stillman's, which produced some of the world's greatest boxers. Jake LaMotta (The Bronx or Raging Bull) is easily the most recognisable thanks to the Scorsese film bearing his nickname. Alex Ramos was also a great middleweight contender. Iran Barkley was a world champion and famous for his fights with Roberto Duran and Thomas Hearns. The Bronx was also home to one of the greatest boxing trainers ever, Cus D'Amato. World heavyweight champions James Braddock and Gene Tunney were born nearby.

Impressive indeed, but there is one small area of London that has produced more national, continental and world boxing champions than anywhere else. An area of roughly 5 square miles immediately east of the City of London, generally referred to as London's East End, has produced boxers who have altogether won almost three hundred top-ranked professional titles. It has also produced countless amateur (ABA) champions. It is a story that dates back almost three centuries and is full of the most amazing characters and stories both inside and outside of the ropes.

One has to ask whether or not the characteristics of such colourful and unique individuals are purely the product of nature rather than nurture. Given the background of the area they were born into, I think it would be fair to say that nurture played a big part. To understand how one small area can produce so many of these special people, you must know something of the area they called home.

Up until the late sixteenth century, London's east side was much the same as any other area adjoining a major city. Due to its proximity to the Thames, on the corridor leading down to its eastern river and coastal ports, the area attracted not only locals looking for work on and around the river but people from nearby

Europe who, for one reason or another, needed to escape across the Channel, away from the many problems that beset the Continent.

By the end of the seventeenth century, Britain was going through a more peaceful period in its history following the upheavals of the Reformation and the Civil Wars. The British Empire was expanding, and within a few years the industrial Revolution would have a big impact on the area.

First to arrive were the Huguenots in the late seventeenth century. The mainly Protestant Huguenots and Walloons, from north-east France and Belgium, were persecuted under the reign of the French king, Louis XIV. Around 50,000 of them fled to England, with many arriving in the Spitalfields area on the eastern borders of the City. They brought with them the trade of silk weaving and began to develop that industry in the area. Some years later they were followed by the Irish weavers.

The Irish weavers had been subject to economic pressure in Ireland, and with East London growing into a hub for the weaving trade they too settled nearby. By the mid-eighteenth century the area was flourishing thanks to its reputation for weaving. However, business has always been at the mercy of the ebb and flow of economic conditions and the weaving trade was no exception.

During a downturn in trade, relationships between the Huguenots and the Irish deteriorated. Disputes broke out. Between 1765 and 1769, conditions worsened and a series of riots broke out at Spitalfields. They were brutally put down, and two men were hanged outside the Salmon and Ball pub in Bethnal Green. This event helped cement East London's burgeoning reputation as a tough place.

Even before this, observers had recognised the area for what it was. In historian John Strype's 1720 *Survey of London*, the capital was described as consisting of four parts: the City, Southwark, Westminster and 'that Part beyond the Tower'. As the description suggests, even then it was an area somewhat looked down upon. In that respect, nothing really changed for the best part of three hundred years! What certainly did change was the society that existed there.

In the 1773 work *A New History of London*, John Northouck wrote:

> These parishes, which are chiefly inhabited by sea-faring persons, and those whose business depends on shipping in various capacities, are in general close and ill-built: Therefore, it affords very little worthy observation.

How short-sighted he was. A few years later, the various ethnic groups that arrived to populate the area were to make this much maligned part of the capital a most interesting place. Notwithstanding the almost endemic poverty, the area became a colourful and vibrant place.

Thanks in no small part to the East India Company, Britain became the world's most powerful trading nation. Vast amounts of goods were arriving at the wharves and docks on the Thames close to the City. It was soon clear that there were insufficient mooring facilities for the increasing number of ships that were coming up the Thames; vessels often had to anchor downstream for several hours, if not days, before they could get a wharf or dock mooring. A couple of large docks were hastily built, the East India and West India docks.

Large numbers of houses were demolished to make way for the new docks, which greatly increased the rental value of those properties left. With the large influx of workers, a housing crisis developed. In 1802, William Hart from Shadwell, a wealthy cooper (barrel maker), wrote that rents from his properties were rising fast because of the London docks development. He reported that in his own home he could easily rent two rooms to a couple of families and keep the biggest and best chamber for himself. He confirmed that whole streets in the area were being demolished to make way for the dock developments. It was estimated that upward of 18,000 people were displaced during this time, adding to the overcrowding in the East End generally.

By the late eighteenth century, with the Industrial Revolution picking up pace, the area welcomed the Ashkenazi Jews from central Europe. Even more Irish poured into the area in the wake of the Irish Potato Famine in the 1840s. The English agricultural industry suffered as the Industrial Revolution took hold, and thousands of labourers from outlying rural areas moved into the area looking for work. Cheap terraced housing and tenement buildings were hastily erected to house this latest ingress of migrant workers.

By the mid-nineteenth century, the roughly 2 square miles from Aldgate in the south-west to Hoxton in the north-west and from Limehouse in the south-east to Hackney in the north-east was a seething mass of cramped, slum-like urban housing. These dwellings were intermingled with small and medium-sized industrial units as well as shops, inns and markets.

Writing for the *Morning Chronicle* after visiting the area around Bethnal Green in 1850, Henry Mayhew, an influential observer of the time, reported:

> Roads were unmade, often mere alleys, houses were small and without foundations, subdivided and often around unpaved courts. An almost total lack of drainage and sewerage was made worse by the ponds formed by the excavation of brickearth. Pigs and cows in back yards, noxious trades like boiling tripe, melting tallow, or preparing cat's meat, and slaughter houses, rubbish piles and lakes of putrefying night soils added to the filth.

The area was notorious for its deep poverty, appalling public health, overcrowding and associated social problems. Crime was rife. Growing up in this environment was very tough, and survival of the fittest prevailed. You either took care of business or starved. Tensions often ran high with such a large ethnic mix. Immigrants continued to arrive in large numbers. Estimates of upwards of 130,000 eastern European Jews arrived in the East End between 1860 and 1900. About 150 synagogues were established in the area.

For generations of young Irish and Jewish men in the area, life was about finding a way out of the appalling conditions they were living in. Many of these men were poorly educated, and they had to make up for this in other ways. Streetwise is what they were, and handy with their fists. The increasing popularity of boxing was the vehicle they would use to achieve their aim.

A Note on Weight Classes

In the very early days, any fights that took place were by and large, restricted to whether or not one man was prepared to take on another man in a boxing match. In theory, a 6-foot, 17-stone man could be matched against a 5-foot, 7-stone man. By the early nineteenth century, boxing matches were split into two divisions: lightweight (under 12 stone) and heavyweight (no limit).

The Marquess of Queensberry Rules, which were published in 1867, focussed on the safety of boxers during a fight and not on who was matched against whom. The weight divisions followed a few years later to ensure that similar-sized opponents were matched up together.

These divisions made for generally closer bouts, which in turn made for more entertaining matches. There were traditionally eight weight divisions in men's boxing, but many more divisions have been added and there are now seventeen weight classes recognised in men's professional boxing. The upper limits of these classes are shown as follows:

Weight class	Maximum weight
Minimumweight	105 pounds (48 kg)
Light-flyweight	108 pounds (49 kg)
Flyweight	112 pounds (51 kg)
Super-flyweight	115 pounds (52 kg)
Bantamweight	118 pounds (53.5 kg)
Super-bantamweight	122 pounds (55 kg)
Featherweight	126 pounds (57 kg)
Super-featherweight	130 pounds (59 kg)
Lightweight	135 pounds (61 kg)
Super-lightweight	140 pounds (63.5 kg)
Welterweight	147 pounds (67 kg)
Super-welterweight	154 pounds (70 kg)
Middleweight	160 pounds (72.5 kg)
Super-middleweight	168 pounds (76 kg)
Light-heavyweight	175 pounds (79 kg)
Cruiserweight	200 pounds (90.7 kg)
Heavyweight	unlimited (super-heavyweight in amateur)

This may give anybody unfamiliar with the sport a reference point to the weights at which the boxers fight.

I

THE EARLY YEARS:
THE GLOVES ARE OFF

Boxing in some form or another has been around for many centuries. Men, and sometimes women, have used their fists to settle arguments since time immemorial. References to pugilism or similar activities can be found as far back as the first century BCE in many cultures, but its origins are most firmly rooted in Greek history and mythology. It is one of the earliest recorded sporting activities.

Specific and reasonably comprehensive references to boxing as well as wrestling can be found in Homer's epic poem *Iliad*, written around 3,000 years ago and purporting to depict events from thousands of years before even that![1] Cave paintings suggest that wrestling dates back almost 18,000 years.

In this country, boxing as a sport began to take off in the second half of the seventeenth century in the form of bare-fisted or bare-knuckle fighting. Prize fights were arranged and matches made. By the turn of the eighteenth century there were four popular and well-established sports in Britain. Three of them – golf, cricket and horseracing – were fairly well regulated and were governed by quite strict rules. The new imposter, pugilism, had no such restrictions. These were completely unregulated and freeform until the introduction of the 'London Prize Ring Rules' and then the more comprehensive Marquess of Queensberry Rules in 1867.

As the popularity of boxing grew, men from all sorts of social backgrounds took up the sport. The poet Lord Byron and the scientist Sir Isaac Newton both practised the sport. However, it was the very poorest of society, living in the squalid conditions of those times, who saw a way to make money out of the sport. The East End of London was home to hundreds of these men, and so a boxing culture began to take hold in the area. Slowly but surely, growing numbers of poverty-stricken young men took up the sport.

From these early years, three boxers emerged who were to take pugilism from a way to settle arguments to a popular and skilful sport. The term 'legend' is often overused when referring to sportsmen. To my mind, you should only apply this term to that handful of sportsmen and women who not only reached the pinnacle of their field but went on to transcend it.

Over the past hundred years or so, only a few sports people have earned this accolade. Muhammad Ali, Pele, Jesse Owens, Michael Jordan, Billie Jean King and Jack Nicklaus can be considered to have done so because their presence in their chosen sport enhanced its development and their achievements both inside and outside of their sport have inspired and influenced a wider public. Perhaps the superstar greats of recent years, such as Tiger Woods, Usain Bolt and Roger Federer, will cement their place as legends too; history will be the judge of that. History has already delivered its judgement on three bare-knuckle boxers from the early years of British boxing, and two of them hail from a small part of London. John Broughton and Daniel Mendoza were at the very forefront of boxing in London's East End.

*

To tell the story of East End boxing, we must first look to the west of England. It was here, near Cirencester, that one **John 'Jack' Broughton** (*c.* 1704–1789) was born and grew up. Little is known about his early life, but he may have indulged in some unofficial prize fights during his early teenage years.

Around 1718 – it is unclear exactly when and why – Broughton decided to move to the Wapping area of East London. It is rumoured that he had been noticed by champion prize fighter James Figg, who may have persuaded the young man to move to London. Whatever the reason, Broughton started work as a waterman on the River Thames. This was the sort of job that would help you develop your upper-body strength. Rowing a boatload of cargo against the Thames tide was hard work.

Broughton was a very fit young man, and competitive. He won a couple of rowing races against other watermen, and in 1720 he won a prestigious annual rowing race held between the Thames watermen for the 'Doggett Coat and Badge'. He was rapidly gaining a reputation. One day he was challenged to a fight for a small wager by a fellow waterman and knocked the poor man out. One or two other successful fights followed, and Broughton soon realised that he could perhaps make more money on dry land than on the water. He started to challenge all comers in street fights in and around the inns and pubs lining that part of the Thames. Two pubs that witnessed these fights, The Prospect of Whitby and The Town of Ramsgate, are still there today.[2]

By this stage it was pretty certain that James Figg would have known Broughton. Figg was now the heavyweight champion of England. He was the first person to hold the title, and retained it from 1719 to 1730. Figg arranged sword fighting, cockfighting and bare-knuckle boxing events at George Taylor's booth in Adam and Eve Court, just off Oxford Street. It was here that Broughton started seriously on his professional career. His prowess and reputation grew. With the growth of the sport, it became common for the landed gentry and aristocrats of the day to 'sponsor' fighters, and Prince William, Duke of Cumberland, became Broughton's patron.

Broughton took on all comers through the 1730s, and went on to become England's third heavyweight champion from 1734 to 1750. Broughton was redefining the sport, and he would later redefine the rules governing it. In 1743 he opened his own amphitheatre for the 'noble art' in Hanwell Street, West London.

In 1741, Broughton fought George Stevenson in a defence of his championship and delivered such a beating that Stevenson died a few days after the bout. Deaths in the ring or shortly after the fight were an occupational hazard in those times, but Broughton, who was an intelligent man, knew that deaths were detrimental to the sport. He actually announced his retirement after that fatality, shifting his focus to training younger boxers and introducing safer fighting methods and rules. The rules he drew up were called the Broughton Rules, and they were universally accepted.

The Broughton Rules formed the basis of the later 'London Prize Ring Rules' that loosely governed the sport until the famous Marquess of Queensberry Rules were adopted nearly a century later. Broughton made his comeback to the sport in 1743.

Although Broughton took the first tentative steps to introduce some structure and regulation to the sport, bare-knuckle boxing was still taking place whenever the opportunity arose. Samuel Johnson, that famous writer and observer of London life, wrote:

> The Fields near Marylebone were a favourite place for bruising matches – that is bare-knuckle boxing. The law (police) broke up one fight between an Irish sedan-chair carrier and an Englishman watched by 500 low and well known wicked ... Irish chairmen, who managed to rescue their man and left the Englishman to face criminal charges alone.

Now, if you think that women's boxing is a reasonably new development, then read on. Dr Johnson goes on to say:

> Sometimes bruising Peg took to the stage who was even more fun to watch as she beat her antagonist in a terrible manner.

Marylebone Fields (now Regent's Park) was a popular venue for the hastily arranged boxing matches. John Broughton had been fighting there since his comeback in 1743.

RULES

TO BE OBSERVED IN ALL BATTLES ON THE STAGE

I. THAT a square of a Yard be chalked in the middle of the Stage; and on every fresh set-to after a fall, or being parted from the rails, each Second is to bring his Man to the side of the square, and place him opposite to the other, and till they are fairly set-to at the Lines, it shall not be lawful for one to strike at the other.

II. That, in order to prevent any Disputes, the time a Man lies after a fall, if the Second does not bring his Man to the side of the square, within the space of half a minute, he shall be deemed a beaten Man.

III. That in every main Battle, no person whatever shall be upon the Stage, except the Principals and their Seconds; the same rule to be observed in bye-battles, except that in the latter, Mr. Broughton is allowed to be upon the Stage to keep decorum, and to assist Gentlemen in getting to their places, provided always he does not interfere in the Battle; and whoever pretends to infringe these Rules to be turned immediately out of the house. Every body is to quit the Stage as soon as the Champions are stripped, before the set-to.

IV. That no Champion be deemed beaten, unless he fails coming up to the line in the limited time, or that his own Second declares him beaten. No Second is to be allowed to ask his man's Adversary any questions, or advise him to give out.

V. That in bye-battles, the winning man to have two-thirds of the Money given, which shall be publicly divided upon the Stage, notwithstanding any private agreements to the contrary.

VI. That to prevent Disputes, in every main Battle the Principals shall, on coming on the Stage, choose from among the gentlemen present two Umpires, who shall absolutely decide all Disputes that may arise about the Battle; and if the two Umpires cannot agree, the said Umpires to choose a third, who is to determine it.

VII. That no person is to hit his Adversary when he is down, or seize him by the ham, the breeches, or any part below the waist: a man on his knees to be reckoned down.

As agreed by several Gentlemen at Broughton's Amphitheatre,
Tottenham Court Road, August 16, 1743.

The Broughton Rules. (Wikicommons)

Broughton was certainly making big strides to introduce greater boxing safety standards. Reports from the time confirm his efforts to introduce greater safety. A piece in the popular periodical *Gentleman's Magazine* gives an insight into this:

> Broughton offered lectures and tuition at his house in the Haymarket so that persons of quality and distinction should not be debarred from entering into a course of those lectures in which they will be given the utmost tenderness. For which purpose they are supplied with mufflers that will effectually secure them from the inconvenience of black eyes, broken jaws and bloody noses.

It was also reported that 'such novices would not be allowed to join in with some of Broughton's "Battle Royals" in which a champion took on seven at the same time, single-handled'.

The mufflers that Broughton designed and used for his training sessions were the forerunner of modern-day boxing gloves and were eventually used for all fights after 1889, when bare-knuckle fighting ceased to be recognised as the official form of the sport.

By the late 1740s, Broughton's powers were diminishing somewhat. Nevertheless, he was goaded into a prize fight by a young upstart called Jack Slack. Slack was an obnoxious, loud-mouthed fighter with minimal boxing skills whose only claim to fame was that he was the grandson of the great James Figg. Broughton had little time to prepare properly, and although he was a lot older than his opponent he entered into the arena on 11 April 1750 very much the favourite.

From the very start of the fight, Broughton imposed himself on Slack. He was delivering a boxing lesson to the younger man when, from nowhere, Slack produced the punch of his life. It exploded Broughton's right eye, which closed immediately. Slack seized his chance and weighed in with everything he had. Semi-blind, Broughton was forced to yield.

The fight was over in less than twenty minutes. Broughton's patron, the Duke of Cumberland, lost a lot of money after betting heavily on his man. Furious, Cumberland withdrew his patronage. Broughton more or less retired from the game after this defeat and dedicated himself fully to training and managing young boxers. There is, however, mention of one last fight as late as 1764; if this is accurate, it meant he fought for a staggering forty-odd years.

Broughton had secured a lasting reputation in the sport as both a great champion and a great innovator. He was appointed a Yeoman of the Guard. He died in 1789 aged eighty-six and his stature was such that he was allowed a burial in the West Cloister at Westminster Abbey, just along from King Henry V, who was also partial to the odd scrap or two – notably against French opposition at Agincourt!

Broughton's legacy grew so that he became known as the 'Father of British Boxing', while his old sponsor, the Duke of Cumberland, has been remembered as 'Butcher Cumberland' for his merciless slaughter of over 1,500 Jacobite Scots during the Battle of Culloden and its immediate aftermath.

*

The first of the great boxers to be born and bred in the East End was **Daniel Abraham Aaron Mendoza** (1764–1836). He was of Portuguese/Jewish extraction and was born in Aldgate. Daniel and his family attended the Bevis Marks Synagogue nearby, the oldest synagogue in Britain and still standing today. Synagogue records confirm Mendoza's presence. He lived in the Bethnal Green area of London as a young man, where he went into the service of a fairly well-off Jewish family, working in a tea shop that they owned.

It was during this time that he attended boxing lessons given by Jack Broughton, and it was while working in the tea shop that he exercised his newly acquired skills. He states in his memoirs:

> It was here that I was frequently drawn into contests with butchers and others in the neighbourhood who, on account of my mistress

being of Jewish religion, were frequently disposed to insult her. In a
short time however, I became the terror of the gentry.

More shop jobs followed, allowing Mendoza to put himself
through boxing lessons and ensuring that he became proficient
with his fists. More fights also followed, mostly backstreet fights
against those who chose to insult him or his religion. One such
fight was witnessed by an established prize fighter of the day who
offered to manage Mendoza. His journey into East End boxing
folklore had begun.

According to the *Ring Record Book and Boxing Encyclopedia*,
Mendoza went undefeated in twenty-seven straight fights prior to
1788. His earliest recorded prize fight was against an opponent
known locally as Harry the Coal-heaver. A few weeks later he
was matched against Sam Martin in Barnet. Martin had made
a number of anti-Semitic comments before the fight, enraging
Mendoza. The fight was well advertised, and the Prince of Wales
was present to watch the proceedings. It was an excellent match
and Mendoza fought with a great deal of skill and determination
to defeat the very experienced Martin.

After the match, the prince congratulated Mendoza and remarked
that he had never seen such boxing skills. As an expression of his
approval, he gave Mendoza an additional £500 above his £50
match win fee – an enormous sum.

Mendoza developed an entirely new style of boxing by
incorporating a lot more foot movement and defensive strategies
that he called 'side-stepping'. He also developed the practice of
moving around the ring, ducking, blocking and avoiding punches.
Using a more scientific approach to the sport, Mendoza identified
and targeted areas of the body which, when attacked, were
more likely to result in an opponent being stopped. This was
a revolutionary development, and through his new techniques
Mendoza was able to overcome much heavier opponents. Mendoza,
more than anyone, elevated the sport to a level that saw it dubbed
'the noble art'.

Beyond boxing, Mendoza was instrumental in elevating the status of the Jews. His efforts both inside and outside of the ring helped lessen the amount of anti-Semitism that prevailed in East London. His influence saw large numbers of young Jewish men taking up the sport, many becoming great champions. After several more professional fights, Mendoza secured the full patronage of the Prince of Wales (later King George IV), marking yet another step in the ascent of boxing in the public eye.

Mendoza had a series of boxing matches against his arch-rival Richard Humphries, one each in the years 1788, 1789 and 1790. He lost the first battle in twenty-nine rounds but won the last two bouts in fifty-two and fifteen rounds respectively.

Although Jack Broughton was referred to as the Father of English boxing, Daniel Mendoza was known as the 'Father of Scientific Boxing'. In 1789 he opened his own boxing academy in Whitechapel and encouraged young Jewish men in the Bethnal Green and Whitechapel area to participate in the sport. He later published *The Art of Boxing*.

Mendoza stood only 5 feet 7 inches and weighed only 160 pounds, yet this did not prevent him from becoming England's sixteenth heavyweight champion between 1792 and 1795. Indeed, he was the first fighter of 'middleweight size' to ever win the heavyweight championship.

In April 1795, Mendoza fought John Jackson for the championship at Hornchurch in Essex. The fight took place in a gravel quarry immediately adjoining Hornchurch's historic church of St Andrews, one Sunday afternoon in April. Several of the 2,000-plus spectators who paid for the privilege to view the spectacle had attended the Sunday service earlier in the day. Jackson was five years younger, 4 inches taller, and 42 pounds heavier. The bigger man won in nine rounds, securing victory by seizing Mendoza by his long hair (Jewish men wore their hair long) and holding him with one hand while he pounded the man's head with the other. Mendoza was pummelled into submission. Thereafter, fighters shaved their heads or wore their hair short.

This and other fights were now widely reported in the press of the time, although this particular fight failed to get a mention in Mendoza's own memoirs. Prize fighting was big news, though. In fact, Mendoza's May 1789 contest against Richard Humphries relegated the news of the growing French Revolution to the inside pages.

Mendoza's fame spread across the nation, and he was often invited to speak all over Britain, as far as Dublin and Edinburgh, where he was presented with a gold medal for his services to boxing and was elected an honorary president of the Gymnastics Society. He was also the first Jewish sportsman to be presented to a British monarch, King George III.

By the early years of the nineteenth century, Mendoza realised his time at the top was coming to an end. He branched out into business, and was appointed a sherriff's officer of Middlesex in 1806. He later became landlord of the Admiral Nelson Public House in Whitechapel. He also had an unsuccessful stint as a recruitment officer for the army, appearing in pantomime and giving boxing demonstrations.

Although the charismatic Mendoza was highly intelligent, having written and published two books, his life became chaotic. By the time of his death, the fortune he worked so hard to accrue had evaporated. After a couple of spells in debtor's prison, he died penniless and depressed in lodgings on Petticoat Lane in 1836.

Mendoza's name goes down in the pantheon of exponents of the noble art of boxing. Figg, Broughton and Mendoza were the superstars of bare-knuckled boxing. Their influence on the sport from 1720 to 1820 was immense, and their legacy lives on.

Samuel Elias (1775–1816), often called 'Dutch Sam', was one of Daniel Mendoza's prodigies and was also known by his fighting name, 'The Terrible Jew'. Born in the Petticoat Lane area of Aldgate, Elias studied boxing at length. With Mendoza as his trainer, he developed several new moves. Like Mendoza, he focused on the technical aspects of boxing. This was just as well, as he would have to fight much larger men in his career.

Daniel Mendoza
Pugilist
1764-1836
English Champion who proudly billed himself as 'Mendoza the Jew', lived here when writing 'The Art of Boxing'.

A blue plaque at Mendoza's Paradise Row home in Bethnal Green. (© Jeffrey Jones)

Elias was quite small, standing at only 5 feet 6 inches and weighing just 135 pounds. In today's terms, he was a lightweight. At that time, then, he would have been fighting opponents up to four weight divisions heavier than him. He perfected the uppercut punch, which meant he could compete successfully with taller men. His first fight was in 1801 and he fought just over hundred fights, losing only twice. Because of his ability to knock men down or out with this punch he became known as 'The Man with the Iron Fist'. That said, virtually all Elias' fights lasted well over thirty rounds, including a couple of sixty-round contests.

Elias began to drink gin very heavily later in his career. It was reported that he was drinking up to three bottles of gin a day, and this began to tell. In December 1814, Elias took on William Nosworthy, aka 'Baker Bill' from Devon, for a prize of £50 at Molesey in Surrey. Once again Elias 'toed the line' as the smaller man. 'Dutch Sam', as Elias had become known, fought thirty-eight rounds that day but received a terrible beating.[3]

JAMES FIGG

J. Ellys Pinx.   *J. Faber fecit*

The Mighty Combatant, the first in Fame,
The lasting Glory of his Native Thame.
Rash, & unthinking Men, at length be Wise;
Consult your Safety, and Resign the Prize:
Nor tempt Superior Force; but Timely Fly
The Vigour of his Arm, the Quickness of his Eye.

Sold by Faber at the Green Door in ye great Piazza Covent Garden.

Sold by H. Overton & J. Hoole at the White Horse without Newgate LONDON.

The Great Triumvirate.
James Figg (opposite), John
Broughton (above right) and
Daniel Mendoza (below right),
bare-knuckle boxing legends.
(Wikicommons)

By all accounts Nosworthy was not a good fighter and should have been easily dispatched. In fact, Nosworthy never won another match. Nor did Elias. This was his last fight, for he retired soon after. The gin had finally taken its toll, and 'Dutch Sam' died two years later, in 1816, aged just forty-one. Baker Bill also died that year.

Elias was bare-knuckle boxing at the height of the sport's popularity, peaking as it did between 1800 and 1850, as documented by Pierce Egan. Egan was the foremost observer of leisure pursuits of the time and described Elias as 'a most fearsome boxer' in the various reports he published on prize fights. In his *Life in London* publications he covered bare-knuckle boxing extensively, with illustrations by Isaac Cruickshank, the preeminent social artist of the day.

Elias had a son, **Young Dutch Sam**. Young Sam was born in 1808, and from birth records it appears he was born outside wedlock. Nevertheless, he lived with his father and was taught to box from about the age of six. He was not quite nine when his father died. He then took the name of Evans and carried on learning to box until he was proficient enough to start prize fighting. At his peak, Young Sam was fighting at 155 pounds, a stone and a half heavier than his father. He too became a formidable boxer.

Although Young Sam boxed for almost nine years, he actually only had twelve officially recorded fights. However, he still managed to go undefeated, picking up the English heavyweight title along the way. His career would have been greater had it not been for the company he kept. He fell in with some aristocratic young men who did nothing more than drink and gamble to while away the time. He eventually went down the same road as his father, drinking himself to death aged just thirty-four.

*

As Mendoza's life in boxing drew to a close, the next great East End pugilist was just starting out. **James (Jem) Ward** (1800–1881) was born in Ratcliff Highway, Shadwell, the son of a butcher.

He worked in the East India Docks from the age of twelve, both on the river and off it, and was also a 'coal whipper'. This was a filthy job, working in the holds of colliers unloading coal.

It is not known how Ward got started in boxing or if he had any formal training. He was, however, a very fit and well-built young man weighing over 165 lbs and standing 6 feet in height. He was a large man for those days. Because of his background working with coal, he became known as 'the Black Diamond'. He was certainly an excellent fighter, going undefeated from 1815 to 1822 and claiming the heavyweight championship.

Ward's defeat in 1822 to Bill Abbott, a vastly inferior fighter, was extremely controversial, with some claiming he threw the match for betting purposes. Witnesses claimed to have heard Ward give instructions to Abbott to hit him, after which Ward staggered around the ring and fell to the floor. An enquiry was launched, and Ward confessed to taking a £100 bribe (it is also suspected that he picked up much more on the betting markets). Banned from boxing, Ward was forced to work the boxing booths and to indulge in the odd backstreet fight to earn a living, often under a false name. Always a crowd pleaser, Ward was allowed to return to the boxing circuit a couple of years later.

Ward got his chance to fight for the championship again in 1825, going up against Tom Cannon. It was a high-profile fight, with many past champions and nobility in attendance. Ward simply had to win if he was to salvage his reputation. The fight took place in mid-July, with temperatures over 32°C. Fortunately, the bout did not take too long as Ward knocked Cannon out within ten minutes to regain the title.

Ward was now looking for an easier life and pursued other activities, but after two years away he was forced to fight again in 1827. He fought and lost to Peter Crawley. The latter retired immediately after the match, however, so Ward claimed the title back by default.

Ward's final match was in 1831 against Irish champion Simon Byrne, whom he defeated. He then retired at the end of that year rather than be forced to fight an eager young hopeful called James Burke. Ward should have relinquished his champion's belt but refused to do so. Instead, he offered to present it to the winner of the upcoming Byrne *vs* Burke fight. Ward was championing his adversary Simon Byrne, and acted as Byrne's cornerman for the contest. Burke beat Byrne in one of that century's most notorious, bloody and brutal matches (of which more later). Rumours were once again rife about Ward's integrity after this fight, and he was forced to flee to France. He took the belt with him, which he kept for another couple of years before agreeing to hand it over to the next champion, William Bendigo Thompson.

Ward retired from prize fighting around 1830 and went on to run several pubs in the Shadwell and Whitechapel areas. It was at this time that Ward witnessed, at first hand, the appalling East London cholera outbreak of 1832. With the area hugely overpopulated, conditions were perfect for an outbreak of this kind. The health authorities had known for some time of the risks of cholera in this part of London but had done nothing. The main sewer was an open one that serviced the area between Spitalfields and Whitechapel before discharging in the Thames at Limehouse. The outbreak could be traced back to colliers arriving from the north-east of the country. Many sailors and dock workers around the wharves were taken ill in late 1831. These included some of Ward's old colleagues from his days working on these types of vessels.

The outbreak spread quickly, and over the next few months thousands were affected. At least eight hundred people died. Many of the workhouses were used as wards for the sick. The open sewer which the locals termed the 'Black Ditch' was blamed for the spread of the disease. Following a further outbreak in 1848, and one in Soho in 1854 which claimed more than six hundred lives, the government was forced to act. A modern sewage system was built between 1858 and 1865, much of it still in use to this day.

Ward himself survived. He was in the right place – it was known that drinking beer was far safer than drinking water in those times.

Ward remained in the pub trade and even developed a passion for painting, with several of his works exhibited. He died at the Licensed Victuallers Asylum on the Old Kent Road.

Although Ward was a great fighter, his run-ins with the authorities over match fixing would tarnish his achievements. He lived to a ripe old age, but this contemporary street ballad, recorded by publisher James Catnach, probably haunted him all his life:

On Thursday, May the 30th day, brave Simon took the ring,
Back'd by Jem Ward the champion, likewise by gallant Spring,
To fight for two hundred pounds, a man of courage bold,
To stop reports that with Ward the battle he had sold

*

One of the last great bare-knuckle fighters of the era, **Tom King** (1835–1888), was born in Silver Street, Stepney. Like so many young boys, King joined the Royal Navy and that's where he learned to box. He was still a young man when he left the navy and settled down in Stepney, where he worked as a docker. Working as a docker was tough, but it was sometimes just as difficult to even get the work. Dock labour in those days was a cutthroat business; no employment contracts back then. King was one of more than 10,000 casual workers who turned up at the London dock gates when cargo ships moored up. They waited for the 'call-on' to be chosen as casual labour by a dock's foreman, or ticket man as he was later known. At the London docks this waiting was called 'Standing on the Stones'.

For the manual labourers, it was often important to get noticed. These men would shout, jostle and even fight each other to make their presence known. For the more skilled stevedores, the 'call-on' was a more civilised affair. King used his physical presence to get noticed by the foremen, and his fists to deter anyone who threatened his livelihood. Although he used his strength to get through the dock gates, this could often backfire; the foremen, acknowledging his physical attributes, often employed him in the heaviest and most dangerous work.

Health and safety were two words never associated with dock work, and Tom had several accidents in the dark and dangerous recesses of ship's holds. From 1854 all dock casualties were sent to the newly built Poplar Hospital. The full name of hospital was morbidly accurate: the Poplar Infirmary for Accidents.

It was at Poplar Hospital that endless streams of casual dockers arrived with crushed and broken bones. They were the lucky ones – many did not make it, or were discharged minus a limb or two. The records of Poplar Hospital make it clear how deadly dock work could be. The older docks and wharves were death traps. By far the worse was the East India Dock, which was often referred to as the 'death dock'. Only coalmining at this time could compare for workplace fatality rates.

Fortunately, King had some brain to go with his brawn. He convinced his bosses that he was best employed keeping troublemakers in order and watching out for dock theft. His skills with his fists had earned him respect and some limited notoriety following several brawls with colleagues. Because of his overwhelming resourcefulness, his bosses took up his offer and he was made a foreman of labourers in Victoria Docks in 1857. One of his first duties at the docks was to sort out a troublemaker and bully known as Brighton Bill. King challenged Bill to a fight and gave him a severe beating.

King's brawling soon bought him to the attention of the retired boxing champion Jem Ward, who started to train him properly. He became known as 'the Fighting Sailor'. His first documented professional fight was against the unofficial dockyards champion, Bill Clamp, and he won convincingly. No more risking life and limb undertaking dangerous dock work. Two more victories followed, and then he fought for Jem Mace's heavyweight title in 1862.

By all accounts this was a terrific fight, lasting forty-three rounds. King gained the upper hand and held the advantage after the first thirty rounds, but the tide gradually turned. The experienced Mace landed some telling blows to the head. In the final round, with King unable to see through two almost completely closed eyes, Mace delivered a huge blow to the neck which made it nearly impossible for King to breathe and he was forced to withdraw from the long and gruelling match.

Such was the clamour for a rematch that another bout between the two took place the following year. On entering the ring, both boxers looked in magnificent condition. They needed to be. The press reported the match as twenty rounds of non-stop fighting. This time Tom King won when Mace, four years his senior, more or less collapsed from exhaustion. King was now the heavyweight champion. With an eye to his future, he became more selective in his choice of opponents and began to fight less.

One of King's last fights was against American champion John Camel Heenan, known as Benicia Boy, in December 1863. Heenan appointed Tom Sayers as his cornerman for the fight. Sayers was regarded as Britain's pound-for-pound best-ever bare-knuckle boxer, and was tactically very astute. Heenan weighed roughly 200 pounds and King a mere 180. It was a close match, but King won in twenty-four tough rounds. Heenan blamed Sayers for the defeat, but it is said that at the time of the fight Sayers was suffering from hypoglycaemia. It was a very prestigious match for both Heenan and King, coming with a massive purse of £20,000.

By 1864, with Mace pressing for a third championship fight, King retired. Now a prosperous young man, he became a successful bookmaker and took up the more peaceful sport of rowing. He became a top athlete in the field. Having become a man of means, he married the daughter of a wealthy shipowner and moved to South West London and then Surrey. He died a wealthy man, with an audited estate worth over £53,000 – a very considerable sum for anybody at the time, and truly astounding for a man of King's humble beginnings.

2

THE EARLY YEARS:
THE GLOVES ARE ON

By the turn of the twentieth century, bare-knuckle prize fighting had all but disappeared in East London, although the discipline has remained popular among the Gypsy and Traveller communities and can still be witnessed today.

From about 1875, gloved contests began to appear with increasing regularity. Championships were still contested with bare fists, but the authorities were beginning to clamp down on some of the less regulated fights. Records of these types of fights were vague, and although the deeds of the top fighters were recorded, very little is known about the many other bare-knuckle boxers of the era.

The name of **Tommy Orange**, a bare-knuckle boxer from the Old Nichol area of Bethnal Green, does crop up in news clippings. From the odd report, it sounded like his character suited his name – he was indeed a colourful individual. Tommy was born around 1857 in the unimaginably grim surroundings of the Old Nichol Street Rookery, the latter word being an old term for a slum. Determined to improve his lot in life, he is first recorded as having fought on a patch of ground on the edge of Hackney

Marshes against somebody called 'Panto'. Apparently, a number of well-known sportsmen from the area made the trip to Hackney, about fifty in all, and they made up the fighting square. Someone from *Sporting Life* was present to record that the fight lasted almost ninety minutes and that Orange was the victor.

Orange then went on to box in bare-knuckle contests at the Five Inkwells and Blue Anchor pubs in Shoreditch. He beat two featherweight contenders, Punch Dowsett and Tommy Hawkins. In 1879 he was matched against the powerful ex-champion George Davis in a fight near the Rising Sun pub in Woodford. Although Tommy was a featherweight, Davis was probably at least a lightweight. Davis also possessed a crippling short and powerful right-hand body punch, often delivered low. Orange was aware of this and took extra precautions in that sensitive area. He also boxed at a distance as he had a slightly longer reach. After some time he managed to produce a stunning right hand to Davis's jaw, apparently lifting Davis off his feet, and ended the fight.

His last recorded match was a gloved championship fight against the experienced Jem Luxton. They knew each other well. The same weight as Orange at 126 pounds, Luxton was the acknowledged English bantamweight champion. Orange was in terrific form coming into the fight, and from the outset he landed blow after blow on the champion. Luxton was overpowered and conceded in the third round. Orange was recognised as the best 9-stone boxer around. Instead of going on to greater boxing achievements, however, he retired.

Despite his name, and unlike many boxers that are to appear later in the book, Tommy Orange did not go into the fruit-and-veg trade. He became a successful timber merchant. He was possibly of Romany heritage, and like many from that background had a passion for horses. His success at prize fighting as well as his business income gave him enough money to purchase and retain a number of top-quality horses, which he used to compete in the sport of trotting, or harness racing.

Joseph Anderson (1869–1943) was one of the last official bare-knuckle prize fighters of the era, and became England's 134-pound champion in 1897. Like Orange, Joe was born into dreadful poverty, in his case on Duke Street in the Spitalfields area of London. Like many others, his family often moved from one local tenement slum to another depending on how much rent they could afford to pay. The alternative was a trip to the workhouse.

The area of Spitalfields where Joe lived was known as the Spitalfields Rookery, and it was a desperate place for a child to grow up. The Georgian poet George Galloway described it as a cluster of mean tenements densely populated by people of the lowest class. There were a number of rookeries dotted around London, like the Old St Nichols Street Rookery that produced Tommy Orange, but the most famous was the Jacob's Island Rookery in Bermondsey, which was the setting for Charles Dicken's *Oliver Twist*.[1] Fortunately for Joe, his father, John, was a carpenter and got work at the small furniture companies that had sprung up and gradually began to flourish in the area during the latter part of the nineteenth century. However, Joe did not acquire his father's handicraft skills – his hands were to be used in other ways.

On leaving school he worked as a porter in the fruit-and-veg market at Spitalfields. Even then, the big London markets were a breeding ground for fighters. Records are slightly vague, but Joe is known to have boxed with and without gloves. He was one of the boxers who bridged the gap between the two forms of boxing.

Joe's first recorded fight was in Shoreditch in 1889, and he fought with some success around the area for a few years before he was booked to fight at what was then the Mecca of boxing, the National Sporting Club at Covent Garden, in 1894. The Sporting Club proved to be a happy hunting ground for Joe, who fought as a lightweight, as he won his first three bouts there. His efforts soon landed him a chance to fight for the title, and his championship fight came in April 1897 against Tom Ireland at the Excelsior Hall in Mansfield Street, Bethnal Green and having already boxed earlier that evening in an eliminator, he duly won.

Joe Anderson only had around forty professional fights in almost eighteen years of activity, so he must have kept working in and around Spitalfields Market throughout his earlier life. However, he seems to have made a good amount of money inside the ring because he retired from the fight game in 1907 and around that time moved to Edmonton, a more pleasant place to live than the squalor into which he was born. His time in the ring and the rare solid silver boxing belt he was awarded for his championship was covered on an edition of BBC's *Antiques Roadshow Detectives* shown in 2015. The belt has been in his family for 120 years.

The unique and impressive solid silver lightweight belt won by Joe Anderson. (© Dave Porter c/o Anderson Family)

A young **Thomas 'Pedlar' Palmer** (1876–1949) would have watched his father, Robert, box gloveless back in the 1880s. One of Robert's fights was against Henry Payne for the unofficial Essex championship at Plaistow. It is suggested that these two boxers were possibly related to each other – the Payne and the Palmer families certainly knew each other as Henry Payne's son Ernest was a financial backer of Pedlar for a while.

Thomas was born in West Ham and spent his early years around the gyms in the area watching his father train and fight. His brother, too, was already boxing. Thomas was a small, slightly built lad but was exceptionally strong for his age and size. One day he went along with his brother and father to Shoreditch's Blue Anchor pub, which had a well-equipped gym in a back room. They persuaded young Thomas to try a three-round workout with one of the gym's top fighters. According to Whipp family research on Palmer, this much more experienced sparring partner was one Fred Johnson. I believe this could have been Fred Johnson of Hackney, a very useful boxer who would go on to hold the British featherweight championship from 1894 to 1897. Whatever the case, Thomas was encouraged to take up the sport.

It's unclear how he got his nickname of Pedlar. Some say it refers to his technical skill while back-pedalling during fights. The jury is out on this particular theory, but there is no doubt that he had ring-craft. For a couple of years, Thomas (now 'Pedlar') and his younger brother Matthew took on all comers at boxing booths and music halls in the East End and beyond. The very impressive Pedlar was spotted by the founder of the National Sporting Club and was invited to fight at their prestigious Covent Garden arena.

Pedlar quickly rose through the ranks, and in 1893 fought for the 'World hundred-pound title' against Walter Croot (this was not an official title). He knocked out his opponent in the seventeenth round. Further matches followed at bantamweight, and he took the British title the next year. He became official world bantamweight champion in 1896 when he beat Johnny Murphy over twenty rounds at the Covent Garden venue. After a couple of successful defences, he went over to New York in 1899 to fight Terry McGovern.

Soon after the boxers entered the ring, chaos ensued. One or two reports say that when Pedlar went to touch gloves, which is a British tradition, McGovern flattened him. Another report says that just as the referee was to start the fight on hearing the bell, the timekeeper intervened by shouting out that he had not yet rung the bell. Both boxers were ordered to retire, but the timekeeper got into an argument and fought with nearby spectators. Attentions were diverted. A bell then rang again and McGovern rushed over to the hapless Pedlar and poleaxed him while the Englishman was still watching the ringside melee. The *New York Times* reported it differently, saying that as soon as the referee signalled the start Pedlar swung both fists at McGovern, missing his man, and then got caught with a powerful punch while the referee's attention was diverted for a split second. Protests were lodged, but the American secured the decision.

Over the next five years, Pedlar fought on with mixed success. He was generally regarded as a very nice person and placid outside the ring, which is why it was sad to see that he managed to get into a fight on a train on the way home from a race meeting he attended. A very large man, Robert Choat, entered the carriage and began to insult some women. Pedlar objected to the language and a fight ensued. He hit Choat hard in the neck, stopping the big man in his tracks. Unfortunately for Pedlar, a clot formed in Choat's carotid artery and he died. The law took a very dim view on professional boxers using their skills on the general public, and Pedlar was initially charged with murder. Following appeals, this was reduced to manslaughter. The trial took place at Guildford Assizes. It came out at the trial that Choat himself had indulged in unlicensed bare-knuckle boxing in and around south London and the boxing booths. On 19 July 1907, Thomas 'Pedlar' Palmer was sentenced to five years for manslaughter.

Pedlar returned to the ring with mixed success after his release, and had his last fight in 1918. He then helped to run a tobacconist shop he had bought with his brother in Barking Road, Plaistow. He moved to Brighton in 1929 and worked as a bookmaker. He died a reasonably wealthy man. He had a son, Billy, who boxed professionally for about ten years; Billy was a decent enough fighter but not in the class of his father. In Billy's defence, he fought in a featherweight division that was brim-full of class boxers and lost to the likes of Harry Corbett, Johnny Curly and George McKenzie.

There was one link that, more than most, bound together the boxers of East London in those earlier years, and that was the poverty into which they were born. However, there was an exception to the rule.

John (Johnny) William Henry Tyler Douglas (1882–1930), known as Douglas, was definitely not your archetypal East End hard nut from the slums. Firstly, he was born in the Upper Clapton

Palmer (left) sparring practice circa 1930. *(© Whipp Family)*

area, which, even by today's standards, is borderline in terms of its East End legitimacy; in the later Victorian era, it was a rather pleasant, quiet, leafy place to live considering it was only a mile or so from Hackney and Hoxton.

More than this, however, Douglas came from a rather privileged background. His family would most certainly have been considered members of the middle/upper class, even in those days. His father was a very successful timber importer, with large timber yards and other premises in the Docklands area and offices in the City. Douglas senior was a keen and competent all-round sportsman. As an amateur, he boxed at middleweight and won the English (Queensberry) Amateur Championships three years running in the 1870s. He later became president of the Amateur Boxing Association (ABA). His name will crop up later as he also had a very distinguished career as a boxing referee. Douglas senior was also a very keen cricketer.

Young Douglas, along with his brother Cecil, was taught boxing. More generally, he was encouraged from a very early age to participate in many sports by his rather 'pushy' father. Douglas rose to the challenge. Although not considered a naturally gifted athlete, he was ruthless and tough, a determined character with a tremendous work ethic. He was sent to the exclusive Felsted School in Essex, where he honed both his boxing and cricketing skills. So dedicated was he that by the age of nineteen he was playing for Essex County Cricket Club. Not content with that, he kept up boxing and twice won the Public Schools Championship. In 1905, he won the ABA Middleweight title.

Douglas's love for boxing ran alongside his increasing cricketing ability, and he represented Great Britain in boxing at the 1908 London Olympic Games. He made it to the gold medal bout and, in a tremendously close fight in which an extra round had to be boxed to produce a winner, Johnny won the middleweight gold medal, defeating the Australian champion 'Snowy' Baker.

Although Douglas appeared the very epitome of the amateur gentleman sportsman, the young Douglas did have his father as an unofficial backer. During his early days with Essex his father stepped in to rescue the Leyton County Cricket Ground from closure by purchasing the lease for the club. Some years later, his father used his influence as a lever to ensure young Johnny was made club captain. His father was also in the background when he was appointed England's cricket captain. That said, Douglas was excellent in the role. The great Yorkshire and England batsman Herbert Sutcliffe was quoted as saying,

> He had a splendid conception of a captain's duty with a fighting spirit second only to Douglas Jardine [captain in the notorious 'bodyline' Ashes series] and was brim-full of the most sterling qualities.

Douglas was to become one of the greatest English cricketers of the first half of the twentieth century, and, as stand-in captain on the Marylebone Cricket Club tour of Australia in 1911, comprehensibly won that Ashes series. He served in the First World War and rose to the rank of acting lieutenant-colonel. He married while on leave in 1916 and he and his wife went to live in Theydon Bois, Essex.

Although a leading name in cricket, Douglas kept up his association with boxing and became a proficient referee, handling some excellent fights. He officiated at about thirty boxing events between 1919 and 1928, including the excellent if somewhat attritional twenty-round fight between Aldgate's Johnny Brown and Plymouth's Bugler Harry Lake for the British Empire and European bantamweight title in 1923. He also refereed the 1928 British featherweight title fight between Bethnal Green's Harry Corbett and Sheffield's Johnny Cuthbert, the last British featherweight title fight to be scheduled for twenty rounds.

Douglas's test playing days finished in 1925 and he played his last Essex game in 1928. After that he mostly worked in the family timber business. Douglas, with his father, was returning from a business trip in Scandinavia in late December 1930 when

Presentation at the Army and Leyton County Cricket Ground, Leyton. The Essex captain, Johnny Douglas (in blazer), looks on proudly as his Essex and England teammate Charles 'Jack' Russell is presented with an award by Mrs Enid Mann of the Whitechapel brewery giants Mann, Crossman & Paulin, later Watney/Mann. Russell was the first Englishman to score two centuries in one test match. (Essex County Cricket Club)

his ship collided with another and sank within a few minutes. Douglas tried unsuccessfully to save his father. Both were lost in the icy sea off the coast of Denmark that night. Douglas was just forty-eight.

As well as his undoubted cricket skills and his boxing prowess, Douglas was also considered good enough to run middle distance at the same Olympics in which he won the boxing gold. Oh, and one more thing – he also played the odd game of football for England as well!

Coincidentally, Johnny's brother Cecil, who was nicknamed 'Pickles' Douglas, also played cricket for Essex before he too became a leading boxing referee, handling contests including Jack Doyle *vs* Jack Petersen, the Primo Carnera *vs* George Cook and both of the epic Len Harvey *vs* Jack Petersen British title fights in 1933 and 1934. The latter fight still holds the British record for a boxing match attendance – just over 90,000 spectators attended this eagerly awaited rematch at the White City Stadium.

Johnny Douglas remains the only first-class cricketer to win an Olympic boxing medal.

Apart from the fact that they were born within a few months and a few miles of each other, Douglas would have had very little in common with **Alfred John Reed** (1883–1941). Douglas was

Left and opposite:
*J. W. H. T. Douglas,
Olympic boxing champion,
Essex and England cricket
captain, athlete, boxing
referee, Corinthian Casual
and England amateur
footballer. (Essex CCC &
Wikicommons)*

born into a wealthy family and had a privileged upbringing, while Alf Reed was born into abject poverty in Canning Town. Douglas was born with a silver spoon in his mouth; Alf Reed was born with an iron shovel in his hand.

Alf's father was a coal porter, shovelling, delivering and tipping coal which arrived in the nearby docks, and although little is known about young Alf's early boxing years, he too shovelled coal in the docks from an early age to earn a living. It appears he drifted into boxing at the turn of the century and fought at the Wonderland boxing arena in Whitechapel.

His earliest records from these fights date back to 1902 and his family still possess a beautiful belt inscribed 'Presented by Mr Joe Smith for the featherweight Championship won by Alf Reed 1903'. He may still have been boxing as an amateur at this time. Nothing much more is known at this stage. He was one of a number of novice fighters that fought in a sponsored tournament for which a belt was awarded but these took place in 1904. Clearly however, Alf was progressing slowly but surely and within a few years he moved up to lightweight and began to box in slightly higher company.

By 1904 he was boxing professionally at the Wonderland and other local venues, going on an unbeaten run of twenty-one fights. Bigger and more lucrative fights were set up, and Alf even went to Paris to fight some top French fighters and European champions of the day. In late 1910 he was signed up by the management of a new East End arena, the Premierland Arena, to fight exclusively there. He had fourteen contests at Premierland throughout 1911 and 1912 and won ten of them. He retired in 1915.

Alf had married in 1908, and he had five children. Two of the children were boys, and they both boxed. One of them, Leslie, became a professional boxer in 1938 and looked to have a promising career ahead of him but it was put on hold after he was called up by the army to fight in the Second World War. Worse still for the Reed family, young Leslie was posted to the Far East, into

Britain's so-called 'Forgotten Army', which fought the Japanese in Burma. He was taken prisoner in 1943 and imprisoned in the notorious Kanu camp (No. 1 camp), Thailand. From here prisoners were worked to death on the Thai–Burma Railway construction and the infamous bridge on the River Kwai. Miraculously, Leslie managed to survive and got back home. By all accounts, he was greatly affected by his experiences. Sadly, he gave up any thoughts of boxing again.

Huge numbers of boxers fought for their country over the years. They were probably considered god's gift to the forces by the officer classes. Fit young men, tough, well used to rigorous training and very accomplished with their fists, many boxers finished up in the forces during periods of hostilities. Up until 1960, when conscription finished, many were either conscripted or called up for national service. However, before 1879 some voluntarily signed up, taking the 'King's Shilling' as one way to survive poverty.

One such volunteer was **William Albert Sharpley**. Sharpley was born in Lamprell Street, Old Ford, Bow, in December 1890. He was a very good all-round sportsman. During his schooldays he boxed, swam and was an excellent tough-tackling full-back on the football field. He must have thought about carving out a living in sports, but instead he decided to join the army, signing up with the 2nd Battalion of the Essex Regiment around 1909. Sharpley kept up his sports during his early years in the regiment, boxing and playing football for the army. He became a regimental champion and boxed for the army in the prestigious Army/Navy Boxing Championships but never won. He made some progress in the army, rising through the ranks to become a sergeant by 1912.

It would appear that football may have been the better choice. In 1912, Leslie was approached by Leicester City's manager to sign 'trial forms' after playing some excellent inter-service matches. Although he was attached to the club for several months, he only made one first team appearance, against Leeds in April that year.

At the outbreak of war in August 1914, Sharpley was back in the army. Being an experienced soldier, he was soon sent to the front line. He fought in the Battle of the Marne in the autumn of 1914. As reported in the *London Gazette* on 4 December 1914, Sharpley had been mentioned in dispatches:

> For conspicuous gallantry in rescuing and bringing in across the open, and under fire, a wounded NCO.

He was also awarded the Medal of St George 2nd class, and in early 1916 he received the Distinguished Conduct Medal. The intelligence summary recorded the act which saw him receive the medal:

> At about 6am on 6 February 1916, Lance Corporal Rogers was severely wounded at an isolated post in front of one of our trenches south east of Hebuterne. It was impossible to reach him except over the open and Sergeant Sharpley, accompanied by a Lance Corporal went out at 7.30am under hostile fire and succeeded in getting Lance Corporal Rogers back to our trenches. Owing to the exposed nature of the ground and the deep mud, it was not until 1.15 pm that this was safely accomplished.

Less than four months later, on the morning of 1 July 1916, William Sharpley went 'over the top' with the 2nd Battalion. It was his part in the first day offensive of Britain's bloodiest ever battle, the Battle of the Somme. The Essex attacked the strongly held Grandcourt Pusieux Ridge. Some 630 officers and men of the battalion went into action, and 438 were killed or wounded. Sadly, Sergeant William Albert Sharpley DCM died that day.

3

TWENTIETH-CENTURY BOYS

By the turn of the century, boxing had come a long way. Although bare-knuckle boxing fights still took place, they were very much restricted to backstreet venues. The Marquess of Queensberry Rules were well established, and boxing was well regulated.

Soon after the new century began, the Victorian Era ended with the death of Queen Victoria in January 1901, ushering in the Edwardian. The last few years of the old queen's reign made for sombre times, but with the dawn of a new century and the coronation of Edward VII, the population of the East End looked forward to better times.

East London was by now becoming the hub of British boxing, with gyms, clubs and venues springing up to accommodate demand for the sport. The new king was known to have been a keen patron of the noble art. The East End had the gyms and boxing clubs to produce good boxers and the venues to showcase their talent. Many promising boxers were coming through. The period either side of the First World War was to become the golden age for British boxing. Across the nation, only association football could rival it for popularity.

Competition within the area was fierce, and those men who threw their hats into the ring fought tooth and nail to earn a living. The fighters from the area began to gain a reputation as hard, durable men.

One such man was a decent boxer from Bow called **Joseph Cohen** (1897–1977). He fought under the Joe Conn. Conn had already been fighting for over six years and was a veteran of well over seventy bouts of boxing when, in 1918, he was matched against one of the world's greatest ever boxers, Jimmy Wilde. Wilde was born in a little mining village in the Rhondda Valley in south Wales and went on to become the greatest flyweight in boxing history. Wilde was very, very small, boxing at a shade under 100 pounds at the lowest possible weight, flyweight. Today he would be able to fight at mini-fly or light-fly. He was totally unbeatable at that weight for many years, and after he ran out of opponents at fly he started being matched against heavier fighters in the bantamweight and featherweight divisions. Jimmy Wilde only lost one bout in his 136-fight career – a phenomenal statistic given the size of some of his opponents.

His rise to fame and his exploits in the ring have been well documented, but over his considerable career he fought many tough East Enders. All were dispatched, unable to match Wilde's brilliance. At the height of his powers, in 1918, he stepped into the ring against Joe Conn. A featherweight, Conn stood almost 5 inches taller than Wilde and was over a stone heavier. He was beginning to run into a bit of form but the press, who had already witnessed a number of Wilde's previous wins against bigger opponents, marked the smaller man as the favourite. However, Conn was a canny, gritty and experienced boxer and was not there to be used as cannon fodder for the superb Wilde.

The match was fought at Stamford Bridge, Chelsea. Thousands of East Enders made their way across the capital for the fight and helped make up a crowd of more than 50,000 spectators.

The promoters wanted to show a big London crowd just how versatile Jimmy Wilde was. It turned out to be one of the greatest matches of the era.

From the bell, Wilde went straight on the attack and Conn was forced onto the retreat, trying to defend himself with the use of his long left. Conn launched a brave counter-attack in the third round, but Wilde still took the honours with evasive tactics that caused most of Conn's attacking blows to miss the target. Conn eventually connected on a number of occasions with some quite telling blows. By the seventh round, Wilde was starting to look distressed and Conn's heavier blows were starting to tell. The eighth round was a bad one for the normally brilliant Wilde, and his eye was cut in the ninth. This general pattern continued into the tenth round, with Conn holding his own, but then, from nowhere, Wilde scored with a hard right which put Conn on the canvas. He got up at the nine count but was put down a further four times before the round ended. With Conn at his mercy, Wilde hit the bigger man at will over the next two rounds. After Conn went down a further seven times, the referee finally stepped in and rescued him.

It was, in all truth, a remarkable win for the Welsh Wizard. Joe Conn was in the running for a shot at the British featherweight title at the time, having won nineteen of his previous twenty fights. It was the sort of fight which underlines the grit and determination that was instilled in East End boxers.

Conn was regarded as a 'journeyman', a solid pro boxer. For the popularity of the sport you needed these types. Often on the undercard at boxing events, they sometimes made it into the limelight but in those days they always knew that they were there to feed and clothe their families. Joe fought 120 bouts after turning pro, and boxed both in Britain and in America.

Wilde and Conn both turned professional in 1911. Unlike the great Jimmy Wilde, however, Joe Conn had a steady if unspectacular career and by 1923 was struggling to compete competitively. After losing five consecutive fights, taking some serious punishment in a

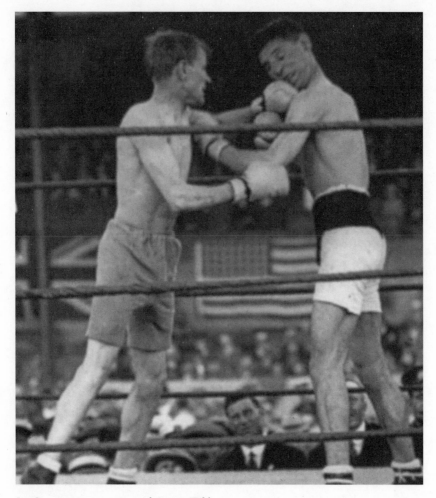

Joe Conn's epic encounter with Jimmy Wilde.

few of them, Conn retired in 1925. Remaining in the Bow area all his life, he spent a lot of his later life working at some of the many boys' boxing clubs in the area.

*

A quick question: What was the name of the man who banged the giant brass gong at the start of the J. Arthur Rank films? The answer: Bombardier Billy Wells.

Actually, Wells was one of three used over the years but it goes to show that those hammer blows were what he might be best remembered for. He was, however, a good boxer and a larger-than-life character in more sense than one. **William Thomas 'Bombardier' Billy Wells** (1889–1967) was born in Cable Street in Stepney. He was the eldest of five brothers and was one of nine children.

At the age of twelve, William left school to become a messenger boy. It was at this time that he started to take an interest in boxing, starting his fighting career as an amateur. In 1904 he was a member of the Old Broad Street Boxing Club and won the Open Lads Competition over 10 stone, marking him as heavyweight champion of the club. However, in 1905 William lost on points after three rounds to Bill Hazel, a member of the City Police, in a men's heavyweight competition. He was just seventeen.

In 1906, Wells joined the Royal Artillery as a gunner. He was posted to India, where he boxed in the divisional and all-India championships with great success. He was promoted to bombardier and began training full-time with the help of a civilian coach. It became apparent that Wells was good enough to make a living from boxing, so in 1910 he decided to buy himself out of the army and returned to Britain. His first professional fight, boxing as Bombardier Billy Wells, took place in June 1910. Fighting against Gunner Joe Mills, he came out the victor on points over six rounds. Eight fights and seven wins later, in April 1911, Wells was fighting for the British heavyweight title against Iron (William) Hague at the National Sporting Club, Covent in Garden. He won by a knockout in the sixth round.

Later that year, in October, Wells was matched to fight the world heavyweight champion, American Jack Johnson, in Earl's Court. The first black heavyweight champion of the world and a hugely controversial figure, Johnson had been touring Europe for several months, fighting in a series of exhibition bouts. He arrived in England in September and set up camp at the Royal Forest Hotel pub in North Chingford. Wells, meanwhile, was labelled the Great British Great White Hope in the press. However, there were strong objections to the fight, led by prominent Methodist ministers and some politicians including the Labour MP and future prime minister Ramsey McDonald. The Home Secretary at the time, Winston Churchill, was initially unmoved but when the Archbishop of Canterbury and Lord Baden-Powell urged him to reconsider, he bowed to the pressure and banned the match. Thereafter, a colour bar for British championship matches remained in British boxing until 1947.[1]

In 1911, Wells became the British heavyweight champion. In doing so, he also became the first heavyweight to win the newly presented Lonsdale Belt. He went on to fight Frenchman Georges Carpentier for the European heavyweight championship in Belgium in 1913, but was defeated. Wells had one further fight against the Frenchman, this time on home turf in Covent Garden, but lost again. He was unfortunate to fight Carpentier, France's greatest ever boxer, at the very pinnacle of his illustrious career. Wells was one of no fewer than nineteen British boxers who tried to beat Carpentier, and not one succeeded.

Wells' boxing was curtailed at the outbreak of war in 1914 when, as an experienced soldier, he re-enlisted in the army. He survived the war unscathed but, tragically, three of his younger brothers did not. One of his brothers, Alfred, was killed shortly after the start of the war. Another, Sidney, was badly gassed at the First Battle of Ypres in 1915 and never fully recovered. A third brother, Albert, was severely wounded that same year. Billy Wells' second-youngest brother, Harold, enlisted in the Essex Regiment while underage around that time. With one son already dead and two more badly incapacitated, their mother, Emily, wrote to the Essex Regiment to ask if Harold could be released from duty as what remained of the family required another member of working age to help with financial support. It is not known if the regiment granted this request.

As for Billy, he still boxed professionally on odd occasions throughout the war. Ten bouts are recorded. At national level he reigned supreme, defending his British crown fourteen times in all. He eventually lost this title to Joe Beckett in 1919, but he boxed on for several years. He ran physical training exercises for the army as well as boxing professionally. Wells' last fight was in 1925, after which he hung up the gloves. Although a fine heavyweight specimen, Wells lacked the killer instinct. After he quit the ring, he admitted that he 'could not hit an opponent whose jaw was sagging and whose eyes were blank'.

Alongside his boxing, Wells was invited to play little cameo roles in silent movies. The first dates back to 1916, when he starred in a British silent film called *Kent, the Fighting Man.* Several more bit parts followed in the silent era. A theatrical impresario was struck by Wells' rugged good looks and presence and thought he might be a natural for the stage. With some earlier screen work behind him, Wells swapped the canvas for the boards. Billy Wells made his debut as Jack Bandon, a fighter and gentleman, and hero of a three-act play called *Wanted-A-Man.* The play opened at the Hackney Empire and, to most people's surprise, Wells came over as a very competent actor. The play was critically acclaimed. One critic wrote, 'Billy scored a singular success as an actor and was something of a surprise. As a boxer, Billy is one of the most nervous people who ever entered a ring, but on the stage, he was confidence itself.'

Not content with treading the boards, Billy became an excellent amateur golfer. By 1930 he held a single-figure handicap and was persuaded to enter the 1931 British Amateur Open Golf Championship at the Royal North Devon Club at Westward Ho!. He was unlucky not to progress to the latter stages after a close match went to an extra hole.

Maybe he had a bit of showbiz in him from an early age, because his acting career continued to thrive. He picked up more small roles in films, starting with Hitchcock's *The Ring* in 1927, and went on to act in some decent films from the likes of Powell & Pressburger and King Vidor throughout the thirties and forties. In 1953, he played alongside Laurence Olivier in Peter Brook's *The Beggar's Opera.* His last screen appearance was in an early British seasonal TV movie called *A Santa for Christmas* in 1957. He had at stint at running pubs and died in 1967.

The Bombardier was a decent enough heavyweight and a good, honest professional. He never fought for a world championship,

Bombardier Billy Wells seen losing to the French superstar boxer Georges Carpentier in Paris. (© Beelden Collectie Belgische)

and in truth he was not in the same class as some of the American heavyweights around at the start of the new century. He was one of the first of those boxers who were to be called the 'horizontal heavyweights', of which there were to be a few over the years.

*

At the lower weights it was a far different story. Lighter-weight East London boxers were a force to be reckoned with. Let's begin with one of the all-time greats.

Much has been written about **Ted 'Kid' Lewis** (*c*. 1894–1970). It is difficult to do justice to this particular East End individual. The 'Kid' was certainly London's greatest ever boxer, and is considered by many aficionados to be among the best English fighters pound for pound and one of the greatest British boxers of all time.

Lewis was born in Umberston Street near Aldgate Pump around 1894 as Gershon Mendeloff. He started boxing at the Judean Athletic Club at the age of fourteen. Winning fights would net him sixpence and a cup of tea. However, he would usually leave with five pence as he gave back a penny for the cup of tea. He eventually won the club's flyweight title, but following that he began his professional career in quite inauspicious fashion in 1909 as he lost his debut to Johnny Sharpe. He was, however, an outstanding talent and went on to win match after match after this early setback. By the age of seventeen, Lewis had won both the British and European featherweight titles against Alec Lambert in 1913. He would successfully defend the latter title against Paul Til in 1914. His reputation increased with each victory.

Just before the outbreak of the First World War, Lewis travelled to America where the prizemoney was considerably higher. He began to earn a reputation for an all-action approach and was offered a shot at the world welterweight championship in 1915. He took the opportunity, beating American Jack Britton to claim the title and becoming the first foreign boxer to win a championship on American soil. He defended his title four times, three of the challenges coming from Jack Britton, who was his closest rival. The 'Kid' was the first British boxer to make a real impact in America. He was also considered to be the first champion to wear a gum shield. He spent a lot of time in the States and became quite a celebrity. He even got to know another expat Brit – Charlie Chaplin. They became great friends, with Charlie named as godfather to one of Lewis's children.

Fights came thick and fast for Lewis over the next six years. He made the jump to lightweight and in 1918 met Benny Leonard, a truly great boxer and widely considered one of the top three lightweights of all time along with Joe Gans and Roberto Duran. The eight-round contest, held in Newark, New Jersey, proved to be a very tight affair and was ruled a draw. In America, to win a fight in those days your opponent had to be knocked out or had to retire, either voluntarily or at the referee's insistence. If none of these things occurred, at the end of the final round a 'No Decision

Contest' would be declared. When that happened, the assorted press covering the match ringside would get together to rule on the match and give a verdict. Should there be disagreement between the press 'judges', a no decision verdict would apply.

Towards the end of his career, Lewis decided to box at higher weights. To help him prepare for this he employed an ageing middleweight boxer whom he knew from his younger days. Born four years before Lewis and just a few streets away, Sid Burns was a very good boxer indeed. In Sid's boxing days he would often use up-and-coming local boxers as sparring partners. When Lewis was just starting out, Sid had sparred with him. He had a reputation for mistreating his partners, and Lewis was no exception; the younger man often suffered at Burns' hands in their sessions. The older man was a big local celebrity, so Lewis suffered in silence. However, the Kid had a long memory.

When Lewis sparred with Burns, he used the opportunity to turn the tables on his old sparring partner and dished out some punishment of his own. Apparently, he also ridiculed Burns during their practice sessions as well. Poor old Sid needed the money he got from these sparring sessions, so he in turn suffered in silence. Coincidentally, looking on during these sessions was Sid's son and namesake, who went on to become a top boxing manager and promoter in the fifties and sixties (more on him later).

Also present was a young up-and-coming boxer called Roland Todd. Todd was carving out a few impressive results of his own but jumped at the chance to spar with the 'Master'. He watched and studied Lewis's strengths and weaknesses. They were to meet a couple of years later for two middleweight title fights; Todd's homework paid off as he gained narrow points victories over Lewis in both fights.

At his peak, Lewis had the ability to lose and gain weight in order to fight anywhere between welterweight and light heavyweight. He fought for the light heavyweight title in 1922 against Billy Wells' old nemesis, the great Frenchman Georges Carpentier. He struggled to get anywhere near a decent fighting weight and, giving away a lot of weight, was knocked out in the first round. As we have seen, he was not the only boxer to fall to Carpentier; losing to the Frenchman was no mark of shame.[2] At the time it was reported that if Lewis had triumphed he would have tried to pile some more pounds to fight the heavyweight world champion, Jack Dempsey. As it was, Lewis decided not to push for heavier weights. He continued boxing at a slightly lower level until 1929, mainly at his favourite venue, Premierland, although occasionally he fought abroad.

The curtain came down on Ted's wonderful boxing career on a cold December night that year. Twenty years previously, he had started on his road to the very top of world boxing by fighting a six-round bout in Stepney. He lost. After travelling all around the world, racking up well over 200 fights in some of the world's greatest arenas, he fought his last match a mile or so up the road at the Pitfield Street Baths in Hoxton. He won!

Lewis finally settled back in England, for good, in 1930. At the start of the 1930s Lewis was, surprisingly for a Jewish man, on the payroll of Oswald Mosley, who would found the British Union of Fascists in 1932. He was retained to train Mosley's bodyguards. Mosley's politics were not overtly anti-Semitic in 1931, and Lewis was actually persuaded to stand for Mosley's New Party in a council election in Whitechapel in that year. However, he failed to register many votes. Mosley soon had his 'Blackshirts' on the streets and his anti-Jewish stance became evident, at which point Lewis parted ways with Mosley. It was rumoured that Lewis, upon realising the depth of the fascist leader's hatred of the Jews, knocked out both Mosley and his bodyguard.

Lewis's record for competitive fights across the weight divisions was astonishing. In his very early amateur days, the Kid boxed at flyweight before winning the featherweight title. As he grew older and larger throughout his teens and early twenties, he boxed comfortably throughout the middleweight range. Later he fought several times at light heavyweight. It is a record for a British fighter that will remain almost impossible to surpass.

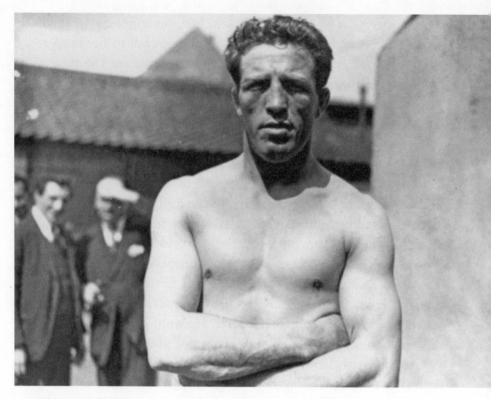

The great Ted 'Kid' Lewis, the East End's finest boxer. (Wikicommons)

Oswald Mosley worked hard to establish his brand of politics in East London, culminating with his much-publicised and infamous march through the East End in 1936. It ended in the violence of the Battle of Cable Street when the local Jewish population and left-wing activists halted Oswald Mosley and his 'Blackshirts'.

Lewis grew up within a stone's throw of Cable Street and was still working in and around the East End then, although it is not known whether he witnessed the event. What is known is that several Jewish and Irish boxers in the area, of which there were hundreds at that time, bolstered the local population's defence against the Blackshirts and the police. The Jewish gangster Jack Spot claimed that he and about twenty of his 'henchmen' fought pitched battles with both the police and the blackshirts.[3]

Ever since Daniel Mendoza had taken a stance against anti-Semitism, the exploits of Jewish boxers had helped lessen the prejudices faced by the Jewish population and instilled in them a resolution to defend their faith. It also helped that many Jewish families ensured their young were capable of physically defending themselves. The Battle of Cable Street was a seminal point in race relations in East London. Any thoughts that Mosley may have harboured about introducing a form of segregation – or worse – was rejected. In the mid-thirties, places like Stepney had a heady mix of Irish and Huguenot descendants living alongside a sizeable Jewish community. Along with them, Afro-Caribbeans, Scandinavians and Germans all lived in relative harmony with the indigenous population. Families felt secure.

The Lazarus family of Stepney were a case in point. Brothers Harry and Lew Lazarus, who boxed under the name of Lazar, were two of seven siblings, including two sisters, all of whom boxed. Harry and Lew carved out decent careers in boxing. They lived most of their lives in the Stepney area in the first half of the twentieth century. They had a younger brother named Mark who boxed at a reasonable amateur level as a young lad. Mark kept his birth name of Lazarus and swapped boxing for football. He enjoyed a long career in his chosen profession, appearing over 400 times for several top professional clubs during the late fifties and throughout the sixties. Talking about his Stepney childhood either side of the war, Mark recalls that he noticed very little anti-Semitic sentiment. In fact, he only faced anti-Semitism after he moved out of the area and to the pleasant and middle-class areas of Essex and Hertfordshire.

Contrary to popular perception, in the years leading up to the Second World War there was very little racial tension in the East End. This fact must have been lost on Oswald Mosley. Apart from losing the Battle of Cable Street, he also failed to register much support at the council elections that took place the next year. Of the ten seats that the fascists contested in East London, only the candidate for North East Bethnal Green Ward attracted more than 20 per cent of the vote (23 per cent in fact).

This was the high-water mark of the fascist movement in Britain, and although it morphed into the National Front after the war, extreme right-wing politics never gained a foothold in the area. Unlike in one or two other areas in London, the absence of this influence has been a defining factor in preventing any serious religious or racial strife in the East End ever since.

4

THE CHARGE OF THE LIGHT BRIGADE

What Ted 'Kid' Lewis achieved across all those weight divisions was the stuff of legend. Most boxers rarely box at more than two or three different weights in their lifetime. The Bombardier was a heavyweight, and the Kid did box at the heavier weights, but the cockney kids who were to follow them into the ring mostly made their mark at the lighter weights.

Spitalfields and Stepney's **Philip Hickman** (1902–1976) boxed at featherweight and bantamweight. Only a handful of readers would know the name. I suspect that even if I told you he fought under the name **Johnny Brown**, not many more would be any the wiser. Brown, as we will refer to him, started boxing at the St George's Club in Stepney. So highly rated was he as an amateur that he soon turned professional. No dim and dark backstreet venue for young Johnny; he was fast-tracked to The Ring for his debut. The Ring was a very prestigious arena in Blackfriars. Things did not start that well for Johnny, however, as he lost a close six-round flyweight contest against another debutant, George Dixon, in 1919.

For Dixon, this was about as good as it got. From 1920, their careers diverged. By 1921, aged just nineteen, Brown was boxing in the States and then in Canada in front of big crowds and gaining lots of experience. George, meanwhile, was fighting at such illustrious venues as the Pitfield Street Baths in Hoxton and the Corn Exchange Rooms in Romford.

In November 1923, Johnny Brown returned to London to fight Bugler Harry Lake for the British/Empire and European bantamweight title and won a great twenty-round contest at the National Sporting Club, Covent Garden. Fifteenth months later he fought the very experienced journeyman boxer Harry Corbett in a title defence and won again. The following year he defended his title yet again to win the bantamweight Lonsdale championship belt outright. Brown fought at all four lightest weights during his time, including a win against future world featherweight champion Andre Routis in a non-championship fight in 1925. Brown was an exceptionally determined boxer and bounced back from some real beatings in his later career.

On a balmy evening in August 1928, Brown climbed into the ring at the Clapton (later Leyton) Orient football ground for his eighty-first fight. Almost 50,000 attended. Sitting patiently in the opposite corner was a young fellow cockney and rising star of the East End. This opponent had some of the fastest fists in the business, and Brown would need all his best defensive skills to keep the younger man off him. As soon as the bell sounded, Brown was immediately on the receiving end of several very impressive left/right straight combinations. He was then on the end of a fierce right-hand hook which sent him crashing to the ground. He recovered but was knocked down again later in the round.

Brown managed to get through to the end of the first round for a brief respite, but that was all it was. He was punished severely at the start of the second round, being hit at will. His cornermen had seen enough. In came the white towel. Johnny staggered back to his corner, then back to his dressing room, and then finally into retirement. So it was that one of the first great modern lighter-weight boxers of the East End relinquished his bantamweight crown to another East Ender. It was handed over to an even more capable pair of hands. The man that sent Johnny Brown into retirement was the 'Pride of Poplar', the truly great Teddy Baldock.

Alfred 'Teddy' Baldock (1907–1971) set out on the same road as Johnny Brown and Billy Wells, but he had a natural talent which would serve him well. He was born in Byron Street, Poplar. His grandfather was a bare-knuckle fighter of some repute who worked the boxing booths, and his father and uncle also had some professional experience. It was a big and talented boxing family from which he came. Young Teddy was slight but quite a handful. He excelled at sports, benefiting from superb reactions and great hand-eye coordination. At school he showed promise at both cricket and football, but under the tuition of his father it was boxing that best showcased his talents.

On leaving school, Teddy got a job at an Epsom racing stables as an apprentice jockey due to his size and athleticism. This did not last long, however, as he gave a fellow apprentice a good hiding after a dispute. In order to curb his waywardness, his father decided to get him into the fight game professionally. Young Teddy began to attend his local boxing club, boxing out of the Port of London Authority Club in Custom House. He became an exceptional young boxer and won the club championship. Indeed, he went undefeated as an amateur. By fourteen he had his first professional fight, when he defeated Harry Makepiece, also from Custom House, at Barking in 1921; he picked up seven shillings (35p) for his efforts. Outside of boxing, Teddy would act as a 'bookies runner' for his bookmaker father. He was later to try his own hand at bookmaking, but with dire results.

Teddy's boxing was going from strength to strength, and within a year he had teamed up with Joe Morris, who acted as his trainer and manager. Morris also handled Mike Honeyman, a previous world featherweight champion. Honeyman got on well with young Teddy, training and sparring with him in a loft above a banana-drying shed on Poplar's Dewsbury Street. Honeyman continued to train with Teddy to hone his skills, and taught the younger man great ring-craft. Under Honeyman's guidance, Teddy very quickly made his way up the bantamweight ladder. His rise to the top was spectacular, with some great wins both in Britain and abroad. He barely broke a sweat dispatching his first forty-three opponents.

By the start of 1925, East London had a future champion on their hands. Teddy was fighting regularly and winning every time. He amassed a huge local following. Hundreds followed him to his fights, hiring dozens of charabancs to take the Poplar faithful to the boxing venues he lit up. The *Sporting Life* correspondent and acclaimed boxing referee Eugene Corri, who had overseen more than five hundred professional fights, wrote in August 1925:

> Not in my long experience of boxing has any young pugilist equaled the record of Baldock. Many times, I have refereed the Poplar boy's fights and have never had occasion to caution him, so clean are his methods. This wonderful boy has the advantage of careful and intelligent tuition of his father who watches over his training and behavior with most noticeable affection. He possesses all the requisite qualities that go to the making of an exceptional boxer. For myself, if ever I felt justified in predicting a world's championship for a coming lad, I do so on this occasion.

A week before this report, Corri was ringside to witness Teddy's fight against Frankie Ash of Plymouth. Ash was an extremely good fighter at the peak of his career. The previous year, Ash was defeated on points after fifteen very close rounds in a fight for the world flyweight championship against the excellent American fighter Pancho Villa in New York. Ash was carrying more weight and a lot more experience than Teddy, so the younger man should have had his work cut out. However, he convincingly won on points. More telling was Ash's verdict on Teddy in a conversation with Corri after the fight:

> A Wonderful boy, very, very clever. For the first five rounds I couldn't keep his straight left out of my face. I held my own

inside but he was all over me at a distance. I looked over to him at the end and he showed no sign of punishment or exhaustion.

In the summer of 1926, Teddy went over to America to fight a series of bouts in preparation for a possible title fight. He was lined up against an up-and-coming fighter named Tommy Lorenzo, whom the promoter expected to give Teddy a few problems. In November 1926, Teddy climbed into the ring to face Lorenzo. If the American boxing public was unaware of this Cockney kid before his visit, they would know him now. The *New Yok Times* reported ringside:

> Only Lorenzo's gameness and recuperative powers enabled the New York's East Side lad to survive the six rounds. He was floored twice during the bout, once in the second round and again in the fourth session, under terrific rights to the jaw, and several times was sent staggering around under Baldock's relentless firepower.

Teddy fought twelve matches on American soil in three months and never lost. By 1927, such was his stature that it was impossible to deny him a crack at the world title. The newly formed International Sports Syndicate offered Teddy three fights at the Royal Albert Hall. If he beat the aforementioned Johnny Brown and the German bantamweight Felix Friedmann, the third fight would be a world championship bout. Teddy duly obliged, knocking out both his opponents. For the Johnny Brown fight, both Jimmy Wilde and the Prince of Wales (later Edward VIII) were in the audience and the match was refereed by East London's greatest all-round sportsman, the somewhat ubiquitous 'Johnny' Douglas (see chapter 2). As promised, Teddy then went on to fight the American Archie Bell, ranked #1 in the world, for the vacant world bantamweight title.

The fight took place at the Royal Albert Hall on 5 May 1927. This great venue was packed out with his East London followers.

It was a tremendous fight, with Teddy starting really strongly and well ahead through most of the match, the American coming back strongly in the later rounds. Teddy just about held on to win what he thought was the world championship. That wasn't quite the case, though. Despite the fantastic win, Teddy was not officially recognised as world champion because the fight took place at the Royal Albert Hall and not at the National Sporting Club in Covent Garden. The National Sporting Club was the controlling body at the time, and claimed that a world championship fight should take place at their own arena. The British Boxing Board of Control (BBBC) had not yet been formed.

The NSC was a very autocratic organisation and was often criticised for its approach to title fights. Outside of their sphere of influence Teddy Baldock was universally recognized as the undisputed bantamweight world champion at just nineteen years of age. The following year the NSC was superseded by the BBBC and Teddy was then recognised as the world champion by all concerned.

Several more successful fights followed, but Teddy started to struggle with a damaged hand and was forced to stop boxing for almost half a year. The bantamweight title fell vacant. Meanwhile, another East End boxer, Alf Pattenden, was rising through the ranks. The East End public was desperate for the two to meet. In May 1929, with the newly installed BBBC taking a more liberal approach to boxing venues, the fight that all of East London wanted to see took place at Olympia. The winner would be crowned the undisputed British champion and receive a Lonsdale belt.

It was later described as one of best British bantamweight fights ever. The two men pounded each other round after round, with Teddy scoring with hooks, jabs and uppercuts. Alf fought on courageously, and although he landed some big punches it was his face that was cut and blooded midway through the fight. Alf was granite tough and kept coming back with big scoring punches. Amazingly, the fight went the distance. Teddy Baldock got the decision. The crowd cheered both men to the rafters and Teddy described Alf as boxing's greatest loser. Teddy went on to move up in weight and successfully boxed at both featherweight and lightweight. He was one of very few boxers to hold three British titles at three different weights. It was during this period of his career that he further damaged his troublesome hand, and he also suffered an eye injury.

Teddy took time out of the ring to marry Maisie McCrea in February 1931 and also underwent an operation to have part of a bone removed from his hand. He resumed training for what was to become the final period of his glittering career. In late 1931 he boxed a non-title match against the very classy and experienced 'Panama' Al Brown. It was a brutal match and Teddy came away defeated and with a recurrence of his hand injury.

Teddy boxed on but was in decline. Large East End crowds still flocked to his matches. Because of the huge crowds he drew he was nicknamed 'The Pride of Poplar'. Despite his success and popularity, once he left boxing he fell on hard times. It is estimated that Teddy made a small fortune boxing. His income was revealed during a court case against the promoter Harry Jacobs in 1927. His last fight was against yet another rising East End star, Dick Corbett, in September 1931. He retired the next day. Having no trade to fall back on, Teddy decided to follow in his father's footsteps and tried a bit of bookmaking. Whether it was bad luck or just bad bookmaking, he lost a lot of money.

Teddy struggled to get any meaningful work after this, drifting in and out of employment, and like many before him he found himself queuing at the dock gates. He often lived in run-down lodgings and occasionally he slept on the streets. He was, by pure chance, photographed queuing for work at the Millwall Docks in 1950. He probably would have got work there, because the London docks were at their busiest in the early fifties. After that, though, he drifted into obscurity.

Teddy Baldock died penniless at the age of sixty- four. As he once said, 'Life is like a boxing match. One round you're looking

Teddy Baldock about to knock out Germany's Felix Friedmann to set up a world bantamweight title fight. (© PA Images)

down at your adversary the next you are looking up at him.' Such are the ups and downs of both life and boxing! Thanks to his grandson, he is remembered in a life-size bronze statue near to his birthplace in Poplar.

*

As the much-loved and popular Teddy Baldock approached the end of his career in the ring, he came up against another East End boxer of note. This was **Richard 'Dick' Truman Ford Coleman** (1908–1943) from Bethnal Green.

Although the family name was Coleman, Dick boxed under the ring name Corbett, which his elder brother used when he boxed. There will be more about Richard's remarkable elder sibling later. Encouraged by his brother, Corbett started fighting professionally in 1926. He was young and hungry for success, fighting no fewer than thirty-seven times in his first eighteen months as a professional. Corbett and Baldock fought each other in a non-title fight in September 1931 at the Clapton Greyhound track. Once again, two great East London boxers squared up to each other. The match was made at featherweight.

Dick Corbett was approaching the peak of a decent career and was about to embark on a magnificent series of bouts for the British and Empire bantamweight title against Johnny King from Manchester. King and Corbett fought five times between December 1931 and October 1934, Dick winning two, drawing two and losing one to his great rival. As he said, 'They couldn't put a fag paper between us.'

Between the King fights, Corbett was retained to fight the current world flyweight champion, Jackie Brown, also from Manchester, in a non-title fight. The weigh-in was arranged to take place in the promoter's office basement on the morning of the fight in December 1932. Brown's manager objected to the venue and to the type and positioning of the scales, but the weigh-in went ahead in the presence of a BBBC representative. Corbett stepped onto the scales and his weight was recorded. Brown's manager immediately disputed the reading, claiming that Corbett was shown to be over the weight, and asked for a re-weigh. This was refused, so Brown's manager refused to put his man in the ring that evening. The promoters lodged a complaint. This resulted in the BBBC revoking the manager's licence, and the promoters also sued for loss of earnings. Lengthy court cases took place. No rematch ever took place. Had the fight gone ahead, Corbett may well have had his chance to progress to a world championship fight. Sadly, it was never to be for this very popular boxer.

The fight against the fading Baldock at the Clapton dog track was an altogether more straightforward affair, and Corbett won comfortably on points. Corbett went on to fight almost two hundred bouts, completing almost 2,000 rounds of professional boxing at flyweight, bantamweight and featherweight. For Teddy, on the other hand, this was the last fight of his amazing career.

Corbett was born and bred in Bethnal Green, and lived there all his relatively short life. He was a likeable and generous man. He possessed quick hands and feet, which meant he managed to keep out of trouble in the ring; perhaps this is why he was able to get so many matches under his belt. Although he impressed in his win against Teddy Baldock in 1931 and also in his series of fights against King, by 1935 Corbett had probably reached his peak. He had one more top-ranked British fight, an eliminator bout for the British featherweight title against a good Scot, Johnny McGrory, in 1935. He lost an excellent match on points. He was also matched against a very good boxer named Pat Crowley for the Southern Area featherweight title.

That was about the end of Corbett's achievements, and with war approaching he found himself in matches billed nearer the bottom of the fight-night posters. He boxed fairly regularly but was rapidly becoming a journeyman. He was still fighting about once a month, mostly in eight- or ten-round fights. With the arrival of the Second World War, Corbett enlisted in the army as a gunner in the Royal Artillery. He still managed to box the occasional match.

On Wednesday 3 March 1943, while back home in Bethnal Green on sick leave, Corbett went out for the evening. Just after 8 p.m. the air raid sirens started. The people of Bethnal Green were well used to German air raids, although by 1943 they had eased off somewhat from the height of the Blitz the year previously. Witnesses said that at the same time as the sirens started, loud bangs or explosions could be heard a short distance away. People usually had a reasonable amount of time to take cover, but people in the area started to panic, thinking that the German bombs were about to land on them. Hundreds rushed to take shelter in Bethnal Green Underground station. Dick Corbett's wife, Rose, and their two children, who lived very close by, went quickly to the station and got in safely. Shortly after Corbett's family arrived, an estimated 1,500 people were trying to get to safety down a single dimly lit staircase.

Corbett arrived at the station entrance a few minutes later and joined the crowd rushing to get off the streets and down into the booking hall. A young mother with a baby tripped over. An elderly man then fell over the pair, which resulted in many people falling down the stairs behind them, blocking the way. Panic ensued in the half-light and an enormous crush quickly developed. Regrettably, Corbett found himself in the thick of it and was crushed to death. He apparently went to the aid of another mother and her baby trapped at the bottom of the stairs. In trying to save the two, he was a tragic victim of that night. Some reports state that, miraculously, when they recovered his body the baby was still alive in his arms. The mother who tripped at the beginning of the crush survived, but alas her baby did not.

Corbett's wife and children survived. It was several hours before his wife was informed of his death. Convinced that Corbett had not made it to the station, she asked her brother-in-law to search the streets and check the hospitals to find him, but alas Dick Corbett was one of the 173 people to die in the infamous Bethnal Green tube shelter disaster of 3 March 1943.[1]

The post-mortem revealed that all 173 victims died of asphyxiation, and it later emerged that the loud bangs people heard had come from nearby Victoria Park, where the army was testing rocket launchers and anti-aircraft guns. The air raid warning was in fact a false alarm.

*

Running up to the Second World War, the East End of London began to spread westward. Before 1930, areas like West Ham, Stratford and East Ham were considered parts of Essex. The Victorian slums of the westernmost areas, including the rookeries nearer the City, were gradually being torn down and redeveloped. The Jewish population had gradually prospered there and began to move on. By 1935, Becontree, just to the east of Barking, was developed to house the exodus of 100,000 East Enders from the slums. It became the largest public housing estate in the world.

One of the last great Jewish East End fighters was **Judah Bergman**, known as **Jack Kid Berg** (1909–1991). Berg was born in Romford Street (off Cable Street), Whitechapel, on 8 June

1909, the second son and the fourth of seven children born to Jacob and Annie Bergman. Life for a family of nine was extremely hard in a flat with neither heat nor hot water in the repressed Victorian slums that still existed, and Berg joined the Whitechapel Boys Gang for something to do. He wasn't averse to a bit of pickpocketing; indeed, he was the Artful Dodger of his day. Getting into and out of scraps would serve him well, and his taste for pushing the legal boundaries would prove to be an omen for the future.

This was a time when there was a great deal of money to be made in boxing; it was somewhat akin to football today. As a result, the criminal underworld paid close attention to the boxing world. In his youth, Berg would have come across the notorious East End gangster Jack Spot. A couple of years Berg's junior, Spot was born a few streets away in Myrtle Street, Whitechapel. Berg started to earn a few pennies working at a nearby barbers, and around that time he joined the Judean Boys Club in Cable Street, the same Jewish boxing club where Ted 'Kid' Lewis learned his craft.

Berg progressed well and started boxing professionally in 1923, at the very young age of fourteen. Jack cut a swath through the local boxing landscape. In his first two years in the paid ranks he won thirty-five, drew three and lost three, the losses coming as decisions to vastly more experienced opponents. In his early days he perfected a fairly orthodox style of boxing, but later his style became a swinging two-handed approach. His character, like his boxing style, was flamboyant and he soon adopted the lifestyle to match. The canny veteran fighter Harry Corbett was one who managed to quell Jack's exuberant style, continuously tying him up in clinches and cunningly pinching his biceps while doing so.

The canny Berg then followed his idol Ted 'Kid' Lewis over to America in 1928 to pursue the dollar. He was nineteen years of age. It was literally a 'tour de force' of supreme, almost exhibition boxing. Going unbeaten in eighteen fights, Jack took on the supremely talented Tony Canzoneri and delivered a fantastic performance in securing a split decision over ten rounds.

The general consensus was that Jack had administered one of the worst beatings Canzoneri ever experienced.

Berg's finest hour on British soil came on 18 February 1930 when he stopped the world champion, American Mushy Callahan, in the tenth round at the Royal Albert Hall in London for the light welterweight world title. Callahan fought bravely but Berg's all-action approach overwhelmed the American. *The Ring* magazine reported the final moments of the fight:

... and then Berg shot a left for the face while driving a right for the body. Callahan plunged at once with a double-handed attack for the mid-section and they were at it like a pair of tiger cats. Fists were flying with the utmost rapidity, with Berg speeding up and lashing out almost faster than the eye could follow. Callahan tried an uppercut, but Berg caught this on his forearms and at once hooked a right to the head and shot a left to the mouth. Again, the Englishman speeded up and, swinging or hooking with all the force and speed of which he was capable, drove the American to the ropes. Smashed up against these the American had to lean on his man and was reproved by the referee.

The end came before the start of the eleventh round, as described in *Boxing Magazine*:

The referee was leaning over the ropes with his back to the ring. A towel appeared like a comet in Callahan's corner. There was a gasp of surprise; then cheers and yells that shook the smoke-laden air. Callahan had retired. His once broken nose had been broken again. His left eye was closed. Misery – dazed misery – was reflected on his badly used face.

Soon after the title fight, Jack was back off to America to continue his path to fame and fortune. It was here that he would face perhaps his stiffest challenge in the form of Cuba's Kid Chocolate. Not only was Chocolate considered the finest lightweight then lacing up the gloves, but many had him as the best pound-for-pound boxer around. Coming in with a stellar record of fifty-five victories and one draw, Chocolate was a massive favourite. On 7 August 1930, before a huge crowd at the Polo Grounds in New York, Berg took Chocolate's unbeaten record and sent a seismic wave through the boxing world. The $66,000 purse he received for beating the Cuban set him up for life. He would repeat the victory two years later.

The year 1930 was an incredible one for the East End pugilist. He defeated the top five lightweight contenders, which is an astonishing feat as there was only one world champion at each weight at the time. By the end of the year, after a string of wins in which he defended his title six times, he was probably regarded as the best pound-for-pound boxer in the world. Berg was coming to be seen alongside Jimmy Wilde and Ted 'Kid' Lewis as one of the three greatest European boxers to be seen stateside.

Paradoxically, although Britain retained a strict colour bar on UK boxing, American society adopted a more liberal approach to fight matchmaking. Boxers of Italian, Irish, Chinese and Polish origins as well as black, Jewish and even Native American fighters were all thrown into the mix. Berg was proudly Jewish and displayed the Star of David on his shorts. His childhood friend Jack Spot, the aforementioned Jewish gangster, remarked that Berg wore a small Star of David when in England and a big one when he was in the States.

Berg's success bore fruit outside the ring also. He was invited into high society circles. He met a wealthy young socialite, Miss Eleanor Kraus, and golden summer days were spent in Florida. He went riding to hounds in Vermont and attended wild parties on Long Island. His flamboyant lifestyle appeared to be not too far removed from that of F. Scott Fitzgerald's eponymous Gatsby. He counted Al Jolson, Rudi Vallee, Eddie Cantor and Johnny Weissmuller (Tarzan) among his acquaintances. It's rumoured that during Berg's first stay in America he even made the acquaintance of Mae West, who had a penchant for younger men.

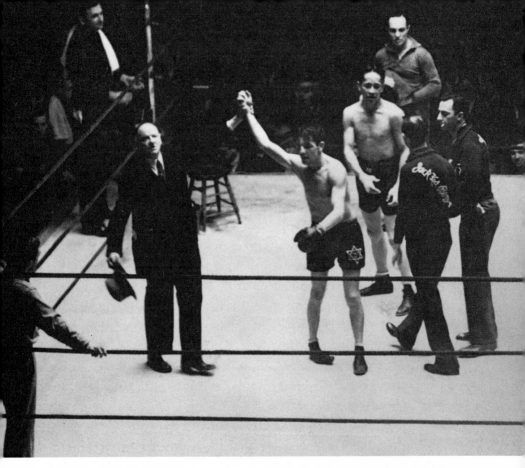

An exhausted Jack 'Kid' Berg gets the verdict over Tony Herrera at Madison Square Gardens in May 1931. Note the large Star of David on Berg's trunks. (© PA Images)

Although details are sketchy, Jack would have met some shady characters in America. It was rumoured that he may have had some involvement on the fringes of Mafia dealings. The notorious Mafia killer Frankie Carbo, who promoted fights for his paymasters, was rumoured to have approached Berg and his trainer about 'fixing' various fights.[2] Berg's trainer and mentor, Ray Arcel, who had taken the young Jack under his wing when he first arrived in America, was a shrewd operator and managed to steer clear of Carbo. Arcel also had to watch Berg carefully as he considered himself 'God's gift to women'.

Arcel recalled a situation that Berg got himself into with the dangerous gangster Jack Diamond. One day, as was his wont, Berg made a pass at a woman. However, this particular female was Jack Diamond's moll. Berg received short shrift from her.[3] Unfortunately, Diamond – known as Legs, either for his prowess on the dancefloor or his ability to evade shootings – got wind of the Englishman's approaches to his girlfriend. Two armed gangsters entered Berg's residence in the Harding Hotel to 'discuss' Jack's foibles and it took incredible mediation on Arcel and Berg's part to placate the henchmen.

In September 1930, Berg was issued a writ by Sophie Levy, another well-connected New Yorker, for breach of promise. Once again, Berg proved as slippery outside the ropes as he did inside them. The young Sophie had to settle for a token amount. Later that year, Berg's engagement to Eleanor Kraus was announced. However, the marriage never happened and by November 1931 the relationship had ended.

In April 1931, after almost a hundred fights with just four losses, Berg fought his old adversary Tony Canzoneri in a defence of his super lightweight title and was surprisingly knocked out in the third round. They had a rematch for the title in September, a much closer affair, but Canzoneri scraped through after fifteen rounds on points. Berg carried on fighting at a very good level for another fourteen years but after the Canzoneri fights he returned to Britain and fought up and down the country for the next two years.

In August 1933 Berg married Bunny Payne, an attractive West End dancer. He was still boxing at a very high level and was now working with Harry Levene, the dominant British boxing promoter in the thirties and a man with the nickname 'King of Fix It'. Berg even managed to star in a couple of films, *Money Talks* and *The Square Ring*. He was still boxing regularly, and Levene set up his 1934 British lightweight title fight with Harry Mizler. In the much-hyped match between two cockney lads, born within a few hundred yards of each other, Berg beat Mizler. Mizler had only lost once in twenty-four fights before this and was a firm favourite. Berg had upset the form book yet again.

Berg had one further lengthy spell in the States between 1938 and 1939 but returned to Britain just after the outbreak of war.

He joined the RAF as a fitness instructor. Here he continued his friendship with the London gangster Jack Spot. Almost as much has been written about Jack Spot as the Krays. He was a nasty piece of work, and Berg did well not to be pulled into his inner circle.

Through a contact in the film industry, Berg managed to get quite a bit of movie work. He appeared in several bit parts in films including Cliff Richard's *Expresso Bongo* and The Beatles' *Hard Day's Night* as well as working on some of the *Carry On* films.

Berg's old adversary **Hyman Barnett 'Harry' Mizler** (1913–1990) was another of the great Jewish boxers born and bred in the area. Mizler was born in an area of Stepney known as St George's and attended the Oxford and St Georges Amateur Boxing Club in Betts Street. Harry had a couple of elder brothers, Moe and Judah Mizler, who also learned to fight there and went on to box at amateur and professional level with some success. Mizler, who was of Polish Jewish extraction, was the only one of his brothers and sisters to be born in England. His mother ran a fish stall and the boys helped out; indeed, for most of his boxing career Mizler used to get up at four o'clock and go with his mother to Billingsgate fish market. He remembers on many occasions wheeling her in the barrow when the weather was bad. Kids in the area remember his mother selling toffee apples through the front window of her house.

The Mizler family were grafters. It was a tough life, but Harry enjoyed his childhood and teenage years and looked back on them fondly. Recalling growing up in Stepney, he remarked that 'growing up Jewish in a Christian country had its advantages. On Saturday, our sabbath, all the shops and markets were open everywhere and then on the Sunday, when everything in Stepney was closed, we would walk a mile or so to Petticoat Lane or Club Row and buy anything we wanted.'

Harry worked hard and played hard. Boxing was his passion and he went on to great things as an amateur in his teenage years. Boxing for the St George's Club, Mizler had the distinction of winning three senior ABA titles in the early

1930s at three different weights. He also boxed for Britain at the 1932 Olympics. Such was his impact at amateur level that he was soon persuaded to turn pro, and in June 1933 he did so under the management of the influential Victor Berliner. He fought his first few professional bouts at the prestigious Ring arena at Blackfriars and won his first ten fights, nine by knockout. Mizler possessed a howitzer of a right hand coupled with a textbook straight left.

Three excellent wins at the end of 1933 and he was offered a shot at the vacant British lightweight title against the excellent Johnny Cuthbert at the Royal Albert Hall in January 1934. The crowd witnessed an excellent fifteen-round scrap which Harry won on points. Mizler defended his title in 1935 before facing his Jewish counterpart and near neighbour, Jack 'Kid' Berg, for a defence of his crown.

Around this time Harry started to experience swelling of his hands after fights and the use of his famed right hand became more

Harry Mizler (right) helping out on his mother's fish stall in Stepney.

circumspect. His match against Berg was tough, but Mizler should have possessed sufficient skill to defeat Berg. However, during the bout Harry managed to break bones in both hands and was forced to retire in the tenth round. Born within a couple a hundred yards or so of each other, Mizler and Berg were two chips off the same block – a granite one! The two met again in 1941. This time the fight was a much closer affair, with Berg shaving it on points over ten rounds.

Harry Mizler boxed on until 1944. He had one more tilt at a British title but lost. But it was two fights in 1935 and 1937 that cemented his reputation as one of the most durable fighters of that era. His fight against the French champion Gustave Humery was possibly one of the great fights of the decade. Humery had held the European crown and was a tough proposition. The Times reported on the contest:

> An absolutely tremendous fight – Mizler floored four times for 9 counts and once for 8 where he was saved by the bell. Battered at least half a dozen times along the ropes Mizler suddenly landed a left-right on Humery's jaw, Mizler still could have lost but he kept his head and with a series of upper-cuts and hooks gave Humery no chance to recover. Humery was iron-barked enough to stay on his feet, but he was now dazed by the rain of blows and blinded by their effects. To all intents he was out on his feet and the only course was the throwing in the towel.

Mizler came through hell to win the match and his hands were the least of his injuries. It took him more than two months to recover. Many people who were present that night witnessed one of the greatest never-say-die performances on British soil.

The other fight was against the tough American Al Roth. Roth had fought for the world championship and was vastly experienced. Punters were aware of Harry's weak hands and all the clever money was on the American. Mizler produced a stunning display of gritty boxing and won a brilliant points decision over ten rounds. Harry's hands held up well; strangely, this was not the case for his opponent, Roth. After the fight it was revealed that the American had broken two bones in his right hand!

Thanks to his brother Judah, Mizler's fight records are exceptionally well documented. Judah accompanied Harry to all his fights and kept a thorough diary of every fight Harry had. His entry for the magnificent Humery fight glows with family pride. Judah wrote:

On a cold October night in London in 1935 Harry set The Royal Albert Hall alight. Harry was up and down about eight times for the first seven rounds. But in the eighth he came out with determination to make a fight of it. He let go with a barrage of one two punches which caught Humery. After that Harry wouldn't let him go because he saw that Humery was out on his feet. Harry kept punching until Humery put his hands up and retired. At the same time as the towel was being thrown in from his corner. Harry had won The Greatest Fight of his career.

It was described as a storybook win.

Harry joined the RAF shortly after the outbreak of war, assisting and performing in many inter-regimental and inter-services boxing events. He rose to the rank of sergeant. After the war he retired from the game and went on to run a fashion shop with his wife.

One other very interesting character born in the early part of the twentieth century was **Stephen 'Johnny' Hicks** (1906–1979). You couldn't really call Johnny a boxer of note. In fact, he only fought about thirty professional bouts in his time and with very mixed results. Johnny was born in the newly built East End Mother's Lying-in-Home on Commercial Road, Stepney. It was an early form of maternity hospital for the poor. The family lived on Bohn Street, Stepney, and Johnny was one of ten children.

Two of Johnny's elder brothers boxed, and he would often watch them sparring against each other in the backyard. Brother Albert was to become a very fine boxer indeed and was an influential figure in the boy's life. When Johnny Hicks was six, his father died. Already exceptionally poor and now with very little income coming into the house, his mother was forced to send him away to a boy's home in Grove Road, Mile End. Johnny hated it but stuck it out for a few years before he eventually ran away. He was rounded up and his mother was called in. With a little more income now coming into the household, he went back home to Bohn Street to live. He was twelve and the war was coming to an end. Shortly after he got home, his mother received the news that his eldest brother had been killed on the front line in France.

A clever lad and an avid reader, Johnny started working odd jobs. Two of his brothers had gotten into the fight game and were doing reasonably well. Johnny followed their progress and that of the other local boxers in the area in the *Sporting Life* newspaper. Watching his brother's fights, he gradually got more interested in boxing and joined his local boxing club at the Stepney Evening Institute where he was trained by Johnny Mann, who was to become one of the great East London trainers. He spent the next year or so learning the craft, but with his keen brain he also tried out the moves he so often saw his brothers make in the ring. He fought around twenty matches as an amateur, losing only three, and according to official boxing records he turned professional around 1927. The records are pretty sketchy and it is possible that he actually boxed for a living earlier than this.

Many of Johnny's matches went unrecorded as in his early career he fought in some very small backstreet venues. According to Johnny himself, his first match was at Manor Hall, Hackney, and ended in a draw. He received seventeen shillings and sixpence (88p) and a badly cut eye for his troubles. He fought a few other unrecorded fights, and he reckons he was nineteen at the time. This means he was actually boxing professionally in 1925. Either way, his overall record as a professional was mixed and even Johnny reckons that he probably lost more fights than he won.

What set Johnny apart from other boxers from the East End were his recollections of both the boxing that took place there and the surrounding social environment. He was fighting during a grim period in Britain. Firstly, there was the General Strike of 1926 followed by the Great Depression of the late twenties and early thirties. His home life reflected this. His elder boxing brother was married with a child, and they lived in the two upstairs rooms at Bohn Street. His mother, two sisters, and his younger brother lived with him in the two downstairs rooms. Johnny's experience was shared by thousands of others in East London in those days. Unemployment was extremely high by the mid-1920s, but with the popularity of boxing in the area hundreds of young men rushed to take up the sport in an effort to make money.

By 1929, Johnny was the main breadwinner in the house and was trying to fight at every opportunity. He was popular in the local area and was much liked by his fellow professionals. He had a series of excellent fights in that year, including a much-advertised bout against the vastly experienced Lew Pinkus, followed the very next day with a match against the up-and-coming Joe Bull. Johnny lost them both. Further losses mounted up, as did his injuries.

Johnny started having problems with his left ear (cauliflower ear) and he started to believe that, in his words, he was 'coming towards the end of my tether'. He was correct. On Whit Monday 1930 he entered the annual open-air featherweight contest at Crystal Palace and fought Harry Brown of Northampton. Johnny talked little about that fight save to mention that he was forced to retire due to an unlucky blow he received to his right eye. His sight did not return after the match had finished, so he visited the Royal Westminster Ophthalmic Clinic the next morning, where they discovered a severe haemorrhage. He was in hospital for six weeks undergoing treatment.

Alas, it was to no avail and he came out of hospital completely blind in his right eye. Minus one eye, he would be unable to box again. Johnny understood the situation. Unable to box and with no trade behind him, Johnny had to do something as the main breadwinner. It was 1930, and there were 2.5 million unemployed in the depressed UK, a little over 20 per cent of the workforce. Unemployment benefit was cut to a pittance. With the help of his brothers and the local boxing fraternity, a couple of benefit boxing shows were arranged to raise some money for him. Johnny had no intention of living off charity, so off he went to the docks to 'stand on the stones' at the dockyard gates.

It was during this time that he witnessed social degradation and the struggles of the working class close up. Articulate and self-educated to a high degree, he was drawn toward their plight. It was when working in the docks that he was exposed to the injustices inflicted on the poorest people in society. Dock labour practices had changed little since the days of the dock's bare-knuckle boxing champion, Tom King. The London docks were huge employers in the first half of the twentieth century and many boxers queued up to gain casual employment there in those days. It was a lottery trying to get work, with fistfights and scuffles breaking out on a daily basis across London's docklands. Being a boxer probably gave you an advantage. Johnny refused to play by these rules. He had a wider vision of it all.

Before today's welfare state was established in the wake of the Second World War, in the broadest terms, if you couldn't turn up for work because you were sick you didn't get paid. There was no free healthcare until the birth of the NHS in 1949. In the docks it could be a 'no win' situation. Don't turn up at the dock gates because you are sick and you go hungry; turn up at the dock gates sick and weak and you get pushed to the back. No work, go hungry. Johnny witnessed all this at first hand. No longer boxing, he was well and truly in the rat race. He penned a poem that sums up the dock gates lottery:

> We could do nought to ease our minds or our tormented souls,
> No sort of labour could we find to keep us off the dole,
> And so with others I had met, I thought that I would go,
> And chance my arm to get some work way down below,
> The Medland Wharf was our first stop, was there we began to grin,
> There was a chance we could cop, cause a boat was coming in,
> But we did not reckon on the score as we got near the scene,
> Standing there were hundreds of men all tensed up and grim and keen.
> Then when the 'ticket man' came to the gates a scramble took place,
> T'was like an all-in wrestling bout but more of a disgrace,
> The ticket man he had no chance, so in his great despair,
> He took one look at the scene, and threw the tickets in the air,
> The struggle really then began, a struggle to survive,
> But me, a disappointed man, got out while still alive.

He could now readily identify with the plight of his fellow cockney workers. He gravitated towards the growing socialist circles in East London. He became a staunch trade unionist and went on several union-organised marches as well as a couple of hunger marches throughout the early thirties. He helped organise local meetings and gatherings to highlight the unemployment situation. In 1936 he helped form the trade union-backed National Union of Boxers. It was during this period that he lost his younger sister to pneumonia in appalling circumstances. This led him to become a firm believer in free universal healthcare. He drifted from one job to another doing mostly manual work. By the outbreak of war, he was working as a fitter's labourer and still living with his mother and his younger brother in Bohn Street.

Socialism, and to a lesser extent communism, had taken a small foothold in the east of London from the turn of the century. Prior to the Russian Revolution of 1917, Leon Trotsky, Lenin and Stalin had visited the area to attend rallies, congresses and conferences at Hoxton and Whitechapel. One congress that was held at a Hoxton church in 1907 formulated plans for the Bolshevik faction, led by Lenin, to lead the fight for change in Russia. Plans were discussed there for the Russian Revolution.

At the outbreak of the Second World War, being a true socialist Johnny tried to enlist to fight Nazi Germany. However, because of his disability he was rejected. Instead he signed up as an air raid precaution warden. During the Blitz his home at Bohn Street was bombed out and he moved into 'digs' in Westminster and was placed on fire-watch duty. He was still working and remained on the fringes of the boxing world. It was during these bleak and blacked-out nights that he developed a talent for poetry. Later in the war, with his younger brother married and his mother moving into a new flat in Stepney, Johnny returned to his roots.

Johnny's mother passed away in 1947, but he remained in the Stepney area for the rest of his life writing volumes of poetry. Initially they were written for his own satisfaction, but gradually they leaked out into the wider world and many of them were published and even performed in public. In 1973, his brother Albert died. Albert was the class act in the family, fighting some of the top boxers of the day including Len Harvey, Harry Mason, 'Kid' Berg and Harry Corbett. Albert had a son who boxed at a very high level as a schoolboy before enjoying a very good career in the RAF.

Stephen 'Johnny' Hicks earned very little from his poetry and not much more from his boxing career. He did, however, earn the respect of his local community and his fellow boxers. Hicks died alone in a single-bedroom tower-block flat in 1979.

The Boxer Speaks by Stephen Hicks
I took up boxing just for sport
and though not very clever
I'm really glad that I was taught
the art of slinging leather.

I was always at my worst
with too many back pedals
And so I started out at first
for cutlery and medals.

So when I learnt to stand my ground
I then began to figure
That I could punch out every round
with all the utmost vigour.

And thus I carried on that way
with very small expense
'til I was brim-full, one might say
of much experience.

The big moment was now at hand
and I was mad to go
To get fixed up at Premierland
as an amateur turned pro.

Needless to say, my luck held out,
for there and other shows
With hard-earned cash from every bout
for punches on the nose.

I've had black eyes and swelled-up ears
and K.O'd. once or twice
But I enjoyed it through the years
a fighter at cut price.

And through it all I say with pride
most boxers are great pals
Because they will stand by your side
if everyone else fails.

Stephen 'Johnny' Hicks, the boxer poet and social commentator. (© Tower Hamlets Arts Project)

5

THE GOLDEN YEARS

Once the dust of the Second World War had settled across the East End, the big clear-up got underway. Throughout the war, the cockney spirit had shone through. Life was still tough, and post-war austerity ensured that for a few years East Enders had to keep their spirits up. Food rationing was still in force. Gradually, things improved. In the 1945 general election, Churchill was rejected and a new, socially minded Labour government came to power. In 1949, Stephen Hicks' dream of universal healthcare would become a reality with the introduction of the NHS.

In 1947, a peacetime conscription system was introduced. Huge numbers of wartime service personnel had been demobbed, so large numbers of able-bodied young men between the ages of eighteen and thirty were drafted into the services to take their place. Each man called up would serve for a minimum of eighteen months. In keeping with the new socialist way of thinking, men from all backgrounds and classes were initially thrown together.

So it was that **Edward Woollard** got his call up in early 1953. Aged eighteen, Eddie had been boxing at the Eton Manor Boxing Club for five years. Like a fair few of the teenage lads that arrived at the army camps that year, he was East End born and bred and had lived through the war. The fitter boys had played football or boxed. Eddie was a cut above and was turning into a good light-heavyweight. You might think that nothing could faze Woollard, a tough and competitive cockney kid, but like most young men at the camp he found it tough to be away from home. Most of the lads were still living with their parents and several had never been out of their mother's sight for long.

Many of the working-class kids in his billet would shed tears of loneliness as they lay in their bunks at night. Woollard admitted that it got to him a bit as well. He recalls consoling some but noticed that one particular lad did not seem to have a problem settling in. In the next bunk to him, a very well-spoken young man had arrived well dressed, groomed and with an air of confidence about him. Eddie, the lad from Hackney, was sleeping next to an Old Harrovian from Hampstead! For the ex-public schoolboy, who spent years away from his parents boarding at Harrow, this place was just a change of scenery. This young man would take it in his stride. He would not be with his working-class brothers-in-arms too long. After a bit of basic training, those of his ilk were singled out for their so-called 'officer qualities' and sent off elsewhere to continue their training.

Eddie continued his boxing with the army. In 1954 he reached the senior ABA championships at Wembley Arena, representing the army, and lost narrowly to Tony Madigan from Fulham. The following year he reached the final once more but was again beaten. Eddie was one of hundreds of boxers who fought for the services during national service.[1] Eddie never made it into the professional ranks but enjoyed an excellent amateur career.

After completing his national service, **Peter Waterman** (1934–1986) competed for the Caius Amateur Boxing Club in the 1952 ABA finals at light-welterweight, which he easily won. After a great amateur career in which he fought a number of excellent international contests, including the 1952 Olympics, Peter turned professional at the end of that year. Peter had been born in Stepney, one of nine children. His father had boxed a little, and one by one so did all the boys in the family. This included Peter's younger brother **Denis Waterman**, known to many as the famous TV actor who starred in *The Sweeney*, *Minder* and *New Tricks*.

The family moved to Clapham soon after the war. Peter went on to win the British welterweight championship in 1956 and the following year gained the European crown by defeating Emilio Marconi in a great fight. Peter Waterman was now at the peak of his powers. He was being tipped for a shot at the world title. In 1958. after successfully defending his British title, Peter was re-matched against Marconi. It was a more attritional match than the first and Marconi gradually gained the upper hand. In the penultimate round, with Marconi ahead on points, Waterman caught Marconi a glancing blow to the left eyebrow and it badly split open. With blood pouring into the Italian's eye, the referee immediately stopped the fight. Waterman thus defended his title. The win was far from convincing, though, and many in the game thought that Peter did not have a big punch in his boxing armoury. He had undoubted world-class boxing skills, but lacked the big knockout punch vital to take on some of the American fighters.

Sadly, Peter's next fight proved a case in point. Pete was matched against the Dartford Destroyer, Dave Charnley. An aggressive fighter, Charnley had just won the British lightweight title. Peter's team got him to shed a few pounds to make the match at lightweight. In theory he should have had enough power at this slightly lower weight to make a big impact, but in this match the reverse proved to be the case. Charnley packed a huge punch, and the term 'punching above his weight' was never truer than on this occasion. Waterman was hit by several very big punches from an early stage and was badly punished in both the fourth and fifth rounds. The devastating shot that thumped into Waterman's head at the end of the fifth round could have been thrown by a big middleweight instead of a lightweight. The referee called a halt to the match and Waterman was led away to the dressing room, where he collapsed and was rushed to hospital. He survived, but there were some signs of brain damage. Peter never fought again.

*

Of all the great East End boxers, the story of the brilliant **Samuel (Sammy) Daniel McCarthy** (1931–) is packed with tremendous boxing feats but has one of the strangest and saddest endings. Sammy was born on Winterton Street in Stepney in November 1931. From an Irish Catholic background, Sammy was one of ten children and by the time he was five his elder brother Freddie was already boxing. His father was also an avid boxing fan. Freddie only boxed as an amateur but won a junior ABA title as well as a Federation of London Boys' Clubs championship. His two younger brothers also boxed a bit. However, it is fair to say that Sammy was the best boxer in the family as he turned out to be one of the most naturally gifted boxers of his generation.

Sammy attended St Mary and St Michael School on Sutton Street in Stepney until the outbreak of war in September 1939. Like many East End children in the area at the time, he was evacuated. Along with three of his sisters, he ended up in Egham in Surrey for the duration of the war. Sammy loved it there but as soon as he returned after VE Day he focused all his attention on boxing. An excellent junior, he entered the senior amateur ranks in 1949, winning eighty-three out of his first ninety fights.

By 1950 his brilliance was being noticed not only by the locals but by boxing observers countywide. Even as an amateur he was attracting large crowds. He boxed at flyweight and featherweight out of the Stepney and St George's Club in Cable Street. He never actually won a junior or senior ABA title but regularly reached the regional finals. He fought on the amateur circuits with four-time ABA featherweight champion Peter Brander, who he regards as the best amateur featherweight he ever saw. He was trained at St George's by Johnny Mann, who himself was an excellent amateur and professional boxer. Sammy looks back on those years with affection and holds Johnny Mann in high esteem as a driving force in his progression through the amateur ranks into professional boxing.

Sammy's younger brother Jackie made pals with Terry Lawless, who was a boxing-mad kid from the area, and Jackie often brought Terry round to the house to talk to Sammy and his brothers about boxing. Terry and Sammy ended up best mates, and as Sammy developed his boxing career he was often accompanied to his matches by the young lad. Lawless never boxed, but that did not stop him carving out a stellar career in the sport; more on Terry later.

After the war, Sammy went to work with his father on the fruit-and-veg barrow in Watney Street market close to his home. Sammy stuck it out through his amateur days, working six days a week. He would be up very early in the morning for the short trip over to Spitalfields to stock up. He worked from very early until late. He admits that it was a struggle for him as he hated the cold and loved his home life. It was therefore an easy step to turn pro, which he did in 1951.

Sammy was signed up by promoters Jarvis Astaire and Ben Schmidt. Sammy worked well with them both. He enjoyed their company and admits that Jarvis helped him quite a bit when he later went into management. By this time he was training at Jack Solomon's gym in Windmill Street, rubbing shoulders with some other great boxers as well as showbiz people and the odd Windmill Girl. Life in 1950s Soho was extremely colourful.

Sammy has always admitted he never found boxing easy, although onlookers could be forgiven for thinking otherwise. He confided in me that he was often petrified before matches but pushed himself to go into the ring. His professional career started sensationally, with twenty-eight straight wins. He knocked out his first opponent, the experienced Hector McCrow, inside a minute. He was just twenty and well on his way. Sammy was quite a shy lad but always went around with a smile on his face. He was nicknamed 'Smiling Sammy' by the press, who featured him regularly.

Sammy had some very hard fights on the way up. The one which sticks in his memory – some of it at least – was a fight at the Mile End Arena against a dangerous opponent, the teak-tough Johnny Molloy from Liverpool. Molloy was a really big puncher, and from the early stages of the match Sammy was being caught by the odd big shot. By the sixth he was bleeding heavily from the nose and left eye. Then, worse still, he got caught by huge right hand from Molloy which sent him crashing. Up on the count of nine, Sammy faced a barrage of two-fisted punches and was forced down again. That was about all that Sammy remembered. According to reports, he dragged himself up and increased his footwork and started using the full space of the ring, throwing out left and right jabs to keep his opponent at bay. Molloy began to tire, and Sammy kept up his boxing until the final bell.

Sammy said later that he remembers hanging over the ropes in the seventh round and then being in the Turkish baths afterwards. He had actually won on points and did not remember the ref raising his arm! He had added grit, determination and durability to his undoubted boxing skills.

Several more tough ten-round bouts followed, including a real blood-and-guts match against the very dangerous Scot Jim Kenny in which Sammy needed all his skill and determination to win a fairly close points decision. Another hard-fought win against Ronnie Clayton would eventually pave the way to a title fight against the same man eighteen months later.

Before his British title fight against Clayton, Sammy was offered a chance at the European title against the Belgian Jean Sneyers at the Harringay Arena in February 1954. Sneyers was vastly more experienced than Sammy and had previously held both the flyweight and bantamweight European titles. Experience told, and although Sammy fought bravely he was outpointed over fifteen rounds of good, clean boxing.

The year 1954 was not all bad for Sammy as he eventually got his chance at the British title and beat Ronnie Clayton to claim the

Sammy, with every reason to smile after taking the British featherweight title. Seen with his friend, mentor and trainer Snowy Buckingham (left). (© PA Images)

British crown in June, the latter retiring with a serious eye injury. Clayton had held the featherweight title for seven years. In 1955, he travelled to Belfast to defend his title. He lost his British title on points in Belfast over fifteen very tough rounds against Billy 'Spider' Kelly and the next year he moved up to fight at lightweight. After a few wins at this new weight, including a brutal and bloody match against Len Johnson, he unfortunately ran up against the aforementioned Dave Charnley in 1956. At this point Charnley was still an up-and-coming lightweight prospect but still came with a reputation as a big hitter. Charnley was to become a thorn in the side for several East End boxers.

The reports on Charnley's power were not exaggerated. Early in the fight, he caught Sammy cold with a right hook flush on the chin. Sammy got up but was obviously struggling. In the third round Charnley hit him with another hugely powerful right hand into the body. Sammy later said, 'I had never felt such pain from a body punch.' He went down again but got up, and, amazingly, began to get back into the match with some crisp and clinical straight punches to the head and body. By the seventh round he had the edge on Charnley. As both fighters tired, the boxing became a close-up affair. Sammy's cornermen were shouting at him to box at distance but Charnley kept it tight and landed the odd blow to earn a narrow points victory. It was one of the great post-war fights.

Sammy in action against Louis Cabo at Earl's Court in 1953. (© Alamy Images)

Sammy McCarthy had one more title shot soon after, but it probably came too quickly for him and he lost to an unpredictable but sometimes durable Joe Lucy. He fought his last fight in January 1957. Sammy had one more appearance in the spotlight when he was presented with 'the big red book' by Eamonn Andrews, being featured on *This Is Your Life* later in 1957. Sammy was the first boxer to be presented with the book, and was the youngest recipient at the time. It was during this TV programme that Sammy announced his retirement. Peter Wilson, the *Daily Mirror*'s boxing correspondent, who was ringside at Sammy's defeat in January when he first concluded that time was running out on Sammy, wrote of him:

> I have never enjoyed this TV programme so much as last night as it was McCarthy's life and during it he announced his retirement from the ring. We may possibly have had a better featherweight champion but never a champion who left behind such a legacy of sportsmanship. In almost six years of professional boxing Sammy set a good example, both in and out the ring for the youngsters who are still to come. Good luck to you Sammy.

Sammy hung up the gloves and looked to pastures new. Married with two children and amply rewarded by the success of his boxing career, Sammy bought a pub, the Prince of Wales (known locally as Kate Odders) on Duckett Street, Stepney.

You might think that Sammy had achieved fulfilment at last, but it was not so. In an interview Sammy gave to me in 2018 he admitted, 'I hated every moment because I like home life and as a publican you are always being called upon. I had a bit of money but unfortunately I spent it all.' Few would predict that within a few years he would be in another kind of fight, this time with the law. He spent the next few years running the pub and doing some boxing management, working alongside Jarvis Astaire for a couple of years, but he struggled with both the pub business and management, saying that the hours made home life difficult.

Then something strange happened. It seems that nobody really knows why; even McCarthy himself is not really sure. For some reason, in a move that was completely out of character, Sammy decided to become a robber. Maybe he was after a greater 'buzz' than running a pub or managing boxers. He obviously rubbed shoulders with a number of dodgy types in both the boxing and pub games, but up until then he had trod a straight and narrow path and people close to him must have been gobsmacked. His great trainer Snowy Buckingham attests to this:

> After 30 year in the fight game there ain't much sentiment left in a man, but when I think about young Sammy I can get a catch in my throat. This London boy was the straightest and most lovable champion of them all. The Smiling kid from Stepney has rightly been called 'every mother's angel' and to me he is a fighter in a million.

In the interview that Sammy gave me in 2018 he said,

> I got talking to some guys who used to come into the pub. They used to have a bit of money on them. One night I asked them what they did for a living and they told me they did the 'Jump up'. Even then I was a bit naive and I had never heard of that sort of job. I asked, what's that? They told me they would follow a lorry until it parked up and then jump up into the back of it and snatch what they could. They said, do you want to come with us on Monday? So, I did. Sounds ridiculous now but when I got back, I was on a high. I have never done any sort of drugs, I've never seen one, but that is what it must have been like. I ain't proud of what I did and I deserved everything I got.

Sammy was in trouble with the law as early as 1963 after being arrested for receiving stolen goods. Three years later, after a few minor convictions, he was arrested again for his part in a restaurant robbery. Sammy was now very much on the police's radar. Finally, he was sentenced to twenty-one months imprisonment in 1968 after he was found guilty of going equipped for burglary and carrying an offensive weapon.

This appeared no deterrent to Sammy, and he gravitated up the criminal ladder and worked with a gang that did banks and

Still Smiling – Sammy McCarthy, Britain's oldest surviving British boxing champion, aged eighty-seven, in 2019. (© Jeffrey Jones, by kind permission of Sammy McCarthy)

payroll delivery robberies. In 1974 he was back in the dock, this time at the Old Bailey, for aiding and abetting the escape of a bank robber. He was jointly accused with his wife, Sylvia, but they were both acquitted. After a couple more heists he finally got nailed for his part in a payroll robbery. He received a six-year jail term. He did his time, but when he got out he was soon up to his old tricks and was arrested for his part in an armed bank robbery. This time he was sent down for fourteen years.

Sammy accepted his fate and knuckled down to do his time. By all accounts Sammy was a model prisoner and was well liked by both cons and screws. Sammy told me that, surprisingly, he was quite comfortable doing a long stretch. However, much to his own regret he had split from his wife by this time and was also separated from his children.

Whether or not he was a sucker for punishment outside the ring I can't say, but Sammy was a much better boxer than bank robber. Nobody who witnessed his journey to boxing stardom could envisage how it ended up for the likeable Sammy. Fortunately, he is now reconciled with his children and lives a quiet and peaceable life in Wanstead, Essex.

*

When West Ham's **Terence 'Terry' George Spinks** turned up in Australia in 1956, the authorities there must have done a double take. The picture in his passport matched, but surely this boy could not be much more than twelve or thirteen years of age. They probably asked where his parents were! This baby-faced assassin was in fact the real deal, and he proved it a couple of weeks later at the 1956 Olympics in Melbourne.

Terry Spinks started young – very young – and had his first amateur boxing match at only nine. A few years later he tried his hand as an apprentice jockey at a Newmarket stable. He boxed as a stable lad and was successful in the annual national stable boys' boxing event in March 1955, receiving a trophy from the great jockey and horse trainer Sir Gordon Richards. Although he showed promise as a jockey, Terry thought he may be a bit better off in the boxing ring. That said, he was no boy prodigy and it took him several years to get near the top of the amateur tree. In April 1956 he defeated Scotland's Paddy Walsh to win the ABA flyweight title, and after 200 amateur bouts he was in the running for a place on the British Olympic boxing team.

Unfortunately, shortly after picking up the flyweight title Terry had a big drop in form, losing five of his next six bouts. He possibly resigned himself to spending the foreseeable future back working as a dustman in and around Royal Docks, near to where he lived in the Canning Town/West Ham area. In fact, Terry would not have made it on the plane to Melbourne had the British Olympic Committee not changed their minds at the last minute about the proportion of English boxers to those from Northern Ireland, Scotland and Wales in the British boxing team. Reg Gutteridge, a noted boxing journalist and commentator, also championed young Terry's cause.

British Amateur boxing was extremely rich in talent at that particular time. With a late injury also hitting the British squad, Terry was rushed out to Australia. He regained his form and reeled off four straight wins and then defeated the Romanian favourite in the final to take home the flyweight gold medal and write his name into East End folklore as the youngest ever British winner of a gold medal. The medal was presented to him by Prince Philip, who was impressed by the youngster. He later arranged for a case of champagne to be sent to Terry's home in Canning Town in preparation for his homecoming party. It is unlikely that Terry's parents had ever seen a bottle of vintage champagne before, let alone tasted any. It was stored beside the stout, brown ale and the bottle of Harvey's Bristol Cream sherry no doubt. Terry's dad was a bookies runner and his mum a charlady, so I don't suppose they developed a taste for it!

Terry Spinks remains the only English boxer to have been schoolboy, ABA, British professional and Olympic champion.

Interestingly, until recently no British Olympic boxing champion had ever gone on to win an outright world professional title.[2]

Terry Spinks and J. W. H. T. Douglas were not the only boxing gold medallists from the East London area. Thirty years earlier Harry Mallins won back-to-back gold medals in the 1920 and 1924 Olympics, and Harry, like JWTH, remained an amateur. Terry Spinks had other ideas, turning pro in late February 1957 around the time that Sammy McCarthy announced his retirement from the ring. Sammy had got to know young Terry in his amateur days, and over the following days and weeks helped Terry prepare for his first professional fight. In fact, Sammy applied for a manager's licence at the end of March and became Terry's manager.

Sammy McCarthy recalls that Terry was an outstanding boxer but could easily be led astray and was always on the lookout for female company. It took all of Sammy's efforts to keep him focused and training properly.

Terry (left) with Sammy McCarthy posing after a training session. (© Alamy Images)

With the experienced Sammy McCarthy and promoter Jarvis Astaire now looking after him, Spinks had his first professional bout in April 1957 against Jim Loughrey at the Harringay Arena, winning on a stoppage for a cut eye. He did enough over the next three years to earn a shot at the British featherweight title against Bobby Neill. In September 1960, Terry beat Bobby Neill at the Royal Albert Hall with a seventh-round stoppage and claimed the featherweight crown.

The rematch with Bobby Neill two months later was a tougher affair that Terry won in the fourteenth round. His form began to dip slightly the following year, and when he faced the great Welsh boxer Howard Winstone in a title defence in May 1961 he was comprehensively out-boxed, retiring in the ninth round. It became clear that Terry was struggling to stay within the featherweight limit. Nonetheless, it came as a surprise to most when he retired relatively early from the game the following year.

Terry spent the next few years just getting by, and at one point he was asked by the Kray Twins to return to the racecourse to ride a horse they had bought. That was a non-starter in terms of his future plans. He did a bit of training work at his old gym, but he gradually drifted into obscurity before he was signed up by the South Korean Olympic Committee to train their boxing team for the 1972 Olympics Games in Munich. Shortly after the games started, he was nearby when members of the infamous Black September terrorist group approached the Israeli athletes' quarters. He saw that they were armed and raised the alarm. Tragically, this did not prevent the subsequent massacre, which resulted in the deaths of eleven of the Israeli team and one German policeman.

After that brief return to the sport, Terry again drifted aimlessly and started to hit the bottle. He lost two marriages and much of his middle age to drink. The lengthy relationship with scotch took its toll; he collapsed and was taken to hospital, where he was told he had only a few days to live. He weighed just 7 stone at the time. A real chirpy cockney, Terry was always humble about his achievements and his slide into near obscurity was sad to see. Fortunately, his fighting spirit saw him through and he recovered.

Terry moved to Romford in Essex and lived with his sister for a while. He started to do some charity work, and after pressure from his family he was awarded a long overdue MBE in 2002, mainly for his later charity work as well as his services to boxing. After his death, a small memorial garden was created near his home in Canning Town.

When Terry came home from the 1956 Melbourne Olympics with a boxing gold, he was one of five British boxers who returned with a medal. It was an outstanding Olympics for the GB boxing team. Terry grabbed a lot of headlines, but the Scot Dick

Terence 'Terry' George Spinks OBE (1938–2012). From dustman to Olympic and British champion. (Royal Albert Hall Archives)

McTaggart also won a gold medal at lightweight. McTaggart was to go on to become Britain's greatest ever amateur boxer.[3]

*

Spinks and McTaggart did not arrive at the Melbourne Olympics as hot favourites for a gold medal; that particular label was stuck firmly to the gloves of **Nicholas 'Nicky' Gargano** (1934-2016).

Nicky was born in West Ham and joined Eton Manor Boys' Club in Hackney around 1948. He was a very talented all-round sportsman and an outstanding schoolboy footballer, playing left wing for London Schoolboys. Although Eton Manor catered for all sports, its boxing set-up was exceptional and produced some outstanding boxers, including the great amateur and Olympic champion Harry Mallins. Nicky's father had boxed a bit in his younger days and encouraged his son to try the sport. He learned his craft as a schoolboy boxer at Eton Manor and became a truly outstanding talent, with lightning-quick hands and exceptional foot speed. Nicky would often go three rounds without feeling an opponent's glove hit any part of his head or body, such was his movement and defence.

When Nicky left school, he started working in the fruit-and-veg trade. At eighteen, he went off to do his national service in the army. He carried on boxing successfully while in the army. By the time the 1956 Olympics came around, Nicky was the three-time British amateur welterweight champion. After losing narrowly to Tommy Molloy in the semi-final of the 1953 ABA finals, he then went on to claim successive titles between 1954 and 1956, the only fighter ever to do so at welterweight. Apart from his British titles, he won gold at the 1954 Vancouver Empire Games (now Commonwealth Games) with some staggering performances. The following year in Berlin, he took the European title, picking up the award for the best boxing stylist of the tournament. This brilliant East End southpaw was rapidly becoming invincible.

When the British team took on a strong US team in late 1955 in the run-up to the Olympics, Nicky was picked to face one of America's rising stars, Walter Sabbath of Detroit. Sabbath had easily won the USA's junior welterweight championships and was tipped for great things at senior level. Nicky completely out-boxed the American, who was reduced to holding on to his opponent for long periods. Nicky therefore set off for Australia as the nailed-on favourite for a gold medal. His first two fights were mere formalities, with comprehensive wins against his Russian and

Argentine opponents. In the semi-finals he went up against the Romanian Nicolae Linca.

Linca was a good fighter and put on a decent performance, but everybody ringside witnessed a winning show from the East Londoner – everybody, that is, except for two of the three judges, who inexplicably called the fight in favour of Linca. To the astonishment of the British contingency, Nicky was out of the final and had to settle for a bronze medal. It was by all accounts an outrageous decision, and the British camp objected vigorously, but to no avail. When he returned home, Nicky found it extremely hard to come to terms with what happened to him on the other side of the world. His faith in boxing had been completely undermined. Both his wife and his mother disliked boxing, and at the end of the year he announced his retirement from the sport.

Nicky is regarded as one of the most skilled British amateurs in the history of boxing. Former BBC commentator Harry Carpenter once said, 'You would never see anyone box like that today because there is no-one around to teach what Nicky knew. He had such skill, such timing and such defence.' Over his career, he had 197 bouts and won 190, reversing five of his losses at a later date. Although he recalls boxing up to five times in one evening as a junior, he was never knocked down or even cut.

Following his retirement, Nicky settled into working at the fruit-and-veg market in Camden Town, the trade in which he had worked throughout his magnificent amateur career. He tried running a pub in the area, and a little later he moved to Guildford and ran a couple of pubs there.

A painting was commissioned by Major Arthur Villiers DSO, an Old Etonian philanthropist who co-founded Eton Manor. The portrait was painted in 1956 following the Melbourne Olympics.

The great Nicky Gargano never turned professional. Several amateur greats did not. In Nicky's case, he found his niche in

Nicky Gargano of Eton Manor Boys' Club. Oil on canvas portrait by William Dring. Nicky Gargano (Eton Manor/British Army), one of Britain's greatest amateur boxers. (© Bonhams 1793 Ltd with the kind permission of the William Dring estate)

the fruit-and-veg trade. Many boxers in the area were gainfully employed in the big food markets in the area. Dozens of top amateur boxers worked as porters and clerks in Smithfield, Spitalfields, Stratford and Billingsgate markets.

*

Another great amateur who worked at Spitalfields Market in the fifties was **Vic Andreetti** (1942–2018). Vic was born in Hoxton, and like so many of our boxers was the son of a talented former amateur and professional fighter. His father, Victor senior, who also worked at Spitalfields, fought almost thirty professional fights and although records are slightly vague Vic reckons his father was only beaten twice.

Vic joined the Lion Boys' Club in Hoxton, winning three ABA schoolboy titles and a junior championship. Unlike Nicky Gargano, Vic was firmly focused on the professional road and duly signed up with Henry Cooper's manager, Jim Wicks. He trained with Henry at the famous Old Kent Road gym/pub The Thomas a Becket. Vic boxed professionally between 1961 and 1970, and he was put into the ring against some exceptional talent during that decade. He acquitted himself well, and after almost seventy tough fights he eventually won the inaugural British super-lightweight title in 1969. Before this he had failed on two occasions to beat the classy Maurice Cullen for the British lightweight title, losing on points both times.

After retirement, Vic and his wife Brenda ran the Spread Eagle pub in Kingsland Road, around the corner from his old fight venue Shoreditch Town Hall. He opened up the Ringside Bar and Diner opposite and also ran the boxing gym above it with his dad. Aside from boxing, Vic managed fledgling bands and musicians, giving a first gig to Kilburn and the High Roads – later known as Ian Dury and the Blockheads – and also supported Spandau Ballet. Vic later emigrated to Florida with his wife Brenda and was employed to help train Florida's police boxing team. He worked with the famous Dundee brothers, Angelo and Chris. While in Florida he trained Nigel Benn to win the WBO middleweight title in 1990 by beating Iran Barkley in Las Vegas in just one round.

Enormously popular, Vic sadly passed away after another long, tough battle. This time his fight was against cancer, which he succumbed to in February 2018.

*

The 1950s were proving to be a great decade for amateur boxing in London's East End. Apart for Terry Spinks and Nicky Gargano, another boxer from the area was also making a name for himself. **Ron Barton** (1933–2018) from West Ham had joined the Royal Air Force just after the war. Already a decent schoolboy boxer, Ron developed his skills in the service and duly won the ABA middleweight championship in 1953, representing the RAF before heading off to represent Great Britain in the European Amateur Boxing Championships in Poland.

The following year he left the RAF and turned professional. He had a sensational start, knocking out his first opponent inside two minutes at Leyton Baths in February. Over the next eighteen months he won another eighteen fights before losing to a useful Italian fighter in the build-up to a British title fight. It was not much of a setback as a rematch was made three months later in which Ron got his revenge. That set up a title fight for the vacant light-heavyweight title against the very experienced Albert Finch of Croydon. Finch had fought at the very top for several years and in his younger days had defeated the great Randolph Turpin, as well as his brother Dick. Finch had also fought Don Cockell for the European light-heavyweight title in 1951 and was a previous holder of the British middleweight title.

The match took place in March 1956 at the Harringay Arena. Although nearly tripping up and falling through the ropes in an early round, Barton boxed very well and soon had Finch in trouble when a nasty cut above Finch's left eye seriously restricted the Croydon man. Despite great efforts from Finch's corner, the ref stopped the fight in the eighth round to leave the East Ender as British champion.

Barton was being tipped for even bigger things and was quickly matched against the Canadian champion for the British Commonwealth (Empire) title a few months later. Barton was a big odds-on favourite for that fight, but in one of boxing's bigger upsets the Canadian won on points over fifteen dour rounds. It was a big shock for Ron and his team, and he decided to take break from the game to plan his next move. Still only twenty-four, Ron obviously thought he had plenty of time on his side. His British title fell vacant, and it was during this time that he was involved in a very serious car crash in which one person was killed and five others, including Ron, were very badly injured. Ron spent several months recovering but eventually got himself back into the ring in January 1959.

His comeback started well, and he won his first four fights, but the old 'snap' was not quite there and when he started to fight better opponents in the following year he struggled badly and began to lose. When he was knocked out by the Bristol fighter Stan Cullis in March 1961, Ron called time on his career. He went on to work at Smithfield Market, remaining there until his retirement at the age of sixty-three. He passed away in 2018, aged eighty-five.

*

Joe Lucy (1930–1991) was born in Mile End. In comparison to others, Joe Lucy had a short but reasonably successful career. He made his professional debut in May 1950. He was managed by Jim Wicks, who also went on to manage Henry Cooper. Lucy won fifteen of his first sixteen fights. In January 1953 he won the Southern Area title, beating Tommy McGovern in what was also a final eliminator for the British title. He was due to meet Frank Johnson in June 1953 for the latter's British title, but Johnson failed to make the weight. The fight went ahead, with Lucy winning on points, and Johnson was stripped of the title. In September, Lucy faced McGovern again for the now vacant British title. Lucy won on points to become champion.

In early 1956, after a failed attempt to win the British and Empire title against the South African Johnny Van Rensburg in Johannesburg, Lucy's focus returned to the domestic title. After knocking out Gordon Goodman in a final eliminator in February, Lucy challenged for Johnson's British title in April. Lucy avenged an earlier defeat, stopping Johnson in the eighth round to regain the title. He made a successful defence two months later, stopping Sammy McCarthy in the thirteenth round. He lost his title to Dave

Charnley on points in April 1957 and subsequently retired from boxing. He went on to run the Ruskin Arms Hotel in East Ham, where he promoted rock concerts. Some of the top bands from the last three decades of the twentieth century played there.

*

Throughout the late twenties and thirties, the living conditions in the East End had gradually improved. However, it was still a very hard place to live and work, and things were about to take a turn for the worse. Not content with the heavyweight 'slugfest' that was the First World War, in September 1939 Germany and Britain fought a rematch. The first fight took place across the Channel; this time the East End would be one of the venues.

There were still many early Victorian terraces and tenements standing in the heart of the East End, but within a few months of war breaking out the German Luftwaffe decided to lend a hand by doing a bit of slum clearance. For the next five years or so, East Enders would be in the firing line.

Conscription into the forces began at the outbreak of hostilities, and a patriotic Mr William Walker from Stepney joined up with the RAF. It was just as well, then, that Mrs Ellen Walker had just given birth to her third son. The bombs soon started to fall. The Walkers evacuated to the Bedfordshire countryside, and all thoughts of extending the Walker Family were put on hold. Mrs Walker's newborn was **William (Billy) Walker** (1939–), and he and his siblings could sleep easy in their beds at night, safely ensconced in the countryside.

Once the German opposition had been knocked out, the family moved back to London and then moved to Ilford on the London/ Essex border. Young Billy left school at sixteen and started working in the printing business, but later his brother George got him a more highly paid job as a porter at London's Billingsgate Fish Market. He also got a job as a bouncer and then as a part-time DJ at his local dancehall, the Ilford Palais. The later disgraced TV personality Jimmy Saville was Billy's boss there at the time. Billy's elder siblings all boxed a bit, and his eldest brother, George, was a very promising young boxer. More about George later.

Billy joined West Ham Boxing Club to keep fit and was eventually persuaded to spar with other members, whereupon he found that he had the talent to box competitively. He had thirty-nine pretty uneventful bouts of amateur boxing until he joined the British team that took on a strong American amateur team in 1960. The bouts were televised that evening at peak time, and Billy defeated the giant American heavyweight hope Cornelius Perry by knocking him out cold in the first round. With his blonde hair and good looks, the press dubbed Billy 'Golden Boy'.

In early 1962, Billy decided to turn professional. He applied for a pro licence and his brother George applied for a manager's licence. This great sibling partnership thus started out on the road to fame and fortune. After a few eye-catching early performances, including two great fights against Birmingham lad Johnny Prescott, Billy was generally being referred to as the successor to Henry Cooper's heavyweight crown.

In 1964, Billy was the subject of a very good BBC documentary called *The World of Billy Walker*. It gave an excellent insight into the fight game as well as Billy and his brother's business activities outside the ring. It shows clips of Walker's fights and covers his only trip to the States, when he spent some time training in the gyms there.

More fights followed, and Billy was drawing big crowds and even bigger TV audiences. A couple of his matches attracted huge viewing figures of about 20 million each. Brother George was selling the 'Brand Walker' to an ever-increasing market. In an interview Billy gave in 1968, he admitted that boxing was a means to an end in order to invest in his business activities. With the entrepreneurial skills of his brother and the publicity the 'Golden Boy' had built, the two started to spend more time on business ventures. Billy could often be seen making cameo appearances on TV, and even released a record. The brothers opened a string of clubs. One, the Upper Cut Club in Forest Gate, hosted some big-name groups and solo artists of the day. It is widely reported that Jimi Hendrix wrote one of rock music's greatest anthems, 'Purple Haze', in his changing room there while waiting to go on stage.

In 1967, Billy fought Germany's Karl Mildenberger for the European heavyweight title. The southpaw Mildenberger proved to be too much for Walker and the German retained his crown via an eighth-round stoppage. Billy's next battle, however, was the one the Great British public had been waiting for. This would be for Henry Cooper's British and Commonwealth heavyweight titles.

Billy was five years younger than Cooper. When they met for their title fight, Billy was in good shape and felt confident. He had a game plan to avoid Henry's famed left hook, 'Henry's hammer', and was sure he would outlast his older opponent and catch him later on. Cooper had a reputation for getting badly cut around the eyes because of the amount of scar tissue he had acquired around his eyes over years of fighting. Walker started well but Cooper, possibly the greatest British heavyweight never to win a world title, managed to get through with a vicious left hook that badly cut Walker's eye and the referee stopped the fight in the sixth round. As Cooper said to young Billy as he sat defeated in his corner: 'Well, that makes a change Bill, I'm normally the one who gets badly cut when winning!'

Billy was spending more and more time in the West End's swinging sixties circles, and the Walker business empire was steadily growing. In 1968, Billy rekindled the hopes of his fans as he clubbed his way to a TKO victory over the once highly regarded American Thad Spencer. However, his boxing career took a back seat. The fight against Spencer would be his last win. He had a couple of heavy losses and had a tendency to bleed heavily from the nose when struck. He obviously had one eye on his good looks and future business deals. In March 1969, Billy suffered a loss in the eighth round to Jack Bodell at Wembley. It would prove to be his last fight.

In 1969, at the age of thirty and after just thirty-one fights, Billy Walker retired from boxing. Thanks to his elder brother he made a tremendous amount of money both inside and outside the ring. Billy held shares in his brother's two garages and a mini-cab firm, and in later years added more clubs and restaurants to his growing business enterprises He appeared in a couple of Frankie Howard comedy films and also had a small cameo appearance in *The Stud*, starring Joan Collins.

As far as Billy's boxing career goes, I think it would be fair to say it was a triumph of style over substance. Nevertheless, Billy Walker

Above and opposite: Boxer and businessman William 'Billy' Walker (1939–). He managed to dodge the German Luftwaffe's bombs, but not always his opponent's fists. (© E.7 Now & Then)

was a big East End name in the swinging sixties and another great cockney character. He retired in comfort, living in the Channel Islands for a while, but now lives back in Essex.

*

If Billy Walker's career was fairly short and somewhat chequered, then that of **John H. Stracey** (1950–) certainly was not. However, you might have forgiven young John for not believing a stellar career lay ahead of him at the end of his first amateur boxing final; both he and it went seriously south that evening. In the ABA lightweight final of 1968, Scotland's outstanding southpaw Jim Watt poleaxed John in the first minute of the first round with a thunderous left to the jaw. Some amateurs are never quite the same again after a reverse of that nature. Very few go on to win professional championships.

Bethnal Green's John H. Stracey was born with East End grit and a will to win. Seven years after his defeat to Watt, in the cauldron of Mexico City, he survived a first-round knockdown to get up and defeat world welterweight champion Jose Napoles to become the new welterweight champion of the world.

Stracey had a steady rather than spectacular amateur campaign, but he was picked for the 1968 Olympic team as an eighteen-year-old. Although he was one of the youngest boxers ever to fight at the Olympics, he boxed extremely well. He actually came very close to beating the eventual gold medallist, Ronnie Harris. After more than a hundred bouts, Stracey turned pro in 1969 and started his road to the top by reeling off sixteen consecutive and comfortable wins. Although he did lose the odd bout, he climbed steadily through the ranks to fight for the British welterweight title in 1973. His fight against Bobby Arthur was all over inside four rounds when a stunning right cross caught an advancing Arthur flush on the chin. Ten seconds later, with Arthur still on his knees, the title was Stracey's. He then went on to take the European title in Paris in May 1974, comfortably beating the excellent Frenchman Roger

Menetrey, who had held the title for three years. Stracey later retained the title against the Swiss Max Hebeisen.

There were an awful lot of very good welterweight boxers around in the early and mid-seventies, but Stracey was reaching the peak of his powers. He had some tremendous matches, including a battle royale against the American Ernie Lopez. Lopez had the nickname of 'Indian Red', and by the seventh round Ernie was living up to the latter half of the name, bleeding profusely from several cuts to his face. The referee stopped the fight.

There is no doubt that John H. Stracey's career reached its climax with the world title fight against the excellent Jose Napoles in December 1975. Staged in a Mexican Bull Ring, the atmosphere was electric. Napoles was a legend and the Mexicans loved him. He had lost only six of his eighty-one fights up until that point and he got off to a flying start against the East End lad. He knocked John down in the first round. Stracey got up in front of the 40,000 Mexican fans that were now baying for this cocky cockney's blood and managed to see out the round. He then started to take control from the third round onward and managed to get Napoles on the canvas. He then gradually dismantled Napoles' defence and gave him a steady beating for the next few rounds, forcing a stoppage in round six with the Cuban-Mexican's eye completely closed. Cut, bruised and battered, Napoles was led off into retirement. One of boxing's biggest upsets left Stracey on top of the world as the new golden boy of British boxing.

Offers poured in and Stracey was soon fighting again. He considers his next fight to have been the toughest of his career. The never-say-die American Hedgeman Lewis took the fight to Stracey for ten rounds, but Stracey was now supremely fit and confident and out-boxed Lewis before earning a technical knockout to retain the title. It was to be Lewis's last fight. John, on the other hand, was still boxing well when he was offered a fight against an American-based Mexican challenger, Carlos Palomino.

Unlike Lewis, who was on the way down, Palomino was very much on the way up. The match was made only three months after the tough Lewis fight, and Palomino was a very, very dangerous opponent with only one loss coming into the match.

The fight took place at the Empire Pool, Wembley, on 22 June 1976. Stracey started well and was ahead after six rounds, but began to wilt under the sustained body attacks Palomino launched throughout a pulsating match. Referee Sid Nathan eventually stopped the fight. Stracey was bitterly disappointed and may well have underestimated Palomino.

Stracey had previously bought a hotel in Bournemouth and decided to spend more time away from the ring, running the business with his wife, Michelle. In fact, following his great win in Mexico in December 1975, John had only fought three

John H. Stracey retaining his world title against Hedgeman. (© Alamy Images)

times between then and March 1977. The pressure was on for him to fight again, and an up-and-coming boxer was lined up for him.

The challenger's name was Dave 'Boy' Green. John was probably ring rusty, and in hindsight Green was probably not the type of fighter he should have tackled at that stage. Green was an all-out aggressive fighter with twenty-three straight wins behind him. From an early stage, Stracey knew he was in a fight. He drew on all his grit and guile to hold off the Green onslaught but ran out of steam in the final rounds of the match, and referee Harry Gibbs stopped the fight in the last round when the older man got a badly cut eyebrow. It was a thrilling fight, but the writing was on the wall for Stracey.

Stracey again took time off to lick his wounds – over a year in fact. He had one further fight in May 1978. Although he flirted with a comeback, giving an interview with the *Mirror* in 1979 in which he claimed to be going to fight stateside, nothing materialised and he called time on his great career.

Looking back on the Napoles fight in later years, Stracey revealed how he had felt let down by the British press at the time. He knew he had a chance against Napoles but felt that the press had given up on him. In an interview he gave to the *Telegraph*'s boxing correspondent, Gareth A. Davies, he lamented:

I got snubbed by the press. I remember a few of the papers weren't going because the editors had said it was a waste of time. That rankled with me. Napoles had been World Boxing Council champion for four years. There were only the WBC and World Boxing Association belts then. It made the victory all the more great.

Since his retirement, Stracey has carved out a decent living as an after-dinner speaker and cabaret singer. For a once rough and tough fighter, the man has a surprisingly good singing voice and is still active today.

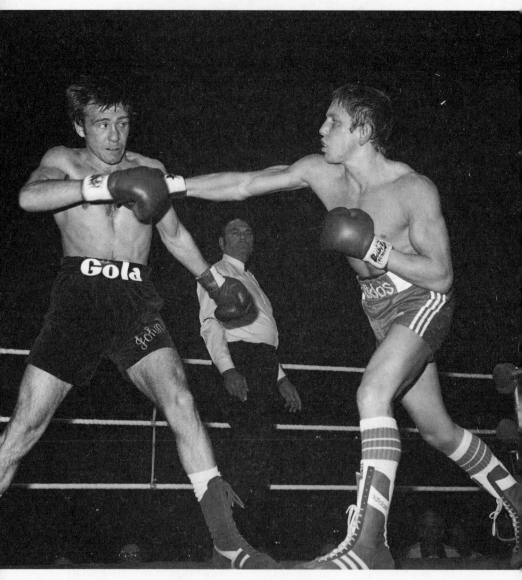

The tough and gritty Stracey just falling short in his match against the precocious Dave 'Boy' Green (Harry Gibbs officiating). (© PA Images)

The Prospect of Whitby. What better way to while away a few hours than by sinking a couple of pints and watching a bare-knuckle fight on a pleasant summer's evening by the Thames. (© Jeffrey Jones)

The Town of Ramsgate. The passageway seen to the right leads onto the historic Wapping Old Steps. (© Jeffrey Jones)

Above left: Joe Anderson being presented with his belt. (Courtesy of the Anderson family)

Above right: Spitalfields Rookery, birthplace of Joe Anderson. Tommy Orange was born close by, in the Old Nichols Rookery. Conditions there were appalling, with a 35 per cent infant mortality rate in the first three years of life. Luckily, Tommy Orange survived.

Above left: A small man with a big reputation – West Ham's Pedlar Palmer on Brighton seafront. (Whipp family)

Above right: The invincible Jimmy Wilde, nemesis of many East End boxers. (Wikicommons)

Bombardier Billy Wells – the 'Gong Man'. (© PA Images)

Another great lighter-weight boxer from the East End, Poplar's Teddy Baldock.
(© PA Images)

Ted 'Kid' Lewis with Charlie Chaplin. (© PA Images)

Playboy boxer Jack 'Kid' Berg. (© PA Images)

Battle of Cable Street.
The East End making a
statement.

The Graffiti generation
committing the
battle to posterity.
(Wikicommons)

Above left: Another great Jewish champion, Al Phillips. (Wikicommons)

Above right: Dick Corbett (Coleman) died in the Bethnal Green Tube station
shelter disaster in 1943. His name appears here on the memorial at the Tube
station with those of 171 others who died that night. (© Jeffrey Jones)

The London Blitz mainly targeted the London Docks. The first bombing raid took place during the evening and night of 7/8 September 1940.

Here, Winston Churchill is seen surveying the destruction in Stepney the following day. Thirty-six hours later the Luftwaffe dropped a bomb half a mile away on a school and almost six hundred died in a shelter there including another young East End boxer.

Right: George Walker: from Billingsgate Fish Market to the Stock Market. (© PA Images)

Below: London Stock Exchange staff training rather than trading on the floor of the Stock Exchange about 1958. (© Alamy Images)

Exterior of the world-famous Repton Boxing Club. (© Jeffrey Jones)

A look inside Repton Boxing Club, showing the famous slogan. (© Jeffrey Jones)

Original site of West Ham Boxing Club. Situated in the buiding to the left of the Black Lion pub. (© Jeffrey Jones)

The visit of the Prince of Wales (centre right) accompanied by the Duke of Kent (centre left) to the West Ham Club in 1931 with Mayor Alderman Sculley (far right). Also attending that evening was Sir Malcolm Campbell. (© West Ham Boxing Club)

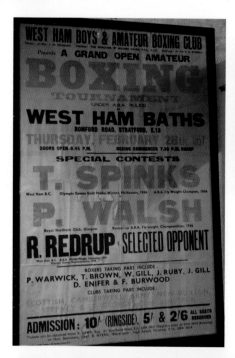

Above: Kevin Lear's WBU world title belt at the West Ham Boxing Club. (Courtesy of West Ham Boxing Club)

Left: A club poster from early 1957 advertising Terry Spinks's last amateur bout of boxing. (Courtesy of West Ham Boxing Club)

Outdoor sparring session at the 'Wilderness', Eton Manor. (© Bishopsgate Institute)

The war effort. Eton Manor's tuck wagon aiding the bomb damage clearup at Hackney Wick. (© Bishopsgate Institute)

The huge Tate & Lyle refinery. (Wikicommons)

Harris Lebus
furniture
company.

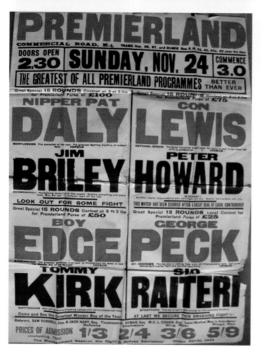

Top: The renowned York Hall, Old Ford (Bethnal Green).

Above right: Inside York Hall for a match. (© Jeffrey Jones)

Above left: Boxing at the Wonderland *circa* 1903. (Wikicommons)

Left: A Premierland poster from 1929. (Wikicommons)

Then and Now

The Changing Face of the East End

Above and below: Spitalfields Market.

Above and below: Billingsgate Market. (© PA Images)

Above and below: The Royal Docks of London. (Wikicommons)

Above and below: Temple Mills railway marshalling yards giving way to the London Olympic Park Complex. (Wikicommons)

6

CHANGING TIMES

By the end of the 1960s, life in East London was becoming reasonably comfortable. There was an air of relative affluence about the place. The dark days of the Blitz and the post-war austerity were swept away by the so-called Swinging Sixties. Employment was high and people had more leisure time. For many, sport would fill the idle hours. Thanks to the eye-catching exploits of West Ham's holy trinity of Moore, Hurst and Peters in 1966, East London was the place to be.

On the other side of the Atlantic, the marketing of boxing was changing, becoming showbusiness as well as big business. Throughout the seventies and early eighties – America's golden age of boxing – several world-class boxers were making global headlines. The line-up of their superstars was astonishing. Muhammad Ali, Joe Frazier, George Foreman, Sugar Ray Leonard, Thomas Hearns, Marvin Hagler, Iran Barkley and Carlos Monzon were all top fighters, and the American promoters made the most of them. This was the birth of the huge gala promotions in Vegas, New York, Miami and Atlantic City, driven forward by larger-than-life promoter Don King.

Britain had to respond. A new breed of managers and promoters started to change boxing in the country, focusing more on the media. The many smaller, more intimate venues prevalent in the first half of the century started to disappear. By the end of the seventies, most boxing venues were large arenas.

The public's taste in boxing began to change, too. It was quality they wanted, not quantity. A new raft of boxers was to emerge to meet the demand. Chris Eubank, Nigel Benn, Lloyd Honeyghan, Jim Watt, Frank Bruno, John Conte and Barry McGuigan were some of the names who played their part in the 'Let's get ready to rumble' era. The East side of London was still producing great boxers, and the grit and determination that had been etched into local boxing was still there to be seen.

*

Possibly one of the toughest boxers to come out of the area after the war was light-middleweight/super-welterweight **James 'Jimmy' Batten** (1955–). Batten was born in Bow on 7 November 1955, and grew up with his parents in his grandparents' Millwall home, one of seven in the house. It was a tough area. Jimmy's dad did a short stint in prison, and his uncle Ronald Bender was sent down for twenty years in 1969 for his part in the infamous fatal attack on Jack 'the Hat' McVitie by the Krays (he disposed of the body).

Although it was a tough neighbourhood and the long arm of the law reached out to grab a couple of his family, Jimmy enjoyed a happy childhood. Growing up in the fifties and early sixties, Jimmy spent many happy hours playing on the bombsites that peppered the whole of the docks area. If nothing else, the Blitz left some great play areas for the cockney kids. Hours spent kicking a football gained him some skills. A little later he was scrapping with local gangs. They used the bombsites as meeting points for 'bundles'. So, Jimmy learnt to handle himself. He certainly had grit and determination. As he says, 'You win fights and you lose fights but you never back down.' It was an ethos that stayed with him all his life. Jimmy was a very good athlete, playing football for Millwall juniors.

Boxing was Jimmy's real passion, and he begged his dad to let him join a boxing club. At first Jimmy joined the Poplar and District Boxing Club, but a few years later he moved over to the West Ham Boys' Boxing Club. His brother Tony also boxed to a high standard, winning a junior ABA title when he was fifteen. Tony gave up the sport soon after, but Jimmy was intent on carving out a career in boxing. After going almost six years unbeaten as an amateur and winning two junior ABA titles in 1971 and 1972, Jimmy turned professional in 1974. He teamed up with the Terry Lawless training camp at the Royal Oak gym in Canning Town and worked his way up the British ranks under the watchful eye of Lawless.

In 1977, after Maurice Hope – another Lawless protégé – vacated the British super-welterweight title, Batten was matched with Albert Hillman. Batten stopped Hillman in the seventh round to win the vacant title. He was just twenty-one years of age, and the future looked bright. He would defend the title twice, with big victories over Larry Paul and Tony Poole, both of whom were tough opposition. Poole in particular was very close to pulling off the win. After a slow start, he suddenly burst into life and put in some big body blows, hitting Jimmy with a savage left hook to put the champion down at the end of the seventh round. The bell saved Jimmy. He recovered and boxed very cleverly, overpowering Poole until the challenger retired at the end of the thirteenth. With that, Jimmy gained the Lonsdale belt outright.

In 1979, Jimmy lost his British title to Pat Thomas in a really tough fight that went ten brutal rounds. There was some talk of retirement, and I think Terry Lawless pressed the point. Nevertheless, Jimmy remained active and competitive. He was still boxing when, in 1982, he decided to make a living in America. He upped sticks and with his wife and children set up camp in Chicago, working in the construction trade while training.

After a fourth-round win in his American debut, Jimmy went to Atlantic City to fight the dangerous, hard-hitting but erratic Mario Maldonado. Jimmy surprisingly got caught cold in the first round and went down. He was dazed but was getting up on the eight count when the referee, looking into Jimmy's eyes, asked him where he was fighting. Jimmy, not being in the country that long, answered, 'Chicago!' Big mistake. The ref stopped the fight.

Jimmy and his team put the setback behind them. They worked hard on getting Jimmy back on track, and he won his next match against Jeff Madison in Chicago. They were now in the running for a match against the famous Roberto Duran. Duran was on the comeback trail after losing his crown to Wilfred Benitez, but at the last minute another British boxer, Kirkland Laing, got the fight. In one of the great upsets in boxing history, Laing beat Duran to put the Panamanian's comeback on hold. Nonetheless, Duran was supremely durable and still very ambitious.

Today Duran is regarded as one of the greatest boxers of the modern era, and he still had plenty to offer at that point. The promoters still had faith in Jimmy, too, so later that year he was matched against the legendary Panamanian in what was supposed to be another straightforward warm up match for the great man. All the clever money was on a Duran win inside five rounds.

Jimmy most certainly had other ideas, and although he was out-boxed in many rounds, in terms of big shots he was giving as much as he was getting. The fight went the full ten rounds, and Duran narrowly won on points. Press and other observers ringside thought it was a generous decision, and many thought a draw should have been called. Jimmy sustained three broken ribs but came away with his head held high. It was a big wakeup call for Duran, who was forced to hold yet another warm-up fight before going after Davey Moore to regain his world title.

Jimmy finished with boxing in 1983 after forty-nine fights, but he kept himself busy. Like a few ex-boxers, he got the odd part as an actor and starred in a short film called *Sixteen Straight*, also doing some TV work. He went on to make reasonable money on the stand-up comedy circuit and also did a bit of singing. He qualified as a masseur and worked with boxers in the gym, and is still around the game today. A few years ago he wrote an autobiography, *The Life and Loves of Lucky Jim.*

*

I don't know how best to describe **Terry Marsh** (1958–). He was undoubtedly a very good boxer; he is also a very interesting if slightly complex character. He was commonly known as the 'Basildon Fireman'[1] although he was born in Stepney.

How good was Marsh? Well, he won the IBF version of the world super-lightweight title in 1987 and defended it once before retiring. His record is exceptional, with twenty-seven wins, one draw and no losses. In fact, in the history of British professional boxing, Joe Calzaghe is the only fighter ever to retire with a 100 per cent record and until recently was the only European boxer so to do.

Given those stats, you would think Marsh would be considered one of the all-time great British boxers; but somehow, he just wasn't regarded in that light. This may be a bit harsh on the man from Stepney. The old sporting maxim 'You can only beat what's put in front of you' certainly applied to Terry. He dealt with all his opponents in clinical fashion, but when you look at those wins and who they were against it may be said that not all of his opposition was of the highest calibre.

Terry Marsh learned to box at the St George's Club near his home in Stepney. He had a mixed junior and senior record for his club. Terry was a clever lad and attended Westminster School, where he became a junior chess champion. He later moved to Basildon. Any move into professional boxing was put on hold when he joined the Royal Marines and he saw active service in Northern Ireland as part of 41 Commando. His boxing dramatically improved as an amateur during his time in the Marines, and the fitness and endurance he developed helped him go on to win three senior national titles while representing the Royal Navy.

On leaving the Navy, Marsh joined the Essex Fire and Rescue Service and was stationed at Tilbury fire station. Now, he was able to turn professional. Firemen have always moonlighted, but not many had a job on the side winning professional boxing titles! He had his first professional fight in October 1981. Six months later, he fought Lloyd Christie to a very close draw. He went on to reach the top of the British rankings when he defeated Clinton McKenzie for the British super-lightweight crown in 1984. The European title followed a year later, and in 1986 Marsh completed the full set with an exceptional win over the American Joe Manley to claim the world title.

In 1987, Marsh was planning to head over to America to box when he suffered a badly cut eye in a non-title fight against a little-known Japanese boxer. This put things on hold for a few months, and a little later he was diagnosed with mild epilepsy, thus ending his boxing career. It also meant the end of his time in the fire service.

Looking back over his boxing career, Marsh maintains his approach to all matches was the same. In an interview he gave me he said,

> I had this competitiveness where I'm not aspiring to win, I'm aspiring not to lose. They are different sides of the same coin in many ways, but at the same time it is different in the sense that I never had the killer instinct the way other fighters have. People say that I went unbeaten but I have always preferred to say I went undefeated.

In an earlier interview he said,

> You must know yourself. You must recognize your weaknesses and in boxing too few fighters do this, but if you don't recognize your weaknesses you are exposed even more. If you recognize that then you can make an allowance for it, this is how I see boxing. I'm not sure if it is 90% mental, but the

defining moment is the mental side of things. I think for me (in my fights), I had the edge mentally. I knew what I was capable of and what I wasn't capable of. No one talks about it in boxing as far as I'm aware, but you have to recognize your weaknesses and thrive through them.

The one thing which tended to run through his matches was his ability to study and outsmart his opponents. He had a keen brain and he used it. His approach to boxing goes some way to explaining how, in well over two hundred bouts of amateur and professional boxing, he failed to knock out any opponent.

After Marsh retired, things got slightly strange. In 1989, he had a falling out with boxing promoter Frank Warren. He was hit by a writ for libel. In November, while leaving a boxing match, Warren was approached by a masked gunman and shot in the chest. Warren survived, and was somehow convinced it was Marsh who shot him. Marsh could not provide a strong alibi and the police arrested him. He spent ten months on remand, but when the case came to court he was acquitted. The feud between Marsh and Warren continued, and a further court case for libel went Marsh's way.

Stranger things followed. In 2010, Marsh changed his name to 'None of The Above X' and entered that year's general election as an independent candidate. It was one contest he didn't win. Apparently, he changed his name as a protest against there being no option to select 'None of the above' on an election ballot paper.

Yet another court case followed when he was charged with fraud and deception over student grant payments. More recently, he was involved in an unfair dismissal claim. It seems Marsh has fought as much in the courts as in the ring! By his own admission he made as much out of winning lawsuits as he did inside the ring. Rumours about him rumbled on, but Marsh was always a bright lad and went on to carve out a decent living in the world of finance.

Marsh also participated in chess boxing. Yes, that is correct. Chess boxing involves playing chess and boxing. As a young

Terry Marsh, the fighting fireman.
(Wikicommons)

boxing *and* chess champion, Marsh was well suited to this strange activity. A chess boxing fight consists of eleven rounds: six rounds of chess and five rounds of boxing. Each round lasts three minutes, regardless of whether it involves chess or boxing. Players alternate between a round of chess and a round of boxing until one is declared winner either by checkmate, knockout or technical stoppage. It was initially only thought to be an art performance but it soon turned into a fully developed competitive sport which is popular in Germany, Great Britain, India and Russia. It really is one of those things you must see to believe.

*

It was the West Ham area of East London that saw the birth of one of the greatest heavyweight fighters of all time and one of the biggest names in this new era of boxing. He was definitely East End born and bred, but not always recognized as such. I am talking about **Lennox Claudius Lewis.**

Lennox was born in 1965 and was a large baby, weighing in at almost 11 pounds. He loved sports and played football as a lad. To this day he still declares his love for West Ham United, but when he was twelve his family moved to Ontario, Canada. Lennox kept up his sporting interests and played soccer and basketball to a high standard. However, it was boxing that he loved the most, and he set out on what was to become a fairly lengthy and gloriously golden amateur career. He competed as an amateur in Canada between 1980 and 1988, culminating with winning the Olympic super-heavyweight title for his adopted country in the Seoul Olympics of 1988.

Lewis always maintained that he considered himself a cockney, even though his accent was distinctly North American. It was natural, then, for him to return to the land of his birth, where he would find it easier to turn professional and pursue a more lucrative career.

He was unbeaten in his first twenty-two professional fights and earned a title bout with Riddick Bowe, whom he had defeated in that his gold medal bout. Bowe, who had become the heavyweight champion, felt uneasy about defending his crown against the 6½-foot, 230-pound giant that was Lewis. Bowe kept trying to sidestep a showdown with Lewis. Being so unforthcoming, Bowe was eventually stripped of the title for his repeated failure to arrange a fight with the man. Thus, the crown was passed to Lewis, who defended his title three times, fighting and beating all the top fighters of the day, including Oliver McColl, Frank Bruno, Vitali Klitschko and Tony Tucker.

In the very last heavyweight title fight to take place in the twentieth century, Lewis entered the ring in Las Vegas against the very talented Evander Holyfield for the much anticipated and long-awaited title unification fight. In a gripping twelve-rounder, Lewis eventually gained the upper hand to become the undisputed world heavyweight champion.

Lewis's defence of his title against the once invincible Mike Tyson showcased all of his skills and physical attributes. He was at his devastating best on that January evening in 2002 at the Pyramid Centre on the banks of the Mississippi. Tyson's career was just starting to draw to a close but he was still a very dangerous opponent for Lewis. Tyson was undoubtedly up for the fight, and there were some lively pre-match comments hurled at Lewis in the run-up to the match.

Tyson started the first round well. It looked like it could turn out to be a tight match. Lewis had other ideas, though. From the start of the second round he employed a withering textbook straight jab to keep the bull-like Tyson at bay. On the odd occasion when Tyson managed to get in close, Lenox delivered some jaw-crunching uppercuts. By the time Tyson came out for round four, he had the look of a defeated man about him. He hardly laid a glove on Lewis. Give Tyson his due – he did battle on gamely

Lennox Lewis, on top of the world after his 2002 fight against the once mighty Mike Tyson. (© PA Images)

for few more rounds. However, Lewis was playing with him. The American was a spent force by the time he came out for the eighth round, and he never saw the thunderous right hand which Lewis delivered thirty seconds before the bell. That, as they say, was that. Lewis had defeated all of the very best, and stood at the top of the heavyweight pile. At the same time, he had effectively finished Tyson's career.

It may have been a long time – 102 years to be precise – since Bob Fitzgerald held the world heavyweight title, but at long last Britain had an undisputed world heavyweight boxing champion again – and he came from London's East End. Some British boxing fans still have trouble accepting Lewis as their own. but his birth certificate does not lie.

Lewis retired at the end of 2003 and went into sports management and music promotion. He was awarded a Member of the Order of the British Empire (MBE) in 1999 and a Commander of the Order of the British Empire (CBE) in 2002. He was inducted into Canada's Sports Hall of Fame in 2008, and a year later was inducted into the International Boxing Hall of Fame.

7

THE GOOD, THE BAD AND THE UGLY

> You see in this world there are two kinds of people, my friend:
> those with loaded guns and those who dig. You dig.
> The Man With No Name, *The Good, The Bad and the Ugly*

Boxing has had its fair share of good, bad and ugly characters and, like it or not, for many it was the East End mentality that pushed them to the top. They wanted to be the ones holding the loaded guns, not the ones who did the digging.

From the early part of the twentieth century, the shadow of London's underworld loomed large over East End boxing. The noble art could be lucrative for all concerned. With the controls and regulations that were in place, match rigging was rare in mainstream boxing. It was still big business, though, so London's criminal underbelly sought to make money in other ways. With the influences of the underworld so near, boxing was sometimes the place where young men strayed from the honest path. Most stayed out of the shadows and enjoyed a career free of bad influences, but for a small minority the underworld was seen as an easier way to make money than stepping into the ring.

Without doubt the most notorious of these men turned bad amid the boxing world were the Kray twins. Three feature films, several documentaries and a million words have been written about them, so they will likely be known to anybody reading here. **Ronald (Ronny) and Reginald (Reggie) Kray** were born in Hoxton in 1933, but by the outbreak of war they were living in Vallance Road, Bethnal Green. It was their grandfather Jimmy 'Cannonball' Lee who influenced them the most, and, with extra encouragement from their elder brother Charlie, the Kray twins got into boxing. They joined the world-famous Repton Boxing Club as amateurs and became proficient fighters. Tony Burns, who boxed and has coached at the club for well over sixty years, sparred with the Krays. He sums their situation up: 'Most boxers reach a crossroad. The twins were reasonable boxers. Reggie was a bit classier than Ronnie. In the end they went their way and I went mine.'

During a lifetime in the game, Tony Burns coached hundreds upon hundreds of kids and young men. He has been recognised for his service to the sport. He's one of the good guys. Not so true of his old sparring partners the Krays. He elaborated that 'Reggie was probably the better of the two, quite classy he was, but Ronnie was by far the more aggressive'. Even this early, Ronnie was already showing the first signs of his psychopathic tendencies.

By 1948, Reggie was the schoolboy champion of Hackney and went on to win the London Schoolboy Boxing Championships, as well as being a finalist in the Schoolboy Boxing Championships. In 1949 he became the South Eastern Divisional Youth Club champion and the London Air Training Cadet (ATC) champion. Brother Ron was also the schoolboy champion of Hackney and won the London junior championships and a London ATC title.

In the early fifties, both turned professional. Ron had six fights, winning four of them and losing two. Reggie had seven fights and won them all. They may have made a career out of boxing, especially Reggie, if they had not been called up into the army a few months later. In the 1950s, boys of eighteen had to do national service. For Ron and Reg army life was short and violent, as they

The notorious Kray twins in their boxing days. (© PA Images)

involved themselves in some serious assaults on other men and NCOs. This ended their hopes of promising boxing careers, and thereafter they sought out the dark shadows of East London's underworld to make their mark. The rest is history.

The Kray twins were forced out of boxing after their run-ins with the 'Red Caps' but they still kept up their interest in boxing. They were now on the outside of the ropes looking in and were regular visitors to gyms and clubs around the East End. They were not talent spotting for future boxing champions but for something far more sinister.

*

Joseph Henry (Joey) Pyle (1935–2007) boxed professionally for about a year or so around 1958 and only had six fights, winning four. He had previously dabbled in low-key criminal activity, and after only six fights he obviously thought he would struggle to make any money from the game and returned to his roots in London's underworld. During his relatively uneventful career as a petty criminal and boxer, Joey started making the acquaintance of some seriously heavy gangsters. The Krays and Bruce Reynolds (of Great Train Robbery fame) had befriended Joey, and with such connections he progressed easily into more organised crime. Picking up work from the Krays, he also managed to become a trusted associate of the Krays' arch-rival Charlie Richardson. Joey still had his fingers in boxing, but he also branched out into the music promotions business and was involved in the so called 'Payola' scandals (money for radio airplays).

Joey Pyle became one of Britain's biggest criminals but managed stayed under the radar. He only ever served one sentence: an eighteen-month jail term for assault. Although he was repeatedly arrested in the years that followed, he constantly managed to escape prosecution. Unlike some of his boxing opponents, the police couldn't lay a finger on him! He was suspected of involvement when Frank Mitchell (the Mad Axeman of Broadmoor) and Jack 'the Hat' McVitie escaped from prison. Both men later died – McVitie's death came at the hands of the Krays while Mitchell's fate is still the subject of speculation.

*

Like a lot of other promising boxers who strayed from the straight and narrow, the Krays and Joey Pyle learnt their craft at one of the many boxing clubs that sprung up all over East London before the war. Another such character is the now acclaimed boxing trainer **James 'Jimmy' Tibbs**. Jimmy was born in Canning Town in 1946 and learned his craft at the West Ham Boys' Boxing Club. Of Irish descent, Jimmy's family were in the scrap metal business. He used to do odd jobs for his father as a kid but at sixteen he got a job in the nearby Royal Albert Docks as a shore ganger. He would be sent into the ships' hulls to remove dunnage (the protective packaging left over after the goods had been removed). Even in more recent times, these workers never wore hardhats, protective boots or gloves. Health and safety had not made it to this corner of the docks yet. Accidents still happened.

Jimmy loved nothing more than meeting up with friends at Rathbone Market and having some banter with many of the stallholders he knew. East End street markets were busy, buzzy places, and Jimmy was a hard-working, fun-loving young teenager. Little did he know when he joined the famous West Ham Boxing Club in Plaistow his life would become a rollercoaster, going from the highs of boxing success to the depths of gangland vendettas and then back to universal acclaim as a great trainer.

Jimmy was a very good amateur boxer in his youth, winning three schoolboy championships and a National Federation of Boys' Clubs title between 1960 and 1963. He was destined for a great future in boxing. On turning pro in 1966 he only lost two of his seventeen fights at light-heavyweight and super-middleweight. He was being managed by Terry Lawless, who had high hopes for him. His fight against fellow West Ham lad Johnny Kramer in February 1970 was a real thriller, and after that win he was probably being tipped for a crack at the British title. As it turned out, fate had other ideas. His last fight was against the Nigerian Roy Hassan in March 1970.

Unfortunately for young Jimmy, his family had a rather shady background. They had built up their scrap metal business after the war when there was plenty of scrap metal to trade in. You have to be tough to survive in that particular industry, and the Tibbs family certainly were. They had a reputation in the area.

In the late sixties, there was a bit of a power vacuum left after the conviction and imprisonment of the Krays. A few different parties were interested in filling the gap, and another East End family, the Nicholls, fancied their chances. For some reason, rightly or wrongly, they perceived the Tibbs family as a threat. When one of the Nicholls hit one of the elder Tibbs men after an argument about 'business', serious violence involving guns, knives and clubs broke out. A gangland vendetta ensued. Attacks on the Nicholls brothers continued. An associate of theirs called Len Kersey was attacked and left for dead. Kersey was lucky to survive, but he needed eighty stitches and was given 6 pints of blood. One of the Tibbs boys had his throat slashed.

Things reached a head in early 1971 when a café and a boarding house owned by the Tibbs family were bombed. Six days later, an explosive device was put under the bonnet of Jimmy's van. Unbeknown to the perpetrator, Jimmy's very young son was in it at the time. The bomb did explode, but fortunately the engine block directed the blast outward. Jimmy vowed revenge, and was soon involved in the gang war. His boxing was put on hold during these gangland hostilities.

Arrests followed, and eight men were called to the Old Bailey in October 1972 for a trial that lasted for forty-three days. A couple of the Tibbs brothers were convicted of attempted murder. Big Jim Tibbs, Jimmy's father, received fifteen years for perverting the course of justice. Jimmy himself received ten years. Boxing career? End of. Jimmy Tibbs accepted his fate, knuckled down in prison and was released in 1981. He returned to civilian life, became successful in business and soon after, when the opportunity arose, became a boxing trainer. Jimmy worked mostly with Terry Lawless, but not exclusively. He helped train some of the country's greatest boxers.

In 1991, Jimmy was in boxer Michael Watson's corner for one of the sport's most harrowing nights, when an uppercut from Chris Eubank saw Watson collapse in his corner after the bell. Jimmy knew soon after the referee stopped the fight that Watson's condition was serious. Watson survived with his life, but only just. Jimmy recently said that he seriously considered quitting the sport that night. Had Watson lost his greatest fight – the one for his own life – Jimmy may well have quit. Ultimately, he stayed on in the game to witness greater safety features being introduced into the sport. He recently retired after well over thirty years of putting prospective champions through their paces.

Jimmy Tibbs' young son Mark, who had a lucky escape when his father's vehicle was targeted, also went on to box. Mark, like his father, had a very decent amateur career, boxing out of the Repton Boxing Club and picking up several junior championships before turning pro in 1988. His time in the professional ranks was

Jimmy Tibbs, East End gangster turned world-class trainer. (© PA Images)

very similar to that of his father, losing only two of his twenty-five contests.

Mark then left boxing to join his father in training up-and-coming fighters. He too became an excellent coach, bringing through several top fighters in more recent years. Working out of the Peacock Gym in Canning Town, he has mentored several top fighters. Current top heavyweight Dillian Whyte is one of Tibbs' protégés. Another couple of very useful boxers who have decamped with Tibbs are Sammy McNess and Tony Baker. With the help of his father, Mark took Billy Joe Saunders to world middleweight glory in 2015.

*

Nobody really filled the void left by the Kray twins until **David Hunt** arrived on the scene. Hunt was born in 1961 on an estate in Canning Town. The youngest of thirteen children, he claims his Christian parents brought him up to embrace a strong work ethic. After leaving school at sixteen, he became an amateur boxer and quickly earned a reputation as a ferocious fighter. Unlike the Krays, Hunt only boxed in the amateur ranks. However, he was another young man who thought that the rackets were better than the rings. Unlike the Krays, however, he set about building up a solid criminal empire while maintaining a very low profile. He became a very shrewd operator, and by the late eighties he had amassed a fortune from prostitution, money laundering, smuggling, theft, fraud, drugs, arms trafficking and extortion.

Although Hunt kept to the shadows, he was not averse to the odd bit of thuggery. It is on record that he seriously assaulted many people who crossed him. An old-fashioned gangster at heart, he was without doubt a major crime boss – and by all accounts a seriously nasty piece of work.

*

Unlike in the United States, serious organised crime never really got a foothold in boxing in this country. However, given the nature of the sport there is always going to be the threat of petty crime occurring on the fringes. A fairly common crime in the past was pickpocketing. During the Victorian era, many pickpocketing gangs operated on the streets of London. By the turn of the century, London's police had drastically reduced the problem in central London and the gangs turned their attention to outdoor sports meetings beyond the City. Horse racing and dog racing were both targeted. Boxing was mostly staged indoors, but when one large event was staged in a Canning Town park in 1909, a crack team of pickpockets known as the 'Sporting Boys' moved in.

In early 1909, American fighter Jimmy Britt arrived in the country for a couple of fights against top British fighter Johnny Summers, who was from Canning Town but had been born in the North East. The two fought twice in London, winning one fight apiece. Summers had won both British featherweight and bantamweight titles, while Britt had fought well against the great American Joe Gans for the world lightweight championship and was ahead before he unfortunately broke his wrist. Both were top-drawer boxers.

When it was suggested that the promoters could hold a decider between these two well-matched boxers on Johnny Summer's home patch, both men readily agreed. Everything was set up for a Saturday in July. The venue had been arranged and the event was well advertised. The sun shone on a park in Canning Town where fifteen bouts of boxing took place during the afternoon and evening in front of several thousand happy spectators. As the sun began to set, however, things took a turn for the worse. It was discovered that some of the take money had gone missing and, worse, as some of the crowd began to leave they were 'relieved' of their wallets, watches, tie pins and field glasses.

The incident was witnessed by a racing journalist who had attended the evening session of boxing after reporting on the horse racing at Alexander Park that afternoon. He too was 'light fingered' and discovered his binoculars gone:

> When I arrived, the entrance and exit area of the arena was congested. As soon as I discovered my glasses gone, I looked around and recognised some of the 'Boys' in operation having seen these faces at the races and knew of them. I retired to a place of safety and a little later noticed their ringleader nearby. The ringleader of this enterprising little outfit was called the 'Master'. He was the Fagin of their gang ... I approached him cautiously, informed him of who I was and complained that I needed my glasses to work. Much to my amazement, this well-spoken man apologised and informed me it was never his intention to lift a man's work tools. He asked me for a description of the glasses and agreed to meet me later. He was as good as his word and showed up with a few pairs of field glasses and asked me to pick which pair was mine. The rest, along with his other ill-gotten gains I suspect, were then off to the local fence.

There were rumours that one of the promoters was complicit in this particular adventure, but this was never proved. Interestingly, outdoor boxing events were never very popular with London crowds, mainly due to the possibility of inclement weather. Incidents like this did little to increase their popularity.

You could be forgiven for thinking that most East Enders involved in boxing were closet villains, but that is certainly not the case. For every one bad penny there are a shilling's worth of good ones. There are an awful lot of people both inside and outside of the ring who have given a lot to their sport and the communities in which they lived. Terry Spinks was awarded the MBE, not only for boxing but for his charity work. Repton's Tony Burns, mentioned earlier, has dedicated his life to the sport. Micky May at West Ham gave years to the club. The sport at grass level would not survive without people like them, many of whom dedicate their time and skills free of charge at many of the gyms and clubs in and around the area. Even those who leave the sport often give something back. Frank Bruno has been honoured recently with an MBE for both his lifetime achievements in boxing and his ongoing children's charity work.

*

Patrick (Pat) O'Keeffe (1883–1960) boxed in the years leading up to and including the First World War. Pat's grandparents arrived in East London in the 1840s, another family escaping the horrors of the Irish potato famine. Pat was born in Bromley-by-Bow. Not much is known about his childhood and how he got into boxing, but records show him fighting professionally around 1902. He fought and won the British welterweight title in 1903 before boxing for the next fifteen years at middleweight and heavyweight, winning the British title in the former weight class. Pat had championship matches against heavyweights Billy Wells and Georges Carpentier and was an outright holder of the middleweight Lonsdale belt. He spent many years fighting in America, and also fought several times in France and Australia before the outbreak of war in 1914. A durable fighter, he had built a very good reputation among his fellow boxers and the wider public.

A patriotic man, Pat enlisted in the 1st Surrey Rifles as a fitness instructor and later became a recruitment sergeant. He continued his boxing during the war and fought two great matches against a fellow 'Tommy', Jim Sullivan, the second being a brutal, bloody affair. Jimmy Wilde, the former flyweight champion, described the fight as the most punishing he had ever seen. Both men fought as though their lives depended on it. The ring and nearby spectators were liberally splashed with blood by the end of the battle. It can be seen from some of the old black-and-white photographs of the event that Sullivan's white shorts were dark with blood by the end of twenty rounds, when the Bromley man gained the decision.

Army life – Pat O'Keeffe demonstrating some training routines circa 1917. A much-admired boxer and a tremendous ambassador for the sport. (© Imperial War Museum)

Pat was very popular with the men, and he often arranged morale-boosting events for the troops when they were on leave from the Western Front. His last fight took place in 1918. He remained a public figure afterwards, working on the administrative side of the sport for many years and participating in charity events on behalf of the sport. He continued to work part-time as an instructor for both the British and French armies, and later in his life he ran a pub.

*

You can't have a boxing match without a referee. Boxing is one of the hardest sports at which to officiate, and there are very few referees who reach the required standard to take charge of the top matches. Even when you go further down the bills, referees shoulder a huge burden of responsibility to ensure the welfare of the fighters. It can be a thankless task.

Sidney 'Sid' Nathan was one of the greatest British boxing referees of more recent times. Born in Aldgate, East London, in September 1922, Sid's first memory of boxing was watching the great Ted 'Kid' Lewis beat Bermondsey middleweight Joe Rolfe at Premierland in 1927. Lewis was a friend of Sid's father, and after the fight Lewis picked up the five-year-old Sid and walked him around the ring. Sid was hooked on boxing then and there; he couldn't wait to start. He left school at fourteen and started work as a messenger boy at the BBC and then as a solicitor's clerk. He began boxing through the Jewish Lad's Brigade and turned professional at the age of sixteen. In his first fight as a flyweight in March 1939, Sid outpointed Mike Constantino over eight rounds. He fought mostly at venues like the Devonshire Club and the Holborn Stadium. While he was a good boxer, even by his own admission he probably would have struggled to get to the very top.

Soon after he started boxing professionally, Sid met his future wife, Lilian Greenberg. By June 1940, Sid had fought fourteen matches and lost just two. However, with the outbreak of war Sid was reluctantly persuaded by his fiancé to give up the sport. He joined the RAF as ground crew and was stationed in Scotland. At the end of the war the couple moved to Watford. However, Lilian could not stop Sid's love of boxing, so in the mid-fifties he decided to become a referee and was subsequently awarded a Star licence, the highest refereeing qualification in British boxing. He handled over 800 fights between 1958 and 1988, among them championship bouts featuring the likes of Ken Buchanan, Nigel Benn, Frank Bruno, Barry McGuigan, Alan Minter, Maurice Hope, John Conteh and Charlie Magri. He regards the last two of these as the best boxers he saw in his time as a referee.

Under the Boxing Board of Control regulations, Sid was obliged to retire as referee at the mandatory age of sixty-five. Sid still wanted to play a part in the sport, however, and so highly was he regarded by the British Boxing Board that they agreed he should become a judge. Sid continued to work until 1996, and died twenty years later after spending half a century in the sport. A great servant.

*

The American referee 'Irish' Wayne Kelly once said, 'Boxers are like prostitutes; they are in the business of ruining their bodies for the pleasure of strangers.' Our next area of focus is testament to this. Well organised, regulated and controlled, British boxing is exceptionally clean when compared with the state of the sport in some countries. However, there does exist an ugly side to the sport. The days of fifty-plus rounds of bare-knuckle, anything-goes boxing matches between mismatched fighters is more or less a thing of the past, but something not too far removed from those days nonetheless lingers on. It is known as unlicensed boxing.

Fights in all sorts of different venues started to attract reasonable audiences in the sixties, and it was no surprise that two of East London's hardest men stepped into the ring at this time. The brutal fights they contested against each other have gone down in East End folklore. Two men, more than any others, helped to define this darker side of the sport.

The first was **Leonard (Lenny) John 'The Guvnor' McLean** (1949–1998). He was born in Hoxton and came from an unimaginably tough and brutal family background. He was often abused as a child by his stepfather, Jim Irwin. Lenny is thought to have taken his nickname from the vitriolic words that his stepfather spat out at him; he would often stand over the badly beaten young Lenny screaming out, 'I am The Guvnor!' Most of Lenny's immediate family was involved in crime and he soon fell into the same world, serving a short prison sentence at eighteen. McLean was a big man and handy with his fists, and in the early 1960s he was offered a chance to fight in an unlicensed match on a used car lot. He won and got paid almost £500 for it. This was a lot of money back then, and the fight only lasted a minute. Young Lenny realised this was the game for him.

In his prime, Lenny was 6 feet 2 inches tall and weighed over 20 stone (280 pounds). He boasted that he could beat anybody, licensed or unlicensed, with or without gloves, and reputedly sent out challenges to many of the famous boxers of the day. He was challenged by King of the Gypsies and bare-knuckle champion Bartley Gorman, but declined. Promoter Frank Warren offered him a professional fight against David Bomber Pearce, the British heavyweight champion from Newport, but again Lenny refused. He has claimed to have been involved in thousands of contests but that is probably a gross exaggeration. He used his fights to help exorcise the demons in his head as a result of his abused childhood.

With his growing fame, McLean also became known as 'The King of Bouncers' around many of the clubs and pubs in London where he was occasionally employed. McLean also held joint ownership of a pub in the East End named Guv'Nors along with Charlie Kray, elder brother to the infamous twins. McLean has also been described as a 'fixer' and a 'minder' for criminals and celebrities. Through his contacts in the showbiz world, he appeared in brief cameo roles in a number of films and even had a small speaking role in Guy Richie's *Lock, Stock and Two Smoking Barrels*. McLean was universally acknowledged as the heavyweight champion of the unlicensed version of the sport. He was often pictured with some of the entertainment celebrities of the day, acting as a bodyguard.

Lenny became the most well-known figure in unlicensed boxing. Not only did he make a lot of friends and fans, but he also gained many enemies. This included some of his rivals' supporters, a few of whom had lost money betting on his opponents. Lenny also made enemies from years of ejecting people from pubs and clubs. Violence followed Lenny around the shady world of unlicensed fighting and the pubs and clubs where he worked. He suffered bullet wounds from two separate shootings and was stabbed on two occasions. He has said that he later tracked down and punished one assailant who had attempted to shoot him at his home while his children were in the house. It is not known what happened to the assailant!

As far as the East End was concerned, it was the brutal trilogy of unlicensed matches Lenny fought with East London's other unlicensed superstar, Roy Shaw, that would go down in unlicensed fighting folklore. **Roy 'Pretty Boy' Shaw (1936–2012)** was a hard, brutal bull of a man and a well-known East End gangster. In their first fight, Lenny lost to Shaw by verbal submission, which he justified by claiming his gloves had been tampered with, thus reducing their manoeuvrability. Lenny beat Shaw in a rematch with a dramatic first-round knockout that sent Shaw sprawling out of the ring. There was a big demand for a decider. Lenny's second cousin was a boxing promoter, and was persuaded to promote the match. In their final bout, Lenny ended the feud with a brutal first-round knockout at the Rainbow Theatre, Finsbury Park, in September 1978.

Roy Shaw was born in Stepney in 1936. You can see by the birth dates that when Shaw and McLean had their showdowns the latter was over twelve years the younger. He also had several inches in height and several stone in weight over Shaw. An armed robber with several blags behind him, Shaw was a close associate of Joey Pyle, who would play a hand in promoting some of his later fights. Shaw was caught and sentenced to eighteen years for armed robbery in 1963. He was aggressive in prison and occasionally assaulted his guards. Moving from prison to prison did not curb his violent behaviour toward authority, and he is known to have slashed the throats of incarcerated police informants. He eventually ended up in Broadmoor with his old mate Ronnie Kray.

On his release, Shaw got into the unlicensed fight game. He was already forty-two but had kept himself fit. He made a fair amount of money from these unlicensed matches and his reputation grew. He wisely invested his fight purses in property. In the early 1980s,

Unlicensed fights. Is this the ugly face of boxing? Lenny 'The Guvnor' McLean (above) and Roy 'Pretty Boy' Shaw (left). (© PA Images)

Shaw stated that he was going legitimate and retired from both crime and unlicensed boxing. He became a businessman and author. With numerous fairly lucrative financial ventures and a bestselling autobiography behind him, he amassed a small fortune and died a wealthy man.

In 2017, the graphic film *My Name is Lenny* was released. It told the story of Lenny McLean, and the infamous Shaw fights featured prominently. In the film, Lenny is shown being trained by the accurately named Johnny Bootnose. This was in fact John Wall from Shoreditch, who was Lenny's cousin, and a very useful fighter indeed. After a decent amateur career, Wall fought professionally and was Southern light-heavyweight champion. In the film he was played by Nick Moran, who starred in *Lock, Stock and Two Smoking Barrels*. Lenny is played by Josh Helman, and mixed martial arts star Michael Bisping plays Shaw.

*

Unlicensed boxing is quite brutal by today's standards, but let's not carried away. While deaths in the ring do regrettably occur, the mainstream game is so well regulated now and the medical backup is so good that deaths are, fortunately, very rare indeed – and unlicensed boxing generally has all the same safety measures in place.

To put things into perspective, here is an account of a British heavyweight title fight. It is the aforementioned bout between James Burke and Simon Byrne:

The match lasted for 3 hours and 6 minutes, during which time 99 rounds were fought, the longest ever recorded championship prize fight in this country. For the most part Byrne seemed to be in control in the early stages of the fight; in the 30th round he trapped Burke against the ropes and battered him severely around the body before throwing him to the ground. Burke fell on his face, vomiting and throwing up blood, and for the next few rounds Byrne looked the more likely winner.

By the 49th round however, Burke had recovered sufficiently to knock Byrne to the ground, whose hands by then were so swollen that he was unable to deliver a finishing blow. By the 93rd round Byrne was reported as 'scarcely able to stand, and rolled before the Deaf'un like a ship in a storm'. Although both men were utterly exhausted Burke continued to 'pepper away at Byrne's body and head', until the 99th round when Byrne collapsed unconscious and could not be revived to take his place once again.[1]

Byrne was carried away to receive treatment but died two days later. Fortunately, this is not a recent match but one which took place in 1833. Both James Burke and Jem Ward, Byrne's

James Burke. (© Alamy Images)

cornerman, were sought by the authorities to answer the charge of manslaughter. Ward fled the country, but neither faced official charges. Thirty years later, the Queensberry Rules were introduced and this most ugly form of the sport was changed forever.

*

To round off this chapter on the good, bad and ugly sides of boxing, I would like to introduce you to a man who could lay claim to possessing all three of these characteristics. **Alan Mortlock** grew up on the East End council estates of the seventies and eighties. He was involved in crime and violence from an early age. A drug dealer and an alcoholic, he fought in the gangs that plagued the streets and the concrete jungles of the inner-city estates. He stills wears the scars today, with a face that has met a boot or two along the way.

Growing up, Roy Shaw and Lenny McLean were Mortlock's idols. He realised that there was a way out of his criminal lifestyle and started to get involved in staging the odd unlicensed fight. At this early stage, his fights would have been extremely dangerous, with few safety procedures in place. Gradually, though, he started to get into some reasonable venues and went about procuring a stable of unlicensed boxers.

Mortlock says that it was around this time that he started to have thoughts about religion and became a born-again Christian. For the following few years he actively promoted God as well as fighting, often both at the same time! He set up sessions in a Pentecostal church in Leytonstone which involved constructing a ring and staging exhibition matches along with preaching. He hit the road to redemption with his stable of boxers, fighting and delivering the word. They called themselves the 'Godfellas'. Mortlock has since become one of the biggest promoters of unlicensed fighting in the country. Quite strange bedfellows, some may think – boxing and the Bible – but that's an argument for another day.

8

AT THE CROSSROADS

Given their background, you could argue that the Guvnor and Pretty Boy gravitated naturally into the sport and were comfortable inside the ropes. However, for some this is not the case. There are several examples of young men starting out on the boxing road only to change direction. Some took the wrong road, like the Krays, but many more took the right path. Two of the most well-known boxing clubs in East London are West Ham and Repton. A steady stream of would-be champions have passed through their doors over the years. Many trod a sure and steady route to the top in the sport, but others reached a crossroad on their boxing path and headed off in a new direction.

Raymond Andrew Winstone was born in Hackney Hospital in 1957 and lived in Homerton. As a boy, Ray loved films and boxing. Again, like so many, his father did a little bit of boxing in his youth. Known to his friends as Winnie, Ray was called Little Sugs at home (his father already being known as Sugar, after Sugar Ray Robinson). At the age of twelve, Ray joined Repton Boxing Club. Over the next ten years he won all but eight out of his eighty-eight fights. He was London schoolboy champion on three occasions, fighting twice for England. The experience gave him a perspective on his later career.

Realising that boxing would be a tough way to earn money, Ray enrolled in a drama school and grabbed an opportunity to audition for a television production playing, unsurprisingly, an East End hoodlum. His love of films spurred him on, and further roles followed. As his acting career began to take off, he turned his back on boxing for the world of film and TV. Ray Winstone is now a household name and graces the big and small screen regularly. Although he moved out of the Homerton area aged ten, he never lost his cockney roots and has been a season ticket holder at West Ham's stadium for many years.

West Ham football Club pops up often when it comes to boxing stories. A few West Ham footballers tried their hand (or hands) at boxing before earning a living with their feet. **Noel Cantwell**, the Irish international footballer who played for both West Ham and Manchester United, boxed as a junior in his native Ireland before moving over to England to enjoy a football career. He played 245 times for the Irons and holds the distinction of being the only Irishman to play senior matches in both cricket and football for his country. A great all-round sportsman.

Another very good football player who went on to be an even better coach was **Dave Sexton**. Dave was another lad born into an East End boxing family. His father, Archie, was a top professional and there will be more about him later. Dave's two uncles, Jim and Billy, also had some professional bouts. He was quite keen to take up boxing at a higher level, and when he went off to do his national service in the army he won some decent inter-regimental boxing matches. Dave reckons his mum was against another boxer in the family as she was only too aware the risks involved. He later admitted that his mum would have gone potty if he had gone into boxing, so she was happy when he decided that football was the game for him. Dave played seventy-seven times for the Hammers between 1952 and 1955.

There were two more Irons who boxed a bit in their teens. One was **Ken Tucker**, whose brother was a very capable amateur boxer and an English international. Ken boxed a little bit and often worked out with his brother. He played for West Ham between 1947 and 1956, making almost 100 appearances and scoring a very creditable thirty-three goals in his time there.

The other was, surprisingly, **Ted Fenton**. Ted Fenton was a great West Ham servant. As a player he turned out for the East End club between 1932 and 1946. Born in Forest Gate, Ted was a good all-round sportsman and a very promising boxer. However, football was his greatest talent. During the war he joined the army as a physical instructor and was posted to North Africa and Burma. He both boxed and played football during his time in the forces. He finished his playing days at the club after 166 appearances, and in 1950 was appointed the Hammers' manager. His tenure at the club was exceptional, and he was instrumental in developing the famous West Ham Academy. He left the club in 1961 after securing the club's place in the top tier of football in the 1957/8 season and having helped to develop the country's greatest footballing son, Bobby Moore.

One last connection concerns West Ham's current co-owner/director **David Gold**. David was born in Stepney before the war but his family moved to Upton Park after their house was destroyed during the Blitz. They lived on Green Street, so David grew up across the road from West Ham's Boleyn Ground. He and his brother both attended East Ham Boxing Club as young lads. David was a reasonable boxer but was a much better footballer, playing schoolboy football at quite a high level. He was actually very close to signing professional forms for West Ham, but his father would not let him sign for the club – instead, fifty years later, he bought it! David's father was a bit of a boxer as a young man but his younger brother **Ralph Gold** was an excellent amateur.

Ralph Gold also boxed at the West Ham Club, becoming an established English international as well as winning the ABA London and regional championships in the early 1960s. Ralph was in the British squad that took on the strong Yankee team that visited in 1960. You will remember Billy Walker made the headlines that night, although it was a great team victory as the

Brits won every single fight that evening. Both Gold brothers went on to become successful businessmen.

On the subject of East End siblings gravitating into business, the Golds followed in the footsteps of the Walkers. Heavyweight Billy Walker had some success in the sport and went on to make a crust in business. Billy had his elder brother, **George Alfred Walker** (1929–2011), to thank for that. George also pulled a pair of gloves on at a fairly early age, and when he did his national service in the RAF he continued his passion for the sport and became a keen and talented amateur light-heavyweight.

After finishing his stint in the RAF, George went back to work in Billingsgate Fish Market as a porter. Boxing out of the Thames Refinery club, he had an outstanding amateur career and became amateur champion in 1951. A long and successful boxing career lay ahead. He turned professional that same year and had several impressive early fights, twice beating Albert Finch, who had fought and beaten some great light-heavyweights in his time. He became known as the 'Stepney Steamroller' and was at one point ranked seventh in the world. After just eleven fights, very early in his career, George was then thrown in for the British light-heavyweight title against the talented Welsh champion Denis Powell. The title had just been relinquished by the great Randolph Turpin and was up for grabs.

The vastly more experienced Powell was excellent, and although George fought bravely and had Powell in trouble several times, the Welshman managed to land a savage blow to Walker's left eye which soon closed completely. Powell's ring-craft came to the fore and he out-boxed Walker for several rounds before the referee stopped the fight in the eleventh. Both boxers had taken a fair amount of punishment, but George was soundly beaten. He fought another five fights but then picked up a long-term injury. George thought long and hard about his future before he decided to call it a day in the ring and try earning a living outside of it. He was just twenty-five years old. It seemed to George that decent money could be made a lot easier outside the law than within it.

Underworld characters were always close by, and George got friendly with Billy Hill. Hill was a serious player in London's underworld. He and the legendary gangster Jack Spot ruled over London's underworld either side of the war. Hill was the idol of the Krays and had his fingers in many pies. He soon realised that George had brains as well as brawn, and put a few deals his way. Unfortunately, one dodgy deal went sour; George got caught and served nine months in jail for stealing £2,000 worth of nylon stockings and woollen goods. Once he was released, he developed his entrepreneurial skills in more legitimate business activities. He took a share in a garage and developed a small transport company before masterminding his talented brother's boxing career. Such entrepreneurial success was a far cry from George's Stepney beginnings as the son of a £2-a-week drayman who had left school at fourteen to work at Billingsgate Fish Market.

By the late sixties, George, with his boxing brother Billy, owned several properties including clubs and a small chain of restaurants. The business was to grow into the huge Brent Walker Corporation, the largest property/leisure business in the country. George and his partners built and operated London's first giant shopping mall at Brent Cross in North London. The much-hyped Trocadero shopping and leisure complex at Piccadilly was developed next, and George became a multi-millionaire soon afterward. No state schools in Stepney for his kids; they were educated at the prestigious Millfield private school in Somerset, and one of his daughters married Prince Philip's cousin George Mountbatten, Marquess of Milford Haven, giving George two titled grandchildren.

*

Another boxing family, the Murphy family from West Ham, had a couple of promising boxers in the house. Dad **Terry Murphy** (1934–) had been boxing for several years before his son Glen came along. In his childhood Terry would often tune into the radio to follow the fortunes of his boxing heroes, and he pulled on a pair of boxing gloves at an early age. He was an accomplished schoolboy boxer, winning the national Schoolboy Boxing Championship for his age group, and went on to win a further two London titles and the national ABA Junior championships. Terry was a huge West Ham fan, and so he was absolutely thrilled to bits when he was presented with an inscribed watch by the Hammers' manager Charlie Paynter after he won his UK title.

Terry turned pro in 1953 and had an impressive early record at middleweight, losing only one of his first twenty fights. He was in fact the first boxer to appear in a live fight on the newly created Associated Television (ATV). After winning two area titles, his form dipped. Within four years, he had retired. He went into the pub game, running several pubs until he landed up at the Bridge House in Canning Town in 1974. Already a popular music spot, Terry turned it into one of London's premier music venues. From 1975 to 1982, the Bridge House was one of the places to be. Heavy metal fans rubbed shoulders with punks, mods, skinheads and goths to watch Iron Maiden, the Tom Robinson Band, Secret Affair, Cockney Rejects and Wasted Youth. The 500-plus capacity pub is where Dire Straits, U2 and the Stray Cats played their first UK dates, where The Blues Band and Chas & Dave recorded live albums, and where Depeche Mode got signed. He later wrote a bestselling book on the iconic pub.

Terry's son **Glen Murphy** (1957–) is best known as the actor who appeared as fireman George Green in the TV series *London's Burning* for almost fourteen years. Glen was born in West Ham. He attended both Repton and West Ham Boxing Clubs and boxed for both. A decent amateur schoolboy boxer, he won a National Schools Championship. He boxed at a semi-professional level before turning his full-time attention to his acting career. Glen is a karate black belt, he gained his Sandan (3rd Dan) in 2016 after training for thirty-three years and still trains in the Kyokushin style today. An accomplished actor, he was awarded the MBE in the 2007 Queen Elizabeth Birthday Honours List for his services to charity and drama. He was also awarded the Freedom of the City of London in 1994 for his charity work in the area. Apart from Glen's dad being a top boxer, his uncle was the aforementioned Joe Lucy.

*

The rather impressively nicknamed 'Assassin from Wapping', **James 'Jimmy' Flint** (1952–), also made the transition from boxing to acting. The son of a docker, Jimmy was born in Wapping and attended the Broad Street Boxing Club in Stepney, the same club where Bombardier Billy Wells learnt his craft. He had a reasonable amateur record and turned pro in 1973. Impressive from the start, Jimmy only lost one of his first twenty-three fights before he met the gifted Pat Cardell in a fight for the British featherweight title at the Royal Albert Hall in 1980. He lost. Jimmy fought on for another six fights but his enthusiasm for the game was dropping off, and he called it a day after he was knocked out by a pretty ordinary journeyman boxer named Steve Sims in 1981.

It is doubtful that Jimmy would have imagined a career in acting was just around the corner, but it was. He became friendly with Ron Peck, a film director who was known for making tough social dramas. Peck was planning to produce a film about East End organised crime and gave Jimmy a small talking part in the film, which was called *Empire State*. It was a reasonable success. Jimmy got his name out there, and several more parts followed. He appeared in films like *Lock, Stock and Two Smoking Barrels*, *The Krays* and *Revolver*, as well as TV shows like *Casualty* and *Kavanagh QC*. He is still very active in film and theatre.

A few years after Jimmy Flint was born, and just a few steps up the road, **Anthony 'Tony' Marchant** (1959–) was starting his life in this tough area. He, like Jimmy, was born on a housing estate. After the war, small and medium-sized housing estates sprung up in this area to make up for the flattened swathes of housing around the docks. The blocks of flats that made up these estates were seen as the answer to the question of mass rehousing. Living conditions had improved by the time Tony came along, but it was still a tough place to grow up.

Tony was a tall lad, and quite sporty. One day he wandered into the Repton Boys' Club in Hoxton and pulled on a pair of gloves. Although he was very tall for his age, with a useful long reach, he was quite slim and boxed at middleweight. Interestingly, both Glen Murphy and Ray Winston were present at Repton at the same time. Marchant developed into a decent schoolboy boxer, becoming a schoolboy champion and boxing in the junior England boxing squad. At one stage, it was felt that Tony could turn into a decent light-heavyweight after filling out. For some time, however, Tony had nurtured a passion for writing alongside his boxing. He got a big break with his writing when his play *Remember Me?* was picked up by the forward-thinking Theatre Royal in Stratford East and turned into an excellent production.

Tony Marchant is now a leading playwright, scriptwriter, author and producer. He is best known for his play about the Falklands War, *Welcome Home*, which was presented at the Royal Court Theatre in London in 1983 after a national tour. He also wrote the excellent *Goodbye Cruel World*, starring Sue Johnson, as well as the 1997 production *Holding On*, starring Phil Daniels. His Channel 4 production *Never Never* owes much to his Wapping background.

Dudley O'Shaughnessy (1989–) from the Poplar/Canning Town area of Tower Hamlets was a schoolboy boxer of some repute. His parents separated when he was quite young, and his early life was split between his father in Canning Town and his mother in Hackney. He attended Brampton Manor Academy in East Ham. His father had boxed a little bit and encouraged Dudley to box, so at the age of nine he joined West Ham Boxing Club. He quickly made his mark on the amateur scene by winning the Federation of Boys Clubs title in 2005, the Junior ABA championships in 2007 and then, a year after finishing runner-up at senior level in 2009, the welterweight senior championship. Despite this success, he was overlooked for international honours.

By 2011, Dudley had reached the crossroads. The thought of turning pro must have been at the forefront of his mind when he was spotted by a local model agency. He was quickly picked up by the prestigious Next agency, and soon the modelling work started to mount up. He was rapidly becoming the new kid on the block. By 2012, he was modelling for Fred Perry, Stone Island and Oswald Boateng. He had swapped the canvas for the catwalk. That year he was crowned male model of the year by *ARISE* magazine.

A rising star in the industry, Dudley nonetheless had other ambitions. Apart from his modelling career, he began to appear in music videos and was centre stage in the video for pop superstar Rhianna's single 'We Found Love'. Rumours were rife after the shoot that the two were romantically linked. More film parts came Dudley's way, and after playing a couple of bit parts in films he landed his first leading actor role in the 2016 film *White Colour Black*. He has since moved to Los Angeles to pursue his acting career.

9

FIGHTING FAMILIES OF
THE EAST END

In addition to producing an inordinate number of individuals with a talent for boxing, the East End has been home to numerous boxing families. The noble art seems to run in the genes of certain families. The East End teems with it. There is no other sport that compares for this. Football is the other big sport in the area, but only a few East End families boasting multiple top footballers spring to mind, including the Redknapps and the Lampards. Not so with boxing. We have already heard about Alf Reed and his sons, Teddy Baldock and his grandad, Terry Murphy and his son Glen, Vic Andreetti and his dad, the Corbett brothers and Kray boys. The middle-class Douglas family stamped their mark on the sport as well. The list goes on and on. There are hundreds. It was not at all uncommon for there to be two, three or even four professional boxers in one household in the East End.

*

The most famous fighting family from the area was the **Lewis Family**. They were more of a dynasty. Lewis was their family's ring name. According to family ancestry, the patriarch of the family, **William Lucioni**, was second-generation London/ Italian and was born in Bethnal Green around 1880. The family was exceptionally poor, wandering from one squalid accommodation to another with longish spells in the local workhouses in between.

In an effort to get out of the poverty trap, a teenage William started to enter prize fights, taking some awful beatings to justify his appearance money. He gradually improved, and by the turn of the century was sometimes boxing three times a week and winning regularly. He had racked up almost three hundred fights before he went off to fight in Flanders fields in 1916. He never returned. He is one of the 72,000 who have no graves and are remembered at the Thiepval War Memorial. William was survived by three sons: Bill, George and Teddy. They all worked in Billingsgate Fish Market and were all taught to box by their father before the war. All three boxed professionally during the 1920s and early 1930s under the great trainer Snowy Buckingham, and Bill became a Southern Area champion. Teddy went on to manage and train boxers.

In 1929, Teddy had a son, **Edward Charles Lewis** (1929–2017). Young Edward was officially to become known as Ted Lewis (not to be confused with Ted 'Kid' Lewis) when the Lucioni name was finally changed to Lewis by deed poll in 1944. Born on Ordell Road, Bow, Ted was a decent amateur and boxed at some events with the young Randolph Turpin. He then moved to Becontree and started to fight out of West Ham Boys' Club. Once he turned pro, he spread his fighting across the popular East End venues and the boxing booths at travelling fairs.

Ted was gradually moving up the ranks and was pressing for a championship match when he fought Johnny Lewis at the Royal Albert Hall. It was Ted's first fight there, and unfortunately it was to be his last. Well ahead towards the end of the third round, he had Johnny Lewis on the ropes but was caught by a right hook to the side of the head which affected his optic nerve, blinding him. Although he boxed on unsighted until the bell, he fell over as he headed for his corner. Not knowing where his corner was, he stayed down. Clearly something was very wrong, and Ted was taken off to hospital. Although he gradually regained his vision, it was discovered that he had developed a small blood clot that had moved to the back of the eye. Ted knew it would be a big gamble to push on for a top title and that he would face some very tough fights. Not wanting to risk further damage, he retired from mainstream boxing but carried on fighting at the boxing booths for a few more years.

*

Most boxers who reach the top of the amateur ranks turn pro at some stage in order to make some money, but not all take this path. The Mallin family was a prime example. **Harry Mallin** was born in Shoreditch in 1892 but moved to Hackney Wick as a boy. His younger brother **Fred Mallin** was born in 1902. They were both sporty, and joined the Eton Manor Boys' Club just up the road from where they lived. The club provided many different sports facilities at which young lads could try their hand. Harry tried boxing, and loved the sport – as did his younger brother Fred when he later joined the club. By the time young Fred joined up, Harry was making a real name for himself in the amateur boxing ranks. He was to become British amateur middleweight champion five years in a row from 1919 to 1923. He was also the amateur world champion in the middleweight class between 1920 and 1928. At the outbreak of the First World War he had already racked up almost 100 matches and was undefeated. He might well have represented Britain at middleweight in the 1912 Olympic Games in Sweden, but boxing was withdrawn from the programme as it was felt the Swedes had little interest in the sport.

Harry joined the Admiralty Police Force at the end of the war and later became a sergeant in the Metropolitan Police. Apart from his ABA and world titles, Harry was also twice All-British Police champion and four-time Metropolitan Police champion. Harry had to wait until 1920 before he could fight at the Olympics for the first time, turning out for Britain in Belgium. He duly won the gold. Thus, Britain retained the Olympic middleweight title, the aforementioned middleweight J. W. H. T. Douglas having taken the title in 1908. Harry wanted to go one step further, and returned to defend the title four years later in Paris. Things progressed well until the quarter-finals when he was matched against the very useful home favourite, Roger Brousse. At this point Harry had gone almost 200 fights unbeaten. The fight became one of the most infamous in Olympic boxing history.

The two men were evenly matched, but in front of a very loud and partisan French crowd Brousse fought a very aggressive match. Harry's boxing skills kept him out of trouble. Later in the fight, Harry appeared to be complaining to the referee. It is unclear whether or not the referee spoke English, but the fight ended with a narrow points win for the Frenchman. Initially, Harry and his corner seemed to accept the decision. However, an eagle-eyed Swedish official made it clear to the referee and the judges that Harry had been badly bitten on his chest and arm. The referee dismissed the complaint, but the Swedish official, Oscar Soderlund, was vociferous in his condemnation and an appeal was lodged.

Harry was later examined by the appointed medical officer. Matters dragged on for another twenty-four hours with claims and counterclaims. The French supporters were enraged, and fighting broke out between the French and members of the British Olympic team which included other boxers, rowers and athletes in and around the Olympic venue. Eventually the medical officer delivered his verdict. He concluded that Harry was bitten by Brousse, and the Frenchman was disqualified. The French do indeed like their British beef rare!

Brousse's supporters were incensed over the decision and when Harry got through to the final the spurned Frenchman arranged for the crowd to carry him into the arena in his dressing gown and deposit him in the ring moments before the final was due to start. They clearly wanted to make the point that their man was the true contender. Pandemonium broke out and the police were called to clear the hall. Harry and his opponent stood quietly in the middle of the ring for almost an hour before order was restored. The fight eventually got underway, and Harry Mallin beat fellow Brit Jack Elliot to become the first and only British man to date to defend an Olympic boxing title.

Mallin continued his career as a policeman following the games. He continued to box but never turned professional. Thanks to that eagle-eyed Swede in Paris, Harry Mallin kept his unbeaten run of bouts, eventually amassing over 300 fights without a single loss. It is an unsurpassed record. His skill, sportsmanship and devotion to the amateur status have been held up as one of the finest examples of the Olympic ideal and the amateur code.

Meanwhile, as Harry was sweeping all before him in a stellar amateur career, his younger brother Fred was well on the way in his own amateur boxing career. He actually equalled his elder sibling's British amateur record of five titles, and went on to represent Britain in the 1928 Olympics in Amsterdam. Fred could not emulate his brother, and just missed out on a bronze medal in what was a disappointing Olympics for British boxers. Fred kept on fighting at a high level and represented his country again at the 1930 Empire Games in Canada, where he won the middleweight title.

It was later reported that the Russian Boxing Federation approached both brothers to train Russian boxers for future Olympics but they both refused. They were a remarkable pair. Their Corinthian spirit and amateur ideals stayed with them, as they were impeccably behaved both inside and outside the ring.

*

Poles apart from the Mallins brothers were the Goodson brothers. These boys were everything the Mallins were not. The Goodson family lived close to Brick Lane, a stone's throw from the Shoreditch home where the Mallin family lived for a while. That's about as close as these two sets of brothers got.

Thomas and Henry Goodson were born in 1852 and 1856 respectively, in the quaintly named Seven Stars Yard in Spitalfields.

Believe me, quaint it ain't! At least, it wasn't in those days. The family were in the haulage business. They were known as 'carmen'. Thomas and Henry were nicknamed Treacle and Sugar, and two less appropriate names you could not bestow on them. It is thought they actually got them from the goods they transported.

The whole family were colourful, especially the elder brother Benjamin, who spent several spells in prison for a number of fairly serious offences. Thomas and Henry also got themselves involved in all kinds of mischief, to say the least. They were not the forerunners of the Krays – far from it – but they were quick witted and handy with their fists. Their early days in boxing are very vague, but it is thought that they may have boxed at Father Jay's Club in Shoreditch. From the 1870s a plethora of various types of social and sporting clubs sprung up in London catering for all interests. Many were little more than drinking dens but some were church driven, like Jay's Club. The clubs in this area were, however, far removed from the gentlemen's clubs which appeared in the more affluent areas of the capital.

Jay's Club was founded by the outspoken Revd A. Osborn Jay of the Holy Trinity Church, Shoreditch, and he encouraged the members, some of whom were known villains and burglars, to improve their lot. He set up games and other sporting activities. The club had a gymnasium in the basement complete with a flying trapeze and, of course, the obligatory boxing ring. Many of the senior clergy took a dim view of boxing and criticised the set-up. Jay fought his corner. Jay's approach to the social problems that beset the area were more aligned to that of the great salvationist William Booth, who had just formed the Salvation Army in nearby Whitechapel in 1878. He made his feelings known to his superiors:

Shoreditch is called the 'Cradle of Pugilism' and its men and boys will box whether you like it or not; if not in this club then some other or worse still, some low booza. As far as most are concerned the knowledge of the art of self defence never harms but raises and improves.

We will never know for sure if a man of the cloth was instrumental in helping the Goodson brothers onto the boxing path. Both fought bare-fisted. Thomas boxed between 1879 and 1884 but Henry boxed a lot longer, between 1878 and 1889. This meant Henry fought from twelve years of age! The family were making a reasonable living hauling goods around the East End, but all the boys liked to scrap. The matches they were involved in were very often fought in the back rooms or back yards of the many back street pubs in that part of London and the prize monies on offer were very small.

Thomas and Harry were active in the transitional period of boxing. Bare-knuckle fighting was heavily governed by the London Prize Ring rules, but by the late 1860s the start of legalised boxing with gloves under the Queensberry Rules was being introduced. These new rules were originally codified to run amateur boxing, and for a time professional boxing was run on amateur lines by the amateur officials. Anything held outside of their jurisdiction was frowned upon by the authorities. Harry, in particular, fell foul of the clampdown on these so-called backstreet fights. As was his wont, the rough-and-ready Harry spent most of his boxing time in conflict with authorities. Mind you, much of it was his own doing.

Family history research shows several brushes with the law. A couple of arrests for disorderly behaviour were accompanied by cautions. In a fairly well-documented case, Harry was arrested for helping to arrange and fight in an unlicensed and illegal match in Tavistock Square in 1882. It caused outrage as it took place in the recently vacated Archdeacon Dunbar's chapel. It was generally believed that this was still consecrated ground, although this might not have been the case. This arrest was followed by assault charges for an attack on his younger brother Edward. Then, early the following year, he was charged and convicted for 'Unlawful Assembly to Fight', as recorded in a report from the time:

Bill England challenged Henry Goodson
Thurs, Jan 11 1884 - Bill England (Canning Town)
Eltham, LOST, STOPPED BY POLICE
Lyme Barn, High Street, Eltham.
Note: Attendance restricted to seventy (70).

This was a 'bare-knuckle' prize fight under LONDON PRIZE
RING rules. Both England and Goodson, plus three others,
Mr James Hull, Mr George Coe, and Mr Thomas Hyams were
arrested, to appear at Woolwich Court the following day, Friday,
January 12, all bailed to Friday, 09 January. The case was
sent for trial at the Old Baily, Wednesday, 30 January, where
both England and Goodson were sentenced to two months
imprisonment without hard labour, for engaging in a 'bare-
knuckle' prize fight.

Like their elder brother, Harry and Thomas were also suspected
of receiving and transporting stolen goods over the years. Their
names came up in a trial involving wholesale theft from the docks.
Dock theft has always been a fairly common occurrence, and in
this case no arrests were made. It seems the brothers sailed pretty
close to the wind.

After the brothers finished their boxing, they settled down.
Both married, and 'Sugar' Harry had a son, Edward (Ted), who
was born in 1880 and also went on to box. Ted fought over
sixty professional bouts in eight years, fighting mostly out of
the Excelsior Hall in Bethnal Green and later at Whitechapel's
Wonderland. Ted was regarded as a much better fighter than
his father, and made a reasonable living. He saw some action in
the First World War and sustained an injury which curtailed his
boxing. He returned home to live in Chingford after the war and
found life a struggle. He was the licensee of the Salmon and Ball in
Lamb Street, Spitalfields and committed suicide there in 1920. He
survived his father by just three years.[1]

⚔ TED GOODSON,
A Clever Youth who Hails from Hackney,
and can Box at 8st 2lb.

Ted, one of the the Fighting Goodsons: carmen, publicans, boxers, market porters and petty criminals. (Wikicommons)

There are countless examples of father-and-son boxers. Back in the day it was normal for parents who lived in small East End homes to share their meagre space with upwards of six or seven children. Billy Wells and Sammy McCarthy both shared theirs with nine others! 'Sugar' Harry Goodman had five sons, so it was no surprise that at least one of them took up the sport. Seven members of the Goodson family boxed a bit at some time or another.

*

As Catholic East End families go, the Quill family was not a large one, but they still managed to produce a couple of good boxers. Stepney-born **Johnny Quill** (*c.* 1908–1935) was the pick of the bunch, but his life was far too short. Johnny was an excellent boxer and boxed professionally from 1926, fighting almost 100 bouts. He was also a talented writer and planned to pursue a career in journalism after retiring from the ring. In 1935 he was on the brink of winning the British welterweight title. He had fought a hard-earned draw before beating his main rival, the tenacious and enduring Billy Bird, in the rematch to set up a crack at the title.[2] Johnny was quick and could deliver a big punch. He trained hard for all his matches, and it was when he was in training for the championship that he fell ill. His conditioned worsened, and he died in the summer of that year. The cause of death was thought to have been pneumonia, but in those days such a label was used for many deaths in which lung issues were evident. He was obviously a fit young man, and it was a great shock.

Johnny's nephew **Eddie Quill** (1932–) did not remember his uncle as he was only three at the time of his death, but he followed in his uncle's footsteps. Although he had a decent amateur career, his professional boxing career lasted only three bouts. He spoke to me about his life and boxing days in the East End, on which he looks back with affection.

Eddie was born on the Isle of Dogs. One night in 1941 he was, along with several hundred others, sitting in a bomb shelter listening to the ack-ack guns. That night the Luftwaffe targeted nearby Millwall Docks. They all but destroyed the Isle of Dogs that night. A large bomb fell just yards away from the young Eddie's shelter and it collapsed. Most of the main roof managed to stay secure, but the entrance was completely blocked. The tenants of the shelter were very lucky indeed, but it took until 11.00 a.m. the next day to dig them out. Homeless, the family went to live with some relatives in Wanstead and Eddie was then evacuated to Northampton. After the war he started working in the fruit and veg trade with his father. Meanwhile, two of his uncles were making a living delivering coal. His father's shop was situated in Cable Street, and Eddie remarked that in those days you could pop into the shop for a cauliflower and four pounds of potatoes and pick up a half-hundredweight of nutty slack at the same time!

Eddie boxed for the St John's Bosco Club in Stepney and was twice the Federation of Boys' Clubs boxing champion. After doing his eighteen months of national service in the RAF, Eddie resumed his boxing and made it to the finals of the senior ABA championships as a regional champion. Eddie got to know Joe Lucy when he was boxing as an amateur. They became good mates and went to West Ham games together. Lucy introduced Eddie to his manager, Jim Wicks, and Eddie turned pro with Wicks in 1955. He trained at Wicks' Thomas a Becket gym on the Old Kent Road with Lucy and the two Cooper brothers, Henry and George. Eddie suffered two very badly cut eyes in his first three fights and, having been injury free for all his amateur career, he was not at all sure if he could continue in the game. He was still making a good living in the fruit-and-veg business, so he called it a day after only three fights. A few years later he followed his uncles into the pub business.

His cousins Patsy and Jimmy Quill were big East End characters and famous faces on the pub circuit. Jimmy Quill had also boxed a bit and could handle himself. You needed to be hard as nails to run one of the notoriously rough pubs in the East End. The two brothers first ran the Two Puddings in Stratford. The Puddings was a real tough pub; I personally witnessed some serious violence there during the sixties. Jimmy and Patsy then went on to become landlords of the Blind Beggar Pub in Whitechapel at the time when Ronnie Kray shot George Cornell there in 1966. Patsy was on duty that night but went down on record as saying he did not see the incident. Bobby Moore and Harry Redknapp were both regulars – Moore held a small stake in the pub – but they were not drinking there that evening.

Eddie has little to say about the Krays. He knew them from his amateur fighting days and was aware of Ronnie's boxing abilities, and he also knew George Cornell. Cornell was a serious hard man and an enforcer for the Richardson Gang. Eddie reckons that if there were no guns in the Beggars that night then Cornell would have left the pub alive and Ronnie would have been flat on the pub floor. Eddie went on to run several pubs over many years, mostly in the Chelmsford area, as well as the popular Ivy House pub on Southend's seafront. He now lives in Wanstead, just up the road from his lifelong friend Sammy McCarthy – two ex-Stepney octogenarians with a mountain of memories.

*

In recent times the sizes of families have greatly reduced, so it is less common that multiple members of the same family take up boxing. There are still one or two recent examples, though. West Ham Boys' Club's Junior 1974 ABA champion **Paul Cook** was born in Stepney and was boxing with likes of Jimmy Batten and Rickie Grover, who later carved out a career in comedy and acting Paul was a decent enough boxer but was a late starter to the professional ranks, having his first fight in 1982. He only boxed twelve times, winning six and drawing one bout. Paul then moved on to coaching and training.

Paul had a son, Nicky, who was also born in Stepney but later moved to Dagenham. A chip off the old block, Nicky took to boxing and was mentored by his dad. Nicky joined the Hornchurch and Elm Park Amateur Boxing Club. A reasonable amateur, he reached the final of the ABA bantamweight championship in 1998 but lost. After that, though, he never looked back. He turned pro later that year and reeled off fifteen blistering wins to take him to a decider for the vacant WBF featherweight crown, which he won inside four rounds. He then won his next ten fights, including two defences of his WBF title, a Commonwealth title with three defences and finally the European crown followed by four defences. All in all, this was a five-year stretch of truly outstanding major international championship boxing. In September 2008, he fought for the WBO title against the defending champion, a Scot named Alex Arthur who was firm favourite. A report ringside summarised the fight:

Cook appeared to win the first three rounds on points by out jabbing Arthur, who came back in the fourth with a lot of left jabs and body shots that landed and had Cook in trouble. Cook won the fifth, Arthur the sixth, Cook the seventh until late in the round when Arthur rocked him with a right hand just before the bell. The battle continued to seesaw back and forth in centre ring and appeared very close through eleven. Cook came out in the twelfth and took the fight to the champion by throwing everything he had left in the tank to try to win the round and the fight and did so.

Nicky's later defence of that title did not go well, and he lost inside four rounds in what was only the second professional defeat of his career. Two fights later, he lost another tilt at the title to Ricky Burns. This time he seemed to have a bad back problem from the outset, and he was floored three times before the towel was thrown in and the referee stopped the fight. Nicky was stretchered off in a great deal of pain with a severe prolapsed disc and never boxed again. His record of thirty wins (fourteen by knockout) and only three losses is tremendous, and his father must have been very proud indeed.

10

NO GUTS NO GLORY

The question isn't who is going to let me;
it's who is going to stop me.

Ayn Rand

Ever since Daniel Mendoza opened up his boxing academy
in 1789, boxing clubs have played a major role in the
development of the sport in East London. The Marquess of
Queensberry Rules were introduced to ensure greater safety
for the professional prize fighters of the day, and gradually this
version of the sport became more organised and controlled.
Back in those days, no real organised amateur boxing existed.
Kids still scrapped on the streets and some of the older boys
joined the many sinister gangs that existed in the East End.
Gradually, on the back of the growing popularity of boxing,
one or two boys' clubs opened. Boxing gloves were becoming
more popular as bare-knuckle boxing declined. Parents saw that
boxing was a good way to get a child off the street and into a
safe place that catered for youngsters.

Not only did these clubs provide the training and support for talented boxers, then, but they also supplied a facility to help get young lads off the streets; in recent years, they have provided the same public service to girls. They can offer hope and direction for a lot of kids who otherwise could well descend into a life of crime, drugs and despair.

Although the vast majority of clubs were set up for the benefit of the working-class youth, some clubs were founded with the leisure of middle- and upper-class men in mind. Many were established during the mid-Victorian period. So-called 'gentleman boxers' would entertain their fellow members in an evening of boxing, often accompanied by gambling activities. These plush venues were a far cry from those in the heart of the East End. Several operated in West London, but there was one that was situated in Clapton.

In 1879, the Clapton Boxing Club was visited by the son of Charles Dickens, also named Charles, who included a description of the venue in his publication *Dickens's Dictionary of London*:

The 'noble art of self-defence' is not, however, altogether neglected, but finds its place among the athletic sports, and the clubs by which it is encouraged may be congratulated on keeping alive one of the oldest institutions, in the way of manly exercise, on record. Perhaps the two most important of these clubs are the Clapton Boxing Club with over 100 members, and the London Boxing Club; the former of which was originally started a couple of years ago among the oarsmen of the River Lea, the latter being an offshoot of the West London Rowing Club.

Boxing, it may be noted, has always been popular with rowing men as a capital exercise for keeping up some sort of condition during the winter months. The Clapton Boxing Club requires an entrance-fee of 5s and an annual subscription of 5s. The election is by ballot at a general meeting, one black ball in five to exclude. The season is from October to March, and the practice-nights are Mondays and Thursdays, when a

professional instructor attends. Valuable prizes are from time
to time offered for competition among gentlemen amateurs.
The head-quarters of the club are at the Swan Hotel, Upper
Clapton, where the hon. sec. may be addressed. With a, perhaps
unconscious, touch of humour, the club has adopted scarlet as
its distinctive colour – delicately suggestive of the 'claret' which
is occasionally 'tapped' at its meetings.

*

London can possibly lay claim to having the three or four top
amateur boxing clubs in England. The oldest of these is Lynn AC
Boxing Club, formed around 1880 in Southwark and still going
strong. Lynn dominated amateur boxing up until the 1920s. Clubs
started to appear in the East End towards the turn of the twentieth
century.

The golden era for East London clubs and gyms came either side
of the First World War. During this time there seemed to be a club,
gym or venue on every other street corner and a boxer in every
other household. Small local clubs like Stepney and St George's,
East Ham Boys' Club, Crown and Manor at Hoxton, Limehouse &
Popular, Fairbairn House and Broad Street Gym produced many
amateur champions and quite a few professional ones as well.
However, two clubs have dominated grassroots boxing in the East
End since the 1920s.

The Repton Boys' Club is the most famous amateur boxing
club in Britain, possibly the world. It was founded in 1884 by
Repton College in Derbyshire as an East London mission for the
underprivileged boys of Bethnal Green and surrounding areas. It is
tucked away behind Brick Lane, deep in London's East End, part
of a converted public bathhouse. It took a few years to develop
into the force in boxing that it was to become.

In its early years, the club was a general boys' social club. It
offered many different activities, including concerts and plays, but
sporting activities prevailed and gradually the club developed its

boxing facilities. In 1971, the Repton School withdrew its support for the club and the club's youth group status disappeared. The boxing division was still very strong, so it was able to transform into a stand-alone boxing club. The name changed from Repton Boys' Club to Repton Boxing Club later that year.

The club is steeped in history. Next to the punchbags hangs a sign bearing the slogan 'No Guts No Glory'. It's been hanging there for a few years. The modern version is 'No Pain No Gain', but when Repton's sign was hung up it was a message to the underprivileged lads that a glorious road could lay ahead for them. It would be a hard road and would take determination to walk it. Many set out, and a quite a few made it.

Repton boasts numerous professional champions among its alumni: Maurice Hope, Audley Harrison, Sylvester Mittee, John H. Stracey and Darren Barker to name but a few in more recent years. Back in the mid-sixties, the club probably thought it had yet another lad coming through to carve out a great professional career. **Michael Carter** from Hackney was a truly great Repton amateur and multiple ABA champion. He joined his clubmate John H. Stracey at the Mexico Olympics in 1968. Carter was more experienced than Stracey and was one of England's big hopes for a gold medal. He stood at the top of the amateur tree that year, unbeaten in five years and with only four losses in almost a hundred fights. The gold medal was beckoning, and to win it would be the cherry on the cake.

In a fight which echoed the heartbreak of Nicky Gargano's Olympic fight in 1956, Carter's hopes were unexpectedly and controversially dashed by a very curious decision by the Japanese referee. Carter was well on top of his Russian opponent when he was slightly winded by a body punch. Being well ahead, he went down on one knee for a breather. Up on the six count and ready to continue, fully recovered, he was inexplicably counted out by the ref. Like Nicky Gargano, Carter was devastated and gave up boxing on his return. It was boxing's loss, but Repton carried on producing great boxers.

Another Repton boxer whose career finished abruptly was **Tom Baker**. Baker, from Chingford, came from Romani descent and grew up on a static travellers' site. He also boxed at the West Ham Club, and appeared in two senior ABA finals. He turned professional in 2012 and trained with the Tibbs father-and-son team. He was considered a very stylish super-middleweight and fought successfully at that weight before stepping up to light-heavyweight. He fought fourteen times at both these weights and went unbeaten, picking up the English light-heavyweight title in 2016. After this win he went on record as saying he was confident of taking the British title within a few months. He fought and beat the polish fighter Bart Grafka in September that year, but then... nothing. It is unclear why such a very promising boxer hung up his gloves, but he relinquished his Southern Area and English titles and gave up the sport.

The Repton Club is not all about how many champions it has turned out or indeed what celebs were once members there.

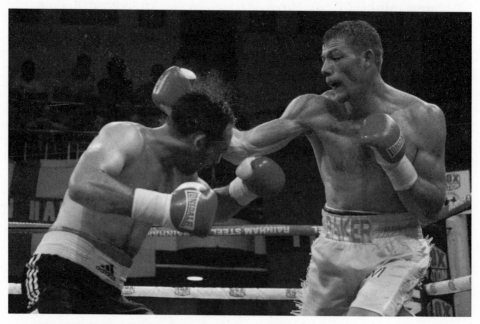

Tom Baker (right) vs Mark Till. His short and successful career came to an unexpected and unexplained halt. (Goodson Family History)

Tony Burns, Repton's lead trainer, has seen it all over the seven decades at the club. As he says:

> Getting kids off the streets is integral to what we do. Our seniors are in the gym three nights a week, sometimes four sessions a week. This is somewhere they can come and they're not getting into trouble. They are actually enhancing themselves, learning self-control as well as learning to box and that's bringing the right stuff out in them.

West Ham Boys' Boxing Club holds the same ethos. Since 1922 it has seen its fair share of champions, and it is still very much a focal point for up-and-coming boxers in the area. It was founded by Captain D. E. Myers and for many years it was situated in Plaistow adjoining the Black Lion, a pub famous for its connection to the many West Ham footballers who used it as their local. Pop in there on a Saturday evening after a game in the sixties and you could stand at the bar with Bobby Moore, Harry Redknapp, Geoff Hurst, Brian Dear and many more. The boxing club, which was briefly threatened with closure in 2010, has recently moved but is still very much active in the community.

It remains a tremendously successful club. Terry Spinks, Nigel Benn, Billy Walker, Mark Kaylor and Kevin Lear all boxed there. Originally the club used a black-and-white kit, but with the area being highly favourable to West Ham FC the club changed its colours to claret and blue. There is, however, no direct connection with the football club although several West Ham players would pop in from time to time and pull on a pair of gloves for a quick workout.

One of West Ham boxing club's earliest prodigies was **Ron Cooper**. Ron won the senior ABA lightweight title in 1948 while doing his national service in the Royal Navy and went on to represent Great Britain at the 1948 Olympic Games in London. Ron was considered one of the best amateur boxers of his generation. He was working in Millwall Docks when he got the call to represent England at the Olympics. It was his good fortune that his boss was a boxing fan and jumped for joy when one of his work force was picked to box at the Olympic Games. At this time Ron was the only breadwinner in the house after his father died quite young. He was asked to go on a fortnight's trip with the British boxing team to train and fight in Switzerland, and his boss generously gave Ron paid leave. Switzerland had been unaffected by the war and was an affluent country. It was an eye-opening experience for Ron. He recalls his time in Switzerland:

> The first night we were there they put a steak in front of me at dinnertime. I hadn't seen a cut of beef like that for over six years. It was over two years after the war had ended and back home we were still getting by on 2oz of bacon, 2oz of sugar, half a loaf of bread and a pint of milk. Most of the nation were still starving.

After the Olympics, Ron turned professional to give increased support to his widowed mother. However, he did not reach the same heights in the professional world that he did in the amateurs, and retired in 1950.

When West Ham born-and-bred **Terry Gill** climbed through the ropes to face the great Nicky Gargano in the ABA welterweight final in 1956, he knew he had his work cut out for him. Gargano was going for his third crown. Terry had reached the latter stages of the competition the previous two years boxing for West Ham, but now was his chance to claim the title. He too was doing his national service, and so he was fighting for the army that night. History shows it was not to be for Terry. Nicky Gargano won a straightforward points decision with some ease. Still, Terry Gill was, in theory, the second-best amateur welterweight in the country.

Rumours were floating around that Gargano might turn professional after the upcoming Olympics. Gill also planned to turn pro, but must have feared he could spend his professional career looking up at the great Gargano climbing the welterweight professional ladder rather than looking down on him. As it turned out, Terry need not have worried. After Gargano's bitter disappointment at the Melbourne Olympics and his family's pressure on him to stop boxing, he quit within a few months. Terry Gill grabbed the chance with both fists and signed pro forms, fighting his first professional bout in December that same year.

When amateur boxers first turn professional, they are normally set up with six-round matches to ease them in. Later they fight a few eight round matches before tackling the longer fights. Gill lost only once in his first seventeen matches over those distances. His first twelve-round match was against Ron Richardson for the vacant Southern Area title at Leyton Baths in February 1958. Gill stopped Richardson in the eighth round. The next month saw Gill fight the first of three matches against Albert Carroll, also at Leyton Baths. Carroll was a doggedly determined fighter from Bethnal Green. On the night, the slightly more experienced Carroll narrowly beat Gill. They were then matched again for a defence of Gill's Southern Area title.

The pair fought a close bout, with Gill just shaving it on a tight points decision. His final match with Carroll came in June the following year, 1959. It was a final eliminator bout for the British welterweight title that Gill had been fighting so hard to get for three years. He was confident, and with no Nicky Gargano around he must have thought the title was so near. The boxing world knew these two East End lads were difficult to split. The BBC, with Harry Carpenter at the mike, covered the fight and he broadcast on another close match between the pair. Carroll did enough in the final few rounds against a tiring Gill to take the win. For Terry, the loss was a bitter pill to swallow and he went out and lost his next match as well. Just like the 1956 ABA final, he just fell short and decided to retire shortly after.

The West Ham club has also rubbed shoulders with royalty over the years. The Duke of Kent was a club patron for a while and it was visited by the Prince of Wales (later to become Edward VIII), who took a keen interest in the club. Although, in keeping with all clubs these days, the club embraces female boxers, it still proudly keeps the title of West Ham Boys' Boxing Club. Kevin Lear's sister boxed for the club and her name can be seen on the honours board there, marking her win in 1990.

Local lad **Ralph Charles** also boxed out of West Ham. He was an outstanding amateur, and on turning professional in 1963 won an incredible thirty-two out of thirty-three fights, taking the British and Commonwealth welterweight title within five years and adding the European title to his impressive cabinet a year later. In March 1972 he took on Jose Napoles for the world title. The brilliant Napoles was just arriving at the very pinnacle of his awesome powers, and although Charles fought quite well for the opening rounds he was caught by a big punch from Napoles in the seventh round and never recovered.

Mark Kaylor had a great amateur record and represented Great Britain at the 1980 Olympics. His professional career started sensationally, with wins in all of his first twenty-four fights. Although he had forty-eight professional fights, he just could not get to the very top, losing five times in European title fights. Perhaps his most famous fight came in 1985, when he defeated Herol Christie in the eighth round of a hard-fought match that was marred by controversy due to a pre-fight scuffle between the pair and death threats directed at Christie by racists. During and after the fight Kaylor and Christie showed great respect for each other, the former saying such values were instilled at him at West Ham.

Kevin Lear was one of the last club members to go on to claim a professional world championship. ABA champion in 1999, Kevin turned professional in September 1999. He had an explosive, brilliant amateur career but a short-lived professional one. Lear suffered from shoulder problems throughout his professional career but this did not stop him from winning all fourteen of his fights, culminating with his victory against the Bulgarian Kirkor Kirkorov for the world super-featherweight title in 2002. It was a great feat given his increasingly troublesome shoulder, and he retired after the fight. Another great amateur to train and box out of the West Ham club was two time All Ireland Champion (1991/2) **Mickey Delaney.**

The late Micky May was West Ham's senior trainer for almost thirty years and personally trained almost two hundred champions at various levels. He prepared dozens of amateur boxers for success at the senior ABA championships and was a holder of the prestigious ABA Coach of the Year award. A true club legend. Mickey's crowning glory was his coaching of two outstanding young amateurs, **Matthew Marsh** and **Kevin Mitchell**. Both boxed for the club around the same time at the beginning of the millennium. Marsh had won the ABA flyweight title in 2001 but both boxers were finalists in the 2003 championships. This time Marsh finished runner up in the flyweight division and Kevin Mitchell won the featherweight title. The following year Marsh regained the flyweight crown. It was some outstanding work by the superb West Ham trainer.

One of West Ham's latest prodigies is the super bantamweight **Lucian Reid.** Reid finished runner-up in the 2013 championships but went on to claim the title the following year. In his short professional career to date, he is undefeated and looks like another East End lad heading for professional glory.

Both Repton and West Ham boxing clubs are still regarded as centres of excellence in the boxing world, and as long as they go on churning out top-class amateurs who go on to compete in the professional ranks they will carry on attracting young talent to their clubs.

*

One other boys' club of note in East London was **Eton Manor Boys Club.** Like Repton, Eton Manor was formed by the philanthropic efforts of others. In Eton Manor's case it was achieved through the works of Eton College and their associated alumni.

In the late 1800s, Eton College founded the Eton Mission to help the underprivileged of Hackney. In 1909, a boy's club was formed.

Initially it was situated above a large coal shop in Hackney. The club was funded and run by four Old Etonians: Arthur Villiers, Gerald Wellesley, Alfred Wagg and Sir Edward Cadogan. These were aristocratic, wealthy and extremely well-connected men. A large and well-equipped club house was built during 1912/13 on the site of the Manor Dairy Farm off Riseholme Street and it was opened on 1 July 1913 by its first and only president, Field Marshall Lord F. M. Roberts VC.[1] A few years later, a large area of land about a mile away close to Leyton was also purchased. It was developed mainly for outdoor sporting activities and was known as 'The Wilderness'.

Virtually every sport and pastime was catered for.[2] Eton Manor produced some excellent sportsmen over the years, mostly amateur. Often current or past top sportsmen would give up their time to coach at the club. Former England footballer and manager Alf Ramsey and former England cricket captain Douglas Jardine were often present at coaching sessions.

It was speculated that an Eton Manor football team of the 1950s under coach Ramsey could easily have competed at a professional level. Competing in the London Amateur League, they won the premiership title three times in four years. A couple of their players were approached by top London clubs. Not one member of the squad turned professional, although a couple of ex-Eton Manor footballers from earlier days did play for top clubs, including Len Wills, who played almost 200 games for Arsenal.

However, it was the boxing setup that was Eton Manor's jewel in the crown, producing a string of truly excellent amateur boxers from its ranks. By and large the amateur champions Eton Manor produced tended to stay amateur, in keeping with the ethos of the club and its founders. Top professional boxer Dick Corbett was engaged as a coach in 1938 and, along with Johnny Thomas and the Mallin brothers, would help train the youngsters.

For many years Eton Manor was considered one of the country's top boxing clubs, and on a couple of occasions it supplied multiple members to British international teams. Nicky Gargano,

Eddie Woollard, Fred Grace and the Mallin brothers were just some of the many boxers who represented the club in junior and senior ABA championships over the years. Fred Grace was a four-time lightweight ABA champion who boxed in two Olympic Games, winning the gold medal at the 1908 edition. Both Gargano and Woollard boxed at the 1954 ABA finals. Although both were Eton Manor lads, they were both doing their national service in the army, so they represented the army at those championships. Nicky won the welterweight title, but Eddie lost in the light-heavyweight final. The following year saw them both back boxing for Eton Manor. Once again Nicky Gargano came away with the winner's trophy and Eddie had to settle for runner-up.

One Manor lad that did make it through the amateur ranks and turned professional was Billy Davis from Bow. A youthful lightweight, he was nicknamed Billy 'the Kid' Davis. Billy turned professional in 1959 and lost just once in his first eighteen fights. He was being tipped for the top when he was matched against Terry Spinks in a featherweight non-title fight. Although he lost

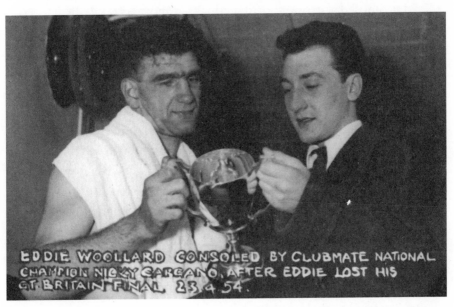

EDDIE WOOLLARD CONSOLED BY CLUBMATE NATIONAL CHAMPION NICKY GARGANO, AFTER EDDIE LOST HIS GT BRITAIN FINAL 23.4.54.

Eton Manor's Eddie Woollard (left) shows Nicky Gargano his runner-up trophy.
(© Bishopsgate Institute)

narrowly on points, a rematch was hastily arranged and on this occasion Billy turned the tables on Spinks. It was a very good result, but then Billy took on Howard Winston, the current British and future world featherweight champion. Although Billy put up a brave fight, he was forced to retire in the seventh round. A few more fights followed with mixed results before he was easily beaten by another British champion, Maurice Cullen, in 1963. He retired shortly after. A rare example of an Eton Manor lad making an impact at a professional level.

Another boxer who was an Eton Manor old boy was Laurie Gold. Gold was a decent lightweight who fought in the 1949 ABA finals for the club and was a Federation of London Boys' Clubs champion. In 1950 he travelled to Israel to participate in the third Jewish Olympics (World Maccabiah Games). These games attract up to 10,000 sporting competitors and Laurie fought some serious opposition from America and eastern Europe to come back as lightweight champion.

Eton Manor eventually closed in 1967, but since its inception it had promoted a strong sporting ethic that most certainly benefitted thousands of young lads from a tough area.

*

In the early 1900s, there was a big demand from Jewish boys and girls for sporting facilities in the area. To meet the demand of Jewish boys wanting to take up boxing, two or three mainly Jewish clubs opened in the area. The Victoria Jewish Boys' Club in Whitechapel was a good base for younger boxers, but the really significant one was the **Judean Athletic Club** in Stepney.

Both clubs had been set up to get young Jewish kids off the streets just after the turn of the twentieth century. Surprisingly, the other sport that caught the imagination of Jewish kids was gymnastics, and several clubs provided facilities for this as well. Quite a few very talented Jewish girls and boys from the area went on to compete at national level in the sport.

Although several future Jewish boxing champions passed through the Judean, it was a relatively short-lived club. It started life in Johnson's Court, Leman Street at the turn of the century and then at Prince's Square, Cable Street where it was housed in a large converted stable loft and regularly drew crowds of up to 1,000 for its events before closing down in 1916. Its most famous sons were Ted 'Kid' Lewis and Jack 'Kid' Berg but other very good Jewish boxers carved out careers after spending time at the club, including British and European bantamweight champion Phil Hickman (Johnny Brown), British and European lightweight and welterweight champion Young Joseph(s) and British light heavyweight champion Harry Reeve.

Joseph(s) in particular had a good, long career, fighting 135 times over twelve years with no fewer than ten fights against East Ender Alf Reed between 1905 and 1912. Josephs was another East Ender who came up against the formidable Frenchman Georges Carpentier and lost.

*

Probably the quirkiest setting for a boxing club was in the City of London. Once the Second World War ended, the East End took stock of the damage and a large rebuilding program began. Some of the older industrial companies relocated or closed, and some of the population moved out into the suburbs and the 'New Towns' that were being built. Although very close to the docks and the industrial units of East London, the City of London itself escaped the very worst of the bombings. Thanks to the herculean efforts of the London Fire Brigade, the financial heart of the country was kept beating. The Square Mile employed tens of thousands of East Londoners in the large numbers of financial institutions situated there.

For those living in the Aldgate, Bethnal Green and Whitechapel areas, the City of London was within walking distance. These people carried on regardless and kept things functioning, often picking their way through bombed-out buildings and rubble-strewn streets to get to the City. One of the largest institutions was the London Stock Exchange, which employed thousands at its Capel Court headquarters – and it was here, just after the war, that permission was granted to set up the Stock Exchange Boxing Club.

You might expect it to have been housed in some smaller nearby building, but you would be wrong. The club was housed on the main trading floor! The members would set up a fully functioning gym, complete with roped ring, following the close of business. After training they would pack it all away again. It was extremely popular, and many East End boxers from this club went on to achieve notable results in amateur championships throughout the 1950s and 1960s. The club produced the 1968 ABA lightweight champion Andy White. It also supplied the ABA middleweight champion in 1964, Bill Robinson, who went on to take the light-middleweight championship the following year.

11

MOVERS AND SHAKERS

Boxing could never exist without the trainers, managers, matchmakers, sponsors and promoters who have supported the sport since its popularity began to grow during the nineteenth century. Harry Abrahams, Micky Duff, Harry Levene, Frank Warren, Mike Barrett and Barry and Eddie Hearn have been big players in the game, but the daddy of them all was the legendary **Jack Solomons** (1900–1979). He was surely British boxing's greatest promoter and matchmaker.

Solomons was born on Petticoat Lane, Aldgate, into a family of fish marketers. After the First World War he helped expand the family business and by the early 1920s controlled much of the fish imports into the south-east. He became a very shrewd operator and had gained a reputation for 'sharp' business practices. He loved boxing and for a while he considered trying to make his name in the ring. He fought a few matches under the nickname of Kid Mears but with mixed results. One night he took his girlfriend to watch him box. What she saw horrified her, and she told him in no uncertain terms that he would have to choose either her or the ring. He decided to choose the ring … and went up to Hatton Garden and got her an engagement one! He settled down working the fish markets. He often quipped that he would rather a fish get battered than him!

Solomons began promoting boxing during the 1930s. He took over operations at the Devonshire Club in Hackney and turned it into a big boxing venue. He was gaining a reputation as a leading name in the sport and started to manage boxers as well. One of his first prodigies was the great lightweight fighter Eric Boon, who held the British title for over three years. Boon was a country lad, born in Chatteris in Cambridgeshire. Solomons signed him up at a very early age, barely eighteen. Solomons had moved on from his Petticoat Lane home and lived in North Hackney, close to his club. Boon used to travel up from the countryside to stay at Jack's house.

One day, Eric asked Jack to show him around London's West End. Jack had promised Eric's parents he would look after the lad. Not wanting to expose him to some of the more eye-popping sites around Piccadilly and Soho, and knowing Eric hadn't a clue of the whereabouts of the West End, Solomons jumped on a No. 35 tram with young Eric to show him the sites. Unbeknown to young Eric, this tram went nowhere near Piccadilly. Instead, as it trundled south, it reached the Narrow Way in Mare Street, Hackney, the borough's shopping centre and home to the famous Hackney Empire Theatre. 'Here it is,' said Jack as they surveyed the mass of shoppers, stalls and stores and the glittering lights on the theatre. Eric was none the wiser!

Although life in the East End had gradually improved since the Great Depression a few years before, young men from the area were still anxious to box professionally. Solomons was a ruthless businessman. Not content with gate receipts at the Devonshire Club, he supplied the venue with many of the fighters from his stable of boxers and took a big cut from their purses as well – not that this practice put young boxers off signing up with him. East Ender Jack Martin, who boxed under the title Kid Nitram, was managed by Solomons and remembered:

I done about six rounds for 2 pounds, If I done eight rounds I got four pounds. If you were top of the bill, you'd get eight pounds. It wasn't bad money. I was born in the East End in 1915 and in the thirties, everyone was out of work. On the Dole I got eight shillings (40p) a week. I hated it. How can you live on that each week?

The Devonshire Club was destroyed in the Blitz during the war, and Jack later moved his base of operations to his gym on Great Windmill Street in Soho. After the war he upped his involvement in matchmaking and promoting with great success. His first big match was the Brian London *vs* Bruce Woodcock British title fight, and soon after he was promoting other great fights. He started using the Harringay Arena in North London for most of his matches.

Throughout his time as a promoter and matchmaker, Solomons was constantly at odds with the British Boxing Board of Control. During 1939 and 1940, a bitter war of words broke out and Jack, together with his fellow Devonshire Club promoter Sydney Hull, resigned from their positions on the board and returned their licences. Hull and Solomons echoed the thoughts of others in the business that the BBBC was becoming far too dictatorial. Many other promoters, trainers and even boxers returned their licences or had them stripped for taking part in unlicensed matches. The so called 'boxing rebels' were supported by the Boxer's Union (Association of British Boxers). The dispute was eventually resolved with some small concessions from the BBBC. Solomons and all the other so-called rebels had their licences returned to them by the summer of 1940, but it was actions such as these that enhanced Jack Solomons' reputation in the game.

The first boxing match to be aired on the BBC was a Jack Solomons promotion featuring his boxer Eric Boon in a British lightweight title match. It was televised from the Harringay Arena in February 1939 in front of a full house of 14,000 punters. It was also shown to additional paying customers in two large cinemas in London. It was a truly epic fight. Jack could not, in his wildest dreams, have imagined that such a tremendous contest could usher in the televised age of British boxing. Not that it would have been watched by that many – the BBC had only started broadcasting three years earlier and at the time of the match less than 5 per cent of British homes had a TV set. Those who did see it, however, witnessed a fabulous match between Eric Boon and Bethnal Green's Arthur Danahar. Both up-and-coming young men in tremendous form. To give Solomons his due, he had done his homework and was confident that these two would be extremely well matched.

The old maxim that the greatest matches are those between an out-and-out boxer and an out-and-out fighter proved to be the case here. It was also, as they say, a match of two halves. Danahar was the skilful boxer and dominated the first seven rounds, using a brilliant defence to counter Boon's aggression and delivering a rapier-sharp left to the face of the oncoming Boon. At the end of the fourth round, Boon's eye was completely closed. His cornermen did a great job to give him some sight through the swollen eye so that he could come out for round five. Boon fought the next three rounds more circumspectly, but Danahar was picking him off regularly.

By the end of the seventh, the Bethnal Green lad was miles ahead and Boon's eye was closing up again. More work for his corner to do. Boon came out for the eighth well behind in the match and decided to go for it full tilt. He rushed in and caught Arthur cold, delivering two huge blows to floor Danahar twice in that round. Groggily, Danahar managed to see out the round and recovered slightly in the break. The following round Boon again got through but Arthur survived. The tide had turned. Boon won the next few rounds comfortably. Arthur was tiring rapidly and was floored three times for the full nine-second count in round thirteen. Showing tremendous determination, Danahar got through that round and, refusing to quit, staggered out for the next round to face the rampant Boon.

Carpe diem. Eric rushed in and smashed a massive right hand through Arthur's feeble left-hand defence, catching him flush on the jaw. Danahar was left flat on the canvas, but to everyone's amazement he slowly began to rise. The crowd were vociferously willing the brave cockney lad to get to his feet and continue. The referee disagreed and stopped the fight. The referee that night was Barrington Dalby. Some will remember Dalby as a great BBC boxing commentator, and he was a big voice in the sport for more than three decades. He would write about the Boon *vs* Danahar fight much later, noting that he regarded it as the best fight he ever refereed.

After the fight, Dalby was talking to Boon in the doorway of the new champ's dressing room. He had just congratulated the victor when a white-haired, middle-aged woman approached Boon and put her arms around him. He recalls the conversation:

> 'Congratulations,' she whispered to Eric and then kissed him on his bloodied cheek. 'I'm Arthur's mum.'
>
> She then turned to me. 'You were right to stop it,' she said. 'My son had had enough.'

Mothers and referees know best ... in that order.

In 1946, Solomons started to attract American talent to these shores. He brought over the very popular Gus Lesnevich to fight Freddie Mills. Probably the greatest fight he put on was the Randolph Turpin *vs* Sugar Ray Robinson middleweight title clash in 1951. Solomons also cashed in heavily on the popularity of the sport by publishing a large number of paperbacks and annuals. He continued to put on boxing productions well into the 1960s, bringing over big American stars like Ike Williams, Archie Moore, Joe Brown, Emile Griffith, Joey Maxim and Sugar Ramos. The relatively unknown Cassius Clay was brought over to fight Henry Cooper in that memorable 'Henry's Hook' 1963 match.

Gradually, with increasing television involvement in the sport, Solomons' productions began to decline. He was awarded an OBE in 1978 and inducted into Boxing's Hall of Fame in 1996. He would promote several hundred fights, including twenty-six

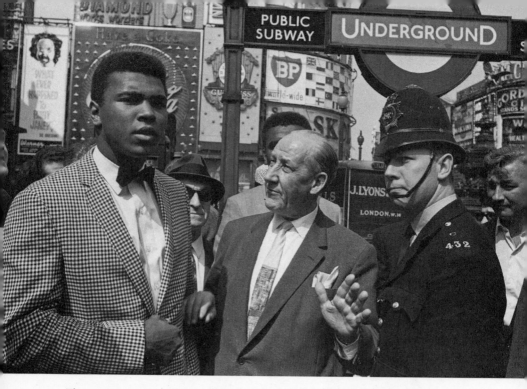

The great man arriving in London for the Cooper fight. The serious-faced policeman is, in fact, asking the planet's greatest ever sporting icon to move on as he is blocking the Piccadilly pavement. (© Alamy Images)

title fights, in over forty years in the game. He worked closely with fellow promoter Sydney Hull, but his right-hand man on his climb to the top was **Sid Burns** (1914–1994).

Sam was the son of the skilled welterweight and middleweight boxer Sid Burns, the British contender who was somewhat contemptuously dealt with by Ted 'Kid' Lewis when he was a sparring partner to the great man. Sam Jnr was born on Cannon Street Road in Shadwell and watched his father train and box when growing up. Boxing wasn't something that he wanted to actively pursue, but he did enjoy the sport. Sam was well educated and got a job at the *Evening Standard* working in their telegraph office. He then moved on to work at *Sporting Life* and reported on both horseracing and boxing.

Given Sam's boxing and media background, Jack Solomons, who knew the young man's father, offered him a job in his rapidly expanding promotions empire. Jack set Sam up in offices opposite his Windmill gym and Sam became his general manager, helping to promote some of the greatest boxing matches around the country in the years after the war. He also went on to manage some terrific boxers himself, including the 'Paddington Express', Terry Downes. Sam split from Solomons in the mid-sixties to concentrate on management and managed the Olympic champion and world title contender Chris Finnegan as well as his brother Kevin Finnegan. The excellent Tony Sibson was also on his roster.

After finishing with his boxing career, Terry Downs stayed in partnership with Sam as joint owners of a chain of ninety betting shops, which they eventually sold to William Hill in the early 1970s. The bookmaker appointed Sam as managing director from 1972 until his retirement in 1981. He was highly regarded and understood boxers as well as anybody in the game. Coincidentally, he died on the same day as Jack Solomons' younger brother Maxie, who also shared some of those great years.

Seventeen years after Jack Solomons was born on Petticoat Lane, and just a stone's throw away, **Nathaniel 'Nat' Basso** (1917–2001) was about to set out on a similar road. Very few people will have heard of Nat Basso south of the Watford Gap, but by the age of forty he was revered in the north, being called 'Mr Boxing' and 'The authentic voice of Northern English pugilism'.

By the early 1920s, boxing was part of the fabric of the East End. Nat grew up with the Premierland boxing venue well established and shows taking place there several times a week. His elder brother smuggled him in to see the fights, and from then on Nat was smitten with the sport. As with so many kids at that particular time, the great Ted 'Kid' Lewis was Nat's idol and he saw Ted box at Premierland regularly.

Unlike Solomons, Nat Basso did not take up the game but he did become quite an aficionado of the sport and when, at the age of eleven, he moved with his family to Manchester, he kept up his interest. He sought out the gyms, clubs and venues in the north-west and followed the progress of boxers in that area. His interest was curtailed for a while during the war, when he served as a machine gunner in the Manchester Regiment and saw a lot of active service. While in the army he helped train some of the men who took part in the inter-regimental boxing matches. After the war he threw himself into boxing, and it was over the next forty years that he earned his tag of 'Mr Boxing' in the north. During this period, Nat trained, managed and promoted all around the north and into Scotland. 'The authentic voice of boxing' was a reference to the long period of time when he was employed as the MC at some of the big northern fight nights.

Nat was elected chairman of the British Board of Boxing's Central Council, serving for forty years, giving him the longest reign by any chairman. At the age of seventy-seven, he became the oldest boxing manager to guide a boxer to a British championship when Carl Thompson took the vacant British cruiserweight title. Over an astonishing career, Nat may have lost his cockney accent for a northern one but he never forgot his East End roots, back where it all started.

If Nat Basso was called the north's Mr Boxing, then the man deserving that title in the south must surely be **Sam Russell**. Russell was born in East London's Limehouse around 1890 and had over 250 amateur and professional fights. Some records of his fights are unclear, but it is possible he only lost four times in his fighting career. It is also reported he managed to inflict sixty-eight consecutive knockouts, although this again is unsubstantiated.

After stopping boxing in 1920, he started to referee matches in and around the area. Working at the Drill Hall in Bow and Premierland in Whitechapel, he gradually earned a reputation for being a very effective referee. It wasn't long before he was officiating at more prestigious venues and in March 1926, he took control of his first British title fight at the Royal Albert Hall. Over the next twenty-five years or so, he handled dozens of British, European, Empire and world professional title fights as well as amateur championships.

Russell's refereeing career finished on a high. His last two matches were Randolph Turpin's British Empire middleweight fight victory in 1953 and the Don Cockell *vs* Johnny Williams British and Empire heavyweight championship fight. After reffing for almost thirty-two years, Russell hung up his boxing bow tie in December 1953 after overseeing more than four hundred bouts across all levels of boxing. Apart from his work inside the ring, he also managed and promoted boxing in the East End. Committed to the sport, Russell stayed within the game for many years after.

Although, on balance, America may have produced the finest boxing trainers, this country produced the finest boxing referees. We know about Sid Nathan, Eugene Corri, Nat Basso and Sam Russell, and in later years the great Harry Gibbs was the man to go to for any big fights. However, for the sheer longevity of his reign inside the ring and the esteem in which he was held, the doyen of them all was **J. H. Douglas**. Does the name ring a bell? Well, almost. J. H. Douglas was the father of J. W. N. H. Douglas, East London's greatest all-round sportsman, whom we covered earlier in the book.

John Herbert Snr boxed to a very high standard as an amateur. He won the amateur middleweight championship, made a small fortune importing lumber from Scandinavia, produced two very sporty sons in John Jnr and his brother C. H. (Pickles) and then went on to become one of the all-time great boxing referees, possibly the greatest of all. As befitted his upper-class status, Douglas wore a top hat while pacing round the ring. He took charge of his first fight in 1890 and went on to officiate on almost 2,200 bouts of boxing up until 1927. He took charge of dozens of British, European and world championship fights, mostly at the prestigious National Sporting Club in Covent Garden. Herbert's last fight was on 19 December 1927, a twenty-round humdinger between Scottish flyweight and future world champion Johnny Hill and the French European champion Emile Pladner at the National Sporting Club. Three years later to the very day, J. H. and his son J. W. N. H. were drowned at sea when their passenger ship, returning from Finland, went down in thick fog in the North Sea.

We have covered the boxing scene of the eighteenth century, when some of the bare-knuckle fighters were 'sponsored' by the aristocracy. They viewed boxing alongside foxhunting, hare coursing and deer hunting. The thrill of the hunt was key, and betting on their charges was an additional indulgence that added some extra spice. All they had to do was to keep their fighters fed, clothed and sheltered.

By the end of the nineteenth century, the Industrial Revolution had resulted in London's eastward expansion as industry looked to develop in areas close to the City. Large companies and organisations set up along the Thames and grew throughout the early part of the twentieth century. In some respects, the role of the aristocracy to sponsor their sporting champions was taken up by these large organizations. Some of these companies and organisations set up social and sports clubs for the benefit of their employees. They had the resources to build impressive training facilities to assist with the development of their employees' amateur sporting ambitions, and boxing certainly benefitted from this. At the forefront were the big industrial complexes of the Midlands and the north. On amateur bills you would often see the companies whom boxers represented. By the late 1930s, large companies like Vauxhall, Rolls-Royce, Electrolux and a couple of the large northern collieries all entered their star boxers into the ABA championships.

To the immediate east of the City of London, the old handcraft industries had been all but swept aside by the Industrial Revolution. By the late nineteenth century, very few weavers plied a trade. In their place, in the particular area in which weaving once thrived, upholstery and furniture manufacturing developed. One of the largest was Harris Lebus. It started life as a small furniture manufacturer in the Old Street/Hoxton area, eventually settling in Tabernacle Street, Hoxton. Harris Lebus later opened a large site in Tottenham Hale, but up into the early fifties they had a giant office and showroom building in the area. The Harris Lebus Boxing Club produced some very good amateur boxers between the late thirties and the early sixties. Mick Pye won the national flyweight title for them in 1962. Both the Tate & Lyle sugar processing company in Silvertown and the Port of London Authority in Custom House had attached boxing clubs producing great amateur boxers.

By the 1920s, the London Docks was the biggest dock complex in the world. It is estimated that at its peak, either side of the Second World War, more than a quarter of a million people worked in and around the docks in some capacity. Casual labour was still very much in evidence. The Port of London Authority administered the running of all the London docks,[1] and the boxing club they set up attracted men from up and down the Thames. They even held their own boxing championships and took part at some prestigious venues. There were lots of aspiring boxers who started work in the many industries in the area, the docks being just one. Several large breweries were big employers. Mann, Crossman and Paulin and the Truman breweries as well as Charrington were big supporters of sports in the area, and a number of boxers found work at their breweries.

Billingsgate Fish Market in Lower Thames Street and Spitalfields fruit and vegetable market off Commercial Street also employed their fair share of up-and-coming boxers. The markets were ideal employers for boxers. Up early and in work by around four o'clock in the morning, most could finish their work by midday, which meant they had ample time to train or fight later in the day. Many boxers were market porters. The manual work that the job entailed kept their fitness levels high. Several employees who left such jobs to pursue professional boxing careers returned to market work after hanging up the gloves.

*

Specialist boxing trainers and managers have been around since the days of Daniel Mendoza in the late eighteenth century. In America, some trainers have achieved cult status which in some cases has eclipsed even some of the champion boxers they trained. Cus D'Amato, Eddie Futch and Angelo Dundee are three such individuals. In East London, the trainers tended to stay out of the spotlight.

Terry Lawless (1933–2009) is probably the most well known of these. Born in West Ham, Lawless started his coaching and management career in 1957. He was based at the Royal Oak gym in Canning Town. His early stable of local boxers included Ralph Charles, Stan Kennedy, Johnny Caiger and Jimmy Tibbs – all good, solid pro fighters who developed under Lawless, but they were to give way to some world-class acts a few years later.

By the early seventies, Lawless had begun to manage boxers as well as training them. Top fighters Silvester Mittee and Maurice Hope joined his growing team. He hired George Wiggs and Frank Black as his training assistants, both of whom stayed with him for more than ten years. Tibbs later re-joined Lawless as a trainer, as did George Francis, with whom he formed a winning team training Frank Bruno. Lawless was in the corner in Mexico City in 1975 when John H. Stracey got off the floor in the first round to beat the great Jose Napoles. He was instrumental in getting Stracey settled in the break between rounds one and two, giving him the necessary instructions to ease back into the fight.

Promoters often pressured Lawless to put his boxers into fights when they were clearly the underdogs, but he never put a fighter into a match he couldn't win. He fell out with boxing promoter Mickey Duff on more than one occasion over this. In his youth, when travelling around to various boxing events with his best mate, the great Sammy McCarthy, he had seen underprepared fighters take severe beatings against opponents who were clearly superior in both fitness and ability. This is not to say that Lawless handled his boxers with kid gloves; after all, the team were in the fight game to make money. But Terry had an instinct about exactly what his boxers were capable of. He took care of his stable of boxers, and they repaid him in the ring. Many used the West Ham Club and the best of them were trained by Terry's old mate Jimmy Tibbs.

In his later years Terry worked tirelessly with Frank Bruno, enjoying somewhat mixed results at the very top. Frank did hold the WBC title for a short while, but he was unlucky to be around at the same time as some very good heavyweights. Of all the big names Lawless worked with, however, his crowning glory was probably his association with **Charlie Magri**. Lawless would frequently visit the local clubs and gyms and kept an eye out for up-and-coming amateur boxers as he had a tremendous eye for spotting young talent. Charlie Magri, however, was not hard to spot.

Although many think Magri was born and bred in Stepney, he was actually born in Tunisia and moved to London at a very young age. A very good schoolboy footballer, he signed a youth contract with Millwall FC, where he played with Jimmy Batten there. He was perhaps, too small to ever make it professionally at football so he turned to boxing. Charlie joined the Arbour Boxing Club. Football's loss was boxing's gain as young Charlie went on to win six ABA championships in seven years. He also represented England and boxed at the Montreal Olympics in 1976.

Magri turned professional after the Olympics and teamed up with the Lawless camp. He hit the professional ground running, stopping each of his first two opponents – quite useful boxers –in the second round. In December 1977 the British flyweight title became vacant. There was a dearth of good flyweights at the time and Lawless fancied Charlie to have a crack at the title. Charlie completely swamped Dave Smith from Eltham inside seven rounds. Lawless knew then that he had some fighter on his hands.

Amazingly, after just three professional fights the Lawless team had a British champion on their hands. Magri went unbeaten for twenty-three fights, picking up the European title and defending it six times. In 1983 he fought and won the world flyweight championship against Eleoncio Mercedes. He had a further two world title fights but was soundly beaten. At this point Magri was still winning the odd British and European fight, but the canny Lawless recognised that by 1985 Magri's dominance was waning fast.

Magri put his European title on the line in 1986 when he was matched against a young and exceptionally talented Duke McKenzie. Magri was mostly out-boxed, and when he went down for an eight count in the sixth round Lawless threw in the towel. After the fight Lawless made it clear to Magri that it had to be the end of the road for him. Although Magri thought he still had further fights in him and fell out with Lawless somewhat over the matter, he eventually decided to hang up the gloves. It was a prime example of Lawless's approach to caring for his boxers, preventing them from going on too long either in a single boxing match or in their overall career.

In the late 1980s, younger, more ambitious managers and promoters came along. Men like Barry Hearn, Frank Warren and Mike Barrett wanted to change the face of British boxing. Lawless slipped slowly into retirement, but he leaves a lasting legacy, having trained or managed six world champion fighters in his time. Jim Watt, who captured the world lightweight crown at the unlikely age of thirty-one, described his former mentor as 'that rare breed of manager who treats his boxers like sons rather than fighters'. This was also borne out by Terry's widow, Sylvia, who explained that his meticulous approach extended to bringing boxers home to stay with them in the days running up to big championship fights. He didn't want to risk his man running into any last-minute problems and thought it best that they stayed with him and his wife. I don't know if the long-suffering Sylvia, who was married to Terry for fifty years, got fed up sharing the bathroom with Frank Bruno or Charlie Magri, but it does give you an insight into the man.

Great Days: Terry with British heavyweight champ John Gardner. (© Alamy Images)

12

NOT FOR THE FAINT-HEARTED

Boxing is a test of strength, power, speed, skill, endurance and the overall ability of boxer to withstand punishment for a long period of time. Boxing is universally acknowledged as the hardest competitive sport in the world. The rewards can be high, but so too can the risks.

On the night Nigel Benn fought the twenty-seven-year-old American Gerald McClellan for the WBC world super middleweight title, Terry Lawless had all but retired. I do not know if he was present to witness what happened that night. If he was there, he would have been appalled. Benn, who was trained by Jimmy Tibbs at West Ham Boxing Club, came from Ilford on the East London border and was defending a world title for the fourth time. McClellan was an outstanding fighter with a big punch. Benn was also noted as a fighter with a big punch, and the match was heavily anticipated in the days and weeks leading up to the fight. Both Benn and McClellan had boxed at middleweight, and both had moved up to super-middleweight.

On that evening of 25 February 1995, one of the most brutal fights ever to take place on British soil in the modern era unfolded before an audience of 12,000 at the London Arena in Millwall's Dockland. In Russell Crowe's gladiatorial words, 'Hell was about to be unleashed'. The half-hour that followed the bell was jammed full of huge punches, both legal and illegal, with many head clashes over ten rounds of relentless, blood-and-guts, no-quarter-given fighting. Benn was knocked through the ropes after just thirty-five seconds in the first round but climbed back in and hit McClellan with a big left hook, shaking the American, who just managed to see out the round.

Both boxers were intent on knockouts, and all the attacks were focussed on the head. This was the pattern of the next few rounds. By the sixth round Benn had been on the canvas and McClellan was looking the more likely to win, but Benn raised his game with some big close-range hits and was catching the American with his head and some 'rabbit punches', both of which were going unpunished by the French referee. Benn was turning the fight into a maul. The American got through again in the eighth and sent Benn to the floor. To the astonishment of the crowd, Benn was up at the eight count and resumed what was now becoming an out-and-out brawl. This suited Benn, who was roared on by the frenzied crowd and encouraged by Frank Bruno, who was standing ringside urging on his former stablemate.

As the fight passed the halfway mark, McClellan began to appear distressed and seemed to be struggling to breathe. His gumshield was hanging out of his mouth. Although McClellan had brought his own cornermen, his team had appointed Brendon Ingle, a very experienced Irish trainer and manager, as the 'bucketman' for the night. He could see that Gerald was looking very distressed, but his cornermen were determined to press on.

Now it was Benn's turn to get on top, and the American began to look increasingly tired. A clash of heads in the ninth forced McClellan down on one knee. At the start of round ten Benn knocked him to his knees again. McClellan took his time rising, watching the referee count, and he looked in big trouble.

The fight continued, with Brendon Ingle looking on horrified. Benn then landed a huge right uppercut and McClellan went down again. He dropped down on both knees looking extremely pained and very disorientated. The US promoter Don King, who was sitting very close to where McClellan had slumped, leaned forward from his front-row seat and shouted in McClellan's ear to stand up and fight. McClellan was completely spent and was unable to continue. After the full count of ten, McClellan struggled to his feet and walked back, badly dazed, to his corner. There was no stool waiting for him in the corner, so he sat down in the ring, propped up against the turnbuckle, and appeared to go to sleep. A crew of medics laid him down gently on the floor and started to administer first aid.

Three years earlier, a very similar situation had occurred in a fight between two of Benn's rivals around that time. Michael Watson suffered brain damage in a fight against Chris Eubank, with the result that improved medical practices had been put in place. An anaesthetist was on standby at the fight, and he gave oxygen to McClellan while a brace was wrapped around his neck. The American was in a very bad way and was rushed to nearby London Hospital, where he underwent surgery for a clot on the brain. The post-match enquiry pointed the finger of blame at the referee, citing his lack of English as prohibiting communications. Others said McClellan's corner was to blame. Either way, McClellan was left virtually blind and badly paralysed for the rest of his life.

Safety rules in boxing coupled with improved medical backup would be one of the reasons McClellan survived – just. Boxing has changed since the bare-knuckle streetfights outside the Prospect of Whitby 250 years ago, but maybe the watching public have not – after the fight Nigel Benn made a telling comment. He said, 'You know what? This is what you wanted to see. You got what you wanted to see.'

*

The Benn *vs* McClellan and Eubank *vs* Watson fights came around the same time as a third, similarly fierce and upsetting contest. This time it was Bow's **Roderick 'Rod' Douglas** who was on the receiving end. Fortunately for Douglas, this match had a slightly happier ending.

Rod Douglas was born in 1964 in Bow and boxed out of the St George's and Broad Street clubs. He was an excellent middleweight/light-middleweight fighter, with four ABA titles and a commonwealth gold medal in his pocket. He fought in the 1984 Olympics in Los Angeles, losing in the quarter-finals. He turned pro in 1987 and fought unbeaten for his first thirteen fights, seven of them first-round knockouts. He blitzed his way through the rankings until he was matched against Herol 'Bomber' Graham for the British middleweight championship at Wembley Arena in October 1989. Graham was a class act with a huge amount of experience behind him; it was always going to be a tough ask for Rod.

Douglas attacked from the start and never stopped coming forward in the first seven rounds, but Graham's ring-craft, footwork, lightning reaction times and defensive skills meant that Douglas didn't really make much progress. By the eighth round Douglas had slowed, and Graham began to pick him off with his greater reach. After Graham put Douglas down twice, it was a case of how long Douglas could last. Not long was the answer, and the referee stopped the match at the end of the ninth. Douglas, looking exhausted but relatively untroubled, retired to the dressing room. A short time later he took a turn for the worse and was rushed into hospital. A blood clot was removed from his brain.

Unlike Watson and McClellan, Rod Douglas was lucky enough to make a full recovery. In comparison with the Watson and McClellan fights, Douglas was under the surgeon's knife within sixty minutes whereas Watson was badly late getting to surgery and specialists had concluded that McClellan could have been worked on earlier as well. Since the early 1990s, the focus has been to get any boxer showing signs of distress admitted to a specialist neurology unit within what is now referred to as 'the golden hour'. This practice has almost certainly saved lives and prevented serious brain damage. Those three fights were instrumental in bringing far more stringent safety guidelines into British boxing.

There is an inherent risk of injury in contact sports; people who take them up realise this. Boxing has, unfortunately, incurred more than its fair share of deaths, and every single one is a tragedy, but in terms of long-term injuries rugby and national hunt racing are equally risky sports.

*

It's very unusual for a boxer to reach the top of the professional ranks with only a little amateur experience; many secure top amateur titles before climbing to the top of the professional ladder. However, there was a young man from Bow who bucked the trend. **Eddie Phillips** (1911–1987) did little or no boxing as a young lad. After leaving school he managed to get a job driving a coach. In those days they were called charabancs. He did runs down to Southend, Clacton and Margate – popular day-trips for East Enders. As a way to keep fit, he joined a local gym and started to box a bit. He was a natural. He sparred with some older, experienced boxers and they taught the young man boxing skills and ring-craft. In 1929 he was spotted by a promoter and given the chance to fight on the undercard of a small boxing event in Rochester, Kent. He fought at light-heavyweight and drew the match.

This spurred Eddie on, and he went back into the gym with a willingness to make boxing his career. He may have had a couple of unlicensed fights the following year but his next official fight was at Olympia in London. The training paid off and he won. He then reeled off six straight wins, including a very bloody fifteen-round fight against a skilled journeyman called Ted Mason at the prestigious Ring arena in Blackfriars.

Phillips seemed to get matched against some superb boxers in the 1930s. In 1932, in only his tenth fight, he took on and beat the very tough Australian Jack O'Malley. Nothing seemed to faze Eddie, which is just as well because he was about to take on two of Britain's greatest-ever light-heavyweights – not just once each but seven times. He fought the great Welshman Tommy Farr in three epic matches and in the third match, after fifteen blistering rounds of boxing, Eddie took the vacant British light-heavyweight title in February 1935. This title had been vacated by the brilliant and durable Len Harvey, who was already a veteran of over 120 fights and another one of those boxers who seemed to be able to box at many different weights. Harvey had already won the Lonsdale British middleweight belt before stepping up to take the light-heavyweight crown.

Eddie Phillips met Harvey on four occasions, the first of which witnessed the pair fighting themselves to a standstill and being judged unsplittable. The rematch was almost as close and a really attritional affair. Both boxers finished badly battered but Harvey shaved the verdict. The third fight took place in October 1935, on Harvey's home patch in Plymouth. Both boxers had moved up to the heavyweight division. Harvey was firm favourite and came out with flying fists. Eddie was caught once or twice but the ring-craft which had been drilled into him years earlier told and he weathered the first few rounds of Harvey's onslaught. Using all his natural ability, Phillips fought back and was level going into the second half of the match. Harvey launched a second wave of all-out attack which Eddie once again survived. Eddie finished strongly and out-boxed Len somewhat. However, it was not quite enough to get the points decision in front of a very partisan crowd.

Eddie decided to box less after this match, but he was still impressive in those matches which came his way. It would be another three years before Eddie and Len met again. In December 1938, they fought for the vacant British heavyweight title. This time, though, it would be a shorter affair as Eddie was disqualified in the fourth round. That was about it for Eddie. A remarkable career for someone who seemed to have little interest in the sport after he left school. Eddie was called up for wartime duties with the RAF in 1940 and then went into acting, appearing in a couple of Will Hay comedy films.

*

Boxing has had its fair share of rivalries over the years. One of the greatest of these was that between the great East End boxer Ted 'Kid' Lewis and the American Jack Britton. They staged a series of epic encounters, the like of which would be unimaginable these days. The pair fought for the first time in March 1915 and went on to fight each other another nineteen times over the next six years!

The second fight between the two, in August 1915, was an absolute humdinger over fifteen stupendous rounds and goes down as one of the greatest fights ever. In 1917 they actually fought four matches between 19 May and 25 June – just thirty-six days. Not only that, but the bouts took place in four different venues, from St Louis in America's Midwest up to Toronto in Canada, and Ted also managed to fit in two other fights in between! Jack and the Kid were evenly matched up until those four fights, when Lewis won all four, with each going the full scheduled ten rounds. Clearly Jack didn't think he was getting the decisions, and over the next few fights a little bit of 'niggle' got into their matches.

On 7 February 1921, at Madison Square Gardens, the two men squared up against each other for the twentieth occasion. This time, there was a world championship at stake. It turned out to be the last of their battles – and the ugliest.

After the bell sounded at the end of the second round, Britton accompanied Lewis to his corner and protested about the mouthpiece Lewis was using. An argument ensued and Britton punched one of Lewis' seconds. The Lewis and Britton camps climbed into the ring and started to push and shove each other. The referee eventually pulled the warring parties apart and told them to get on with the fight otherwise he would abandon the match. Order was eventually restored and the fight was resumed. The match continued with the next six rounds being fought toe to toe while Britton mouthed obscenities at Lewis. Britton then felled Lewis with a punch and hit him again before he could rise. Once up, several low blows from both boxers followed. Lewis was probably more ring savvy than the American, and made sure he was out of sight of the ref when landing some of his own 'dodgy punches' as it appeared that only Jack Britton was warned.

In the last round, both boxers were out on their feet. They were both well into their careers at this stage and age was catching up to them both, although this did not stop them trading big head blows until the final bell. Lewis lost on points over the fifteen rounds. Ted quipped later that he had spent more time with Britton than with his wife, Elsie!

Fighters such as Ted Kid Lewis, Rod Douglas and Nigel Benn were obviously tough as teak and lived to tell the tales of their exploits inside the ring. All boxers go into the ring knowing that they run the risk of getting hurt. For one fighter, though, the ring could be a safer place.

John Lewis Gardner (1953–) is not a household name, although some may remember him as an excellent boxer from the 1970s. He is generally regarded as a forgotten man in the heavyweight ranks of that era. By the time Gardner turned pro in 1973, the likes of Henry Cooper, Billy Walker, Brian London and Jack Bodell had retired or had left their best days in the ring behind them. The division was looking for a new champion, and Gardner was a rising star. How he even made it into the ranks was something of a miracle given his background.

Gardner was born in Hackney. He had a viciously violent father who gave him and his brother regular beatings. Young John often went to school bruised, and because his home life was so appalling he often spent hours playing in nearby London Fields to avoid his father's fists. One time his mother stepped in to prevent his father trying to drown the boy in the sink. His father was an alcoholic and an inveterate gambler. His mother worked twelve-hour days to feed the family and his father spent the same amount of time in the pub or in the bookies.

John recalls that as a young lad he shared the bath water with his brother and used old newspapers as toilet tissue. He was a large lad, and most probably both mentally and physically scarred by his experiences. Many mothers of neighbouring lads knew of the family and warned their offspring to stay away from John. His only real childhood pal was the family dog. It was an extremely grim childhood, and when he got into his teens Gardner joined a local boxing club and used his build to good advantage. He won an amateur regional title before turning professional.

Gardner hooked up with Terry Lawless and his excellent training team and won his first twenty-four fights in a row as a pro, going undefeated for almost five years. He won most of his fights by technical knockouts. He defeated Neville Meade, the Welsh heavyweight champion, but he was knocked out in the first round in 1977 by an American boxer. He earned his first title shot later that year when he defeated Denton Ruddock by another TKO for the Southern Area British heavyweight championship.

Gardner was now a contender for the vacant British and Commonwealth heavyweight championship, and in 1978 he defeated Billy Aird to take it. He went on to defend his title against the notorious Paul Sykes in 1979. Gardner then defeated Rudy Guawe in 1980 for the vacant European heavyweight championship. Gardner was rapidly approaching world class and knocked out Lorenzo Zanon in his first title defence in 1980 after five rounds. Gardner, who never lost a title fight during his career, vacated the European title in hopes of a world title.

In 1981, Gardner signed a contract to fight Muhammad Ali, the legendary heavyweight champion of the world. The fight was scheduled to take place in Hawaii, but Ali backed out of the deal at the last moment and announced his retirement. After that disappointment, Gardner went on to fight the fast-moving American Michael Dokes and was knocked out in the fourth round. A fight or two later, he decided to hang up the gloves.

After stepping out of the ring relatively unscathed, Gardner was about to face a violent retirement. He moved to the north-east of England and with his wife ran a couple of pubs in the area, including taking over one of Gateshead toughest pubs, The Three Tuns. One evening he threw out a notorious drug dealer. Unfortunately, the dealer was hell bent on plying his trade at the pub. It was reported that Gardner and his wife Michele tried to shut him out, but he kept coming back. Then, on one Halloween night, an attacker came into the pub wearing a ski mask and armed with an eight-inch knife. He was later identified as the drug dealer. Gardner describes the horrific ordeal in vivid detail:

He thrust the blade into my chest and I felt a warm trickle run down my stomach. He stabbed me in the abdomen and I went down. He was a maniac, screaming and shouting, jabbing the knife in my neck. He was butchering me, slicing me up. I was hitting him on the top of the head, but the blade came down again and again and again. Blood was squirting out of me. My intestines were sticking out like cauliflower. I was screaming out.

His wife tried to stop the attack but was slashed four times before the masked man ran off. The emergency services arrived and the couple were taken to hospital, where medics fought to save his life. The nurses called him 'the Wonder Boy' after his miraculous survival.

Fourteen stabs to the major organs and I'm still breathing. I was finally allowed out with nothing more than a dose of painkillers and a friendly wave goodbye.

Rehabilitation was slow and painful and Gardner was left with a massive scar running from one side of his stomach to the other.

His attacker was put before the courts and received a fourteen-year prison sentence. After the trial, Gardner left the north-east to live in Suffolk and latterly Lancashire, but during this time he has had to battle cancer as well.

Many regard Gardener as one of the best heavyweight boxers to come out of this country. He has come close to death on two or three occasions, but never once as a result of boxing His style very much mirrored that of the legendary Rocky Marciano, and it is thought that if the match against Muhammad Ali had gone ahead the great man would have had his work cut out to stop this East End all-action fighter. Alas, we will never know.

13

THE JOURNEYMEN

We fight, get beat, rise and fight again.

Major General Nathanael Greene,
Continental Army, 1777

For some, the path to success can be swift. For naturals like Ted 'Kid' Lewis, Charlie Magri and Sammy McCarthy, early proof of ability saw them fast-tracked to glory. The East End had their fair share of these characters. For most, though, the road to the top would be a long, hard journey. A few reached it; most did not. These were the journeyman boxers, and they were in for the long haul, fighting in small venues up and down the country on the undercard of midweek shows. Most realised that boxing was just an income for them; they had no illusions. They treated success and failure, those two impostors, just the same.

For many, you really have to wonder if all the hard work was worth it. **Johnny Greaves** (1979–) from Forest Gate was a prolific journeyman of recent years. He had a fairly short and not too successful amateur career and had a few fights on the unlicensed circuit before he turned pro in 2007. To say he had an inauspicious start to his professional career is a huge understatement. Travelling all the way from East Ham to Middlesbrough for his debut, he lost convincingly on points. Nine more fights were to follow, and he travelled up and down the M1 and M6 only to lose all nine. However, things looked like improving when he won his next match in Newark with a first-round KO. Brimming with new determination, he travelled to Stoke for his next match. Although he put up a good show, he lost on points.

Another twenty-five matches later, having travelled as far afield as Plymouth and Glasgow, Greaves had failed to register a single win. In fact, poor old Johnny fought exactly 100 matches – thanks to his very last bout, which produced a very rare win, his final record reads: won four, lost ninety-six.

Johnny's was a lonely and thankless task. He knew at an early stage that he would never make it to the top of the bill, let alone to a title fight, but his East End grit and determination to keep trying is an inspiration in many respects. His career was eminently forgettable, and indeed it would have been forgotten had it not been for BBC Sport picking up on it and making a documentary – *Cornered* – about his life on the long and lonely boxing road. This documentary would perhaps be the only reason you had heard of him – unless you witnessed one of his many failures.

Mike Honeyman (1896–1944) was born in North Woolwich and has already been briefly mentioned as a mentor to the great Teddy Baldock. Mike, though, had an impressive career himself. He had his first recorded professional fight in 1914. He won most of his early bouts, but in March 1915 he was knocked out in the second round by Charlie Hardcastle and his form dipped. Over the next year or so he lost more fights than he won. But Honeyman was not a quitter. He had a steely-eyed determination, and that gimlet eye was firmly fixed on the top spot in British boxing.

Notwithstanding the fifty-odd fights he had beforehand, between 1917 and 1926 Mike fought another 105 matches! During that time his determination and ring-craft earned him the British

Johnny Greaves: 'Turn up, fight, lose, get paid, happy days.' Johnny taking another one flush on the chin during his unsuccessful travels, this time from Cromer's Ryan Walsh. (© PA Images)

featherweight crown in 1919, which he defended. He fought for the European title in 1920 and had some impressive non-title fights against some very good opponents over the next couple of years, boxing in France and Germany. In 1923 he joined the newly formed Royal Air Force as a boxing instructor but was still boxing professionally up until 1926 when, after suffering six straight defeats, he retired. He then concentrated on training. His work with the young Teddy Baldock was exceptional, and the experience that Mike gained over his long career was passed on to Baldock – with devastating results for Baldock's early opponents.

Whether or not **Henry William Coleman** (1904–1957) from Bethnal Green loved boxing is hard to say. Maybe someone who fought 223 professional matches must have some affection for the game. As he was born into a boxing family on Valentine's day, perhaps he did. Coleman was better known as **Harry Corbett** and was the elder brother of Dick Corbett, who, as mentioned earlier, had died so tragically in the war. It is hard to think of another boxer who travelled such a long, hard road as Harry Corbett did. It was a road full of the potholes of failure but it was eventually to take him to the top of British boxing. Whatever Harry lacked in his fighting armoury, his perseverance more than made up for it.

Harry fought his first professional match in 1921, and for the first seventy fights or so it was a case of two steps forward, one step back. Just when he looked like he was heading towards a title fight, he came up against somebody just that little bit better. He would often string a dozen or so winning performances together only to lose to some other journeyman pro. Eventually, at the start of 1925, after nine eye-catching wins including a tremendous and tightly fought match against rising star Johnny Brown, Harry was matched to fight Brown for the British, Empire and European bantamweight title. It was another great fight. Set for twenty rounds, Harry was forced to retire in the sixteenth.

Harry decided to move up to featherweight. Nineteen fights and a year later, he was still boxing well and was offered another shot at a title. He went into the match after good wins against Johnny Cuthbert and Jack 'Kid' Berg. He fought a very tough boxer, John Curly, over twenty rounds. They fought to a virtual standstill but again Harry lost, this time somewhat unluckily on points. In March 1928, Harry again fought for the championship. It was the 143rd fight of his career and it was against an old adversary of his, Johnny Cuthbert. The fight itself was like his career: one long slog. It went the full twenty rounds, and Harry nearly collapsed when the referee, the aforementioned J. W. H. T. Douglas, raised Harry's arm. He had finally won the British championship.

He fought and retained the title only once before losing it. He then moved up the weights again and fought with some success at lightweight, losing a title eliminator fight and later a European championship fight. By the start of 1932, Harry had fought 192 bouts when a fairly bad eye injury stopped his boxing for a while.

He returned the following year, but he had limited and somewhat blurred sight in his left eye. He fought on bravely for a couple more years. Corbett was clearly – or, in his case, not so clearly – reaching the end of a remarkable career.

One sunny June evening in 1936, after losing a third consecutive fight and with failing eyesight, the great East End journeyman stepped out of a ring in the Devonshire Club in Hackney for the last time. He was still only thirty-two. Harry drifted in and out of odd jobs for the next few years and died quite young in 1956.

Back in Corbett's time, it was quite common for journeymen boxers to use what little money came their way from boxing to supplement their day-job wages. Those boxers who worked as porters at Smithfield, Spitalfields and Billingsgate markets readily accepted that less money from fights meant more early mornings at the market. It was the same with the stevedores, watermen and labourers around the docks.

Jimmy Davis (1927–2008) not only fought almost one hundred boxing matches but from the age of fifteen he worked for over forty continuous years in Spitalfields market. It is possible that Jimmy's poverty-stricken childhood spurred him on to work hard and earn money. Born in the West Bethnal Green slums during the depression years, Jimmy moved with his family from place to place throughout the East End.

Jimmy boxed for the Webbe Institute club as a lad. This was another club founded by a Victorian philanthropist, Herbert Webbe. After losing a closely fought ABA welterweight final in 1944, Jimmy started his professional boxing career in 1945 and between 1945 and 1955 fought at all sorts of venues for a living. Mostly fighting in and around London, his boxing was occasionally showcased at such places as Brighton FC's Goldstone Ground, amateur football club Walthamstow Avenue's ground and its near neighbour, Leyton Orient's Brisbane Road stadium. He boxed almost half his fights at the various London baths that were popular venues during the mid-twentieth century, as well as the idiosyncratic Mile End Arena. Occasionally, though, he appeared on boxing bills at some top London venues like Seymour Hall, Earl's Court and the Royal Albert Hall. It was at the latter that he appeared on the same bill as all three Kray Brothers, the only officially recognised bill of boxing which featured Ronnie, Reggie and their older brother Charlie in one night of boxing.

Jimmy Davis was a touch better than your average light-heavyweight. He had a prodigious left hand by all accounts. He fought for a couple of Southern Area titles but narrowly came off second-best. He was certainly good enough to be matched with some of the greatest British boxers of that era, and proved this by taking on the likes of Randolph Turpin, Ron Barton and the nemesis of a lot of East London fighters, South London's Albert Finch.

It may be a little harsh to put **Ronald Redrup** (1935–2013) in this section. His record does have the look of a journeyman about it at first glance, but this does not tell the whole story.

Featuring the underwhelming boxing skills of the Krays, the overwhelming boxing skills of Lew Lazar and the solid if unspectacular journeyman boxer Jimmy Davis. (Royal Albert Hall Archives)

Ron was born in Skiers Street, Stratford and was a decent footballer. His classmate Freddie Cooper was even better, captaining England Schoolboys and going on to play for West Ham. Ron dropped soccer and joined West Ham Boys' Boxing Club around 1952. He made quick progress. He was good mates with Terry Spinks, and the two would train together at the club before spending Saturday afternoons at Upton Park watching their beloved West Ham. Ron was a grafter and worked as a milkman in the week. Finishing his round by lunchtime, he was training down the club in the afternoon.

The year 1956 was golden for the West Ham club. They had two great young boxers in that year's ABA finals: Ron Redrup, the milkman, fought for the middleweight title while Terry Spinks, the dustman, fought for the flyweight title. The dustman and the milkman both won. Both were then called up by the Great British boxing team for the 1956 Olympics, and it was after this that one was fast-tracked onto a short but stellar career while the other began to tread the long road of pain and ultimate failure.

Spinks won gold at the Games, but Redrup was eliminated in the first round. Spinks came home as the 'Golden Boy', turned pro in 1957 and was a British professional champion inside three short years. Redrup also turned pro in 1957, but he was in for the long haul. By early 1962, after thirty-four bouts, Ron had only won sixteen of them. His road was taking him from Leyton Baths in London to Paisley Ice Rink in Glasgow in pursuit of his dream. It was during this period that the term 'journeyman' applied to Ron as, apart from travelling up and down the A1 trunk road, he also fought further afield in Sweden, Germany and Italy. Ron came very close to real success; unfortunately, he never quite got there.

In August 1958, Ron fought an eliminator for the light-heavyweight title at Shoreditch Town Hall against the experienced Arthur Howard. Harry Carpenter was ringside for the BBC in one of his earliest commentaries and found it hard to call the winner. Ron lost on points. He had one more chance for glory in 1963, when he got a crack at the British title against Chic Calderwood in Blackpool. The milkman started well but picked up a nasty cut above his eye. The cut got worse, and for poor old Ron the fight was over well before the ref stopped it in the eleventh round.

Redrup continued on his way, but with very mixed results. He eventually retired from the professional game in 1968 after stepping into the ring for a fifty-third time at the Drill Hall in Northampton. There was no pot of gold at the end of this boxing rainbow. He obviously didn't make enough money from the game to retire permanently as he dabbled in the unlicensed fighting business. He also spent a period at sea in the Merchant Navy.

*

Many East End boxers travelled a fair bit in pursuit of various boxing titles. Jack 'Kid' Berg and Ted 'Kid' Lewis were often back and forth across the Atlantic chasing the Yankee dollar. Some plied their trade across the Channel. In the second half of the last century, air travel made it a lot easier for boxers to ply their trade in other countries. Before that, journeys were slow and uncomfortable. Some of the top fighters of the day could afford a bit of luxury, but for the less fortunate journeymen it was an arduous life.

In that respect, one **Jack Hare** (*c.* 1875–?) was the daddy of them all. It is estimated he may well have had as many as three hundred bouts, although some were possibly unlicensed and many more unrecorded. He started boxing in the late 1890s.

Records are not clear, but it is possible that Hare may have been born around 1875. Thanks to census records, we do know that he was living in Young Street, Plaistow around the age of four or five. His parents were both Scottish. Young Jack's father was a ship's cook. Like so many young lads, Jack longed to go to sea. One day, when his father went off to sea, he secretly followed his parents down to the nearby docks and crept aboard his father's ship and hid. The ship sailed later that day, with Jack fast asleep and hidden behind some hay bales on the deck. God only knows what his poor distressed mother went through when she got back home and discovered Jack gone.

The following morning, Jack woke up out at sea and became increasingly seasick. He was discovered throwing up over the side and hauled before his apoplectic father and a livid ship's captain. They were America bound, and the captain agreed Jack could stay on board and help his father. Jack spent the rest of the voyage peeling potatoes. The youngster arrived in New York in August 1885 and Jack saw a poster on the quayside advertising a fight featuring possibly the greatest bare-knuckle fighter of all time, the legendary American fighter John L. Sullivan.[1] Jack liked the odd scrap as a kid in Plaistow and enjoyed boxing, as did his father. He slipped off the boat and went to Franklin Hall, where the fight was due to have been held.

Hare patiently waited to see Sullivan, but when the great man came out a crush developed. Another boy trod on Jack's foot and then pushed him. Jack hit the boy, and a scuffle broke out. Sullivan had seen the scuffle, and came over to give Jack a few coins. Picking up on his cockney accent, the fighter asked Jack where he came from. Jack said, 'I am from Plaistow and I'm going to be a fighter like you when I grow up.' Jack was true to his word. His boxing went hand in hand with his travelling. His life on the road started in 1890 when he stowed away on a ship to Australia and had his first recorded match against Bill Mullins in the silver-mining town of Broken Hill, way out in the New South Wales outback. He had four further fights, travelling from Melbourne to Sydney before hopping on a steamer to California, over 7,000 miles across the Pacific, to fight three times in San Francisco.

He returned to fight Bill Mullins again in Perth in 1892, and over the next two years he fought in New Zealand, the USA and Brazil before arriving back home in Plaistow at the end of 1894. He fought around England and occasionally abroad until 1896, when he heard about fighters being paid in huge diamonds for fights in South Africa, so off he went again. The years Hare spent in the ring had toughened him up considerably. He became both resilient and resourceful.

Hare arrived in Cape Town in 1897. His account of what happened next, found in his book *Gladiators of the Prize Ring and My World Travels*, sums up his approach to earning a living at boxing:

On the night of May 1st when the Transvaal mail train left Adderley Street Station in Cape town, bound north, I left with it hidden under the seat of a coach. Fifty miles out, at a place called Paarl, I was put off and walked towards a light which turned out to be a farmhouse. I found a place in the barn and laid down and slept. I was awakened with the sun shining on my face through a hole in the roof, and an Africander boy told me it was 2 o'clock. I had a feed at the farmhouse and told them I had come out from England to fight.

I walked into Beaufort West on June 10th at 7 am. After buying two pairs of veldtschoons (Africander boots) on June 14, I left again on a bullock wagon. This was the first ride I had since I was put off the Transvaal mail train at Paarl.

I passed Goemansberg, Fauresmith, arriving at Jaggerfontein on September 20th, six hundred and eighty two miles from the breakwater. I stayed there ten days and heard that the brothers Denny (Martin and Tom), two great Australian boxers, were at Bloemfontein, where I arrived on October 10th, 1897. If rags had been the fashion, I should have been the Beau Brummel of the capital of the Free State. My worldly possessions were a piece of looking glass, a cake of soap and a comb with two teeth in it, one at each end. My pockets were full of fresh air.

I found Tom Denny, whom I had spoken to in Sydney. Tom treated me well. I had a Turkish bath a good clean up and they brought me a ready made-up suit. I had a good time for a couple of days and then started to train to fight Martin Denny (Tom's brother). Martin had fought a 20-round draw with Griffo five years before, the outlook for me was not bright.[2]

We met at the Town Hall, Bloemfontein, on October 28th, 1897, and I lost on points. I made a good impression with the

Free Staters. Martin was much heavier than me and I believe he was not trying. If he had been, I do not think I should have gone the full distance with a classic performer like him.

Hare goes on to account for the next part of his travels:

I got twenty-five pounds for the loss with Martin and forty pounds for my draw with Tom. I would not think of riding now, as I had walked three parts of the way, so I wanted to walk the rest. I arrived in Kroonstadt at 11 pm on November 14th. I had covered nine hundred miles from Adderley Street Station in Cape Town. I boxed a four-round contest on November 16th at this place with Kid Abel, a black boy, and told him if he was in Johannesburg when I got there, I would fight him if he could get the job. At 2pm on December 11, 1897 I walked up Commissioner Street in the city of the diamond kings after my walk through the wilderness of South Africa.

Jack Hare returned to England and fought more matches, including some bare-knuckle fights. One resulted in a broken nose, two broken ribs and a serious injury which left him with poor vision in his left eye. Unperturbed, he set off to South Africa once more in 1899.

It was to be the peak of his career. After a couple of fights there, he fought Jim Darrell for the South African bantamweight championship on 3 December 1899. Jack beat Darrell over twenty-five rounds. Jack headed back home again but still managed to pick up another couple of fights on the way to Cape Town. Back in Plaistow he spent the next few years fighting and, following in his father's footsteps, by working the occasional stint as a ship's cook. Hare fought sporadically all over the world for the next twenty years. In his last recorded fight, in Port Said, Egypt, in August 1924 at the age of fifty, he gained a stoppage win over Private Vine.

Hare's fighting record is fairly vague at both ends. I found that most records show he only had between seventy-two and ninety-eight recorded fights. The huge amount of travelling he undertook and the ad-hoc way in which prize fighting was arranged in some of these countries meant that many fights either went unrecorded or have been lost to posterity. Between 1910 and 1924 he would have boxed scores of prize fights while working as a cook on dozens of voyages around the world. It is feasible that Hare could have competed in upward of 250 fights!

14

INTO THE RING

Ever since boxing started to grab the attention of the public, boxing promoters and managers were quick to arrange matches. A few boxing halls and boxing arenas had been around since the eighteenth century, but with public demand growing, more venues had to be found or built. In the East End of London there were a number of insalubrious venues around that staged fights but by the end of the nineteenth century a couple of purpose-built halls started to appear in the area.

One of the first to appear was the **Wonderland Arena** at No. 100 Whitechapel High Road. It was originally used as a venue for light entertainment and featured all sorts of weird and wonderful 'human attractions' on the bill. Ten years earlier, on the opposite side of the road at No. 123, the self-styled showman Tom Norman had exhibited John Merrick, the Elephant Man, in the rear of his shop. The Wonderland building had suffered from a couple of fires over the years. Theatres were prone to such things as the lighting was all supplied by candles and oil lamps. Following one such fire the building was actually rebuilt in 1897. After that some electrical power was installed.

Wonderland's boxing matches were run by local boxing promoters Harry Jacobs and Harry Woolf and started in earnest at Wonderland in early 1900. It was a great place for up-and-coming boxers in the area to showcase their talents, and many British and world champions fought there back in the day. The Wonderland never changed its name after boxing began, so the name on the outside of the building appeared at odds with what went on inside. Alice never watched a fight there, and the Mad Hatter never hosted an afternoon tea party at the place either!

Boxing nights were held regularly on Mondays and Fridays, and later Saturdays were added to meet the demand. A seemingly endless supply of boxers climbed between the ropes over the years. A few fighters fought the majority of their careers there. An honest enough pro called Bert Adams, a featherweight and lightweight boxer from Spitalfields, fought 140 times there in a six-year period between 1900 and 1906. Almost once a fortnight!

Harry Jacobs in particular was convinced that boxing was the game to be in, and he was to become an influential promoter. In February 1908 he brought over the Canadian heavyweight champion Tommy Burns to fight British Empire champion Jack Palmer at the Wonderland for the world heavyweight title. It was a coup for the promoters and a major event in the East End. A large crowd was expected. Jacobs and Wolfe were shrewd businessmen, but even they would have looked on amazed and possibly even impressed when Burns, who was as sharp with his brain as with his fists, insisted on opening only one of the three turnstiles at the arena. Standing to one side, he proceeded to count every paying customer coming through! He then counted out his agreed split of the receipts and headed back to his dressing room with his purse. The match started an hour later than billed, and Burns entered the ring and duly knocked out Palmer in the fourth round.

Interestingly, this fight remains one of only nine undisputed world heavyweight championship fights ever to be held on British soil. The Wonderland survived until 1911, when the boxing arena was gutted in yet another fire. Shortly after, Jacobs and Woolf fell out with each other. The number of great champions who started out fighting three- or six-round bouts at the bottom of a weekday bill at Wonderland was impressive. Nipper Pat Daly, Pedlar Palmer, Tom Ireland and Pat O'Keeffe all climbed into the Wonderland's ring at an early age. The Bombardier fought his first recorded UK professional fight there in 1908 after buying himself out of the Army in India a year before. The charismatic Aldgate boxer Jewry Smith made his professional debut there in a six-round bout. Multiple champions Digger Stanley and Kid McCoy appeared at the venue many times throughout their time in the sport.

The boxer who, more than most, made the Wonderland his own was the aptly names **Charlie Knock** (1880–1939) from Stratford. Charlie fought on one of Wonderland's earlier boxing bills in 1901, and in a career spanning thirteen years and 130 fights he fought at the Whitechapel arena almost 100 times. In 1903/4, Charlie fought three successive matches against Charlie Allum from Notting Hill. He won two and lost one. Unfortunately for Knock, the one he lost was for the English welterweight title. Both boxers retired just before the outbreak of war. Both joined up to fight for King and Country, but only one survived. Knock came through it, but Allum died in July 1918 while knocking out German machine gun nests. After destroying a couple, he stumbled through into German lines by mistake and by all accounts started fist-fisting German troops before he was shot. He was posthumously awarded the Military Cross for extreme bravery.

Around this time, the **Premierland** arena opened a short distance away at the corner of Commercial Road and Back Church Lane. It was a similar set up to the Wonderland but was larger and much more professionally run by promoter Jack Callaghan. The property was first built in 1906 on the site of a former fish market and was originally called the People's Arcade, catering for the Jewish community. It soon changed its name to the Premierland

and was granted a licence in 1910. It was completely refurbished in 1914 and heavily promoted as East London's answer to the prestigious Ring venue in Battersea.

This boxing venue thrived for the next fifteen years until bigger and better venues opened. After the First World War it staged some seriously good fights. It hosted three or four boxing bills each week, sometimes two on Sundays. All the great fighters of the day boxed there often, including Ted 'Kid' Lewis, Harry Mizler, Teddy Baldock, Len Harvey and the Corbett brothers. From 1924 to 1930, the legendary boxing promoters Victor Berliner and Manny Lyttlestone promoted shows there. Berliner also managed a couple of boxers and they worked hard to make Premierland successful. Although they did not stage any world championship fights there, several British and Empire bouts were fought at the venue.

On 21 May 1930, just a few months before Premierland closed, a much anticipated British and Empire lightweight title match was fought between Albert Foreman (of whom more later) and Fred Webster. Webster was an excellent young boxer from Kentish town. Foreman was several years older. Although born in Whitechapel and raised in West London, the young Albert emigrated to America and then Canada in his early twenties. It was under the maple leaf flag that he fought Webster. The press at the time anticipated a long, close fight – wrong! Foreman hit an advancing Webster flush on the chin with a perfectly executed powerful left hand and it was all over inside a minute. It goes down as one of Foreman's greatest victories.

One boxer defined Premierland, and that was Jack 'Kid' Berg. He made his professional debut there on 8 June 1924, and between then and November 1925 he fought continuously at Premierland, a total of thirty-seven bouts with only two losses. His all-action style was a crowd pleaser, which in itself helped promote the venue.

Bethnal Green's Alf Pattenden, who held the British bantamweight title briefly in 1928, fought over half of his seventy matches at the venue. With most of the top East End boxers on the bill there, the place was often packed out. Betting on matches was rife and an integral part of the shows. Boxer Dick Corbett recalled his first bout there against Kid Froggy:

> The betting element was terrific. Feelings always ran high and large sums of money passed hands every night ... As I sat in my dressing room waiting to go out to meet Kid Froggy, a couple of ugly looking customers managed to walk in. I was told in no uncertain terms that it would be just too bad if Froggy doesn't win tonight ... 'Ever had a good hard kicking?' they said.

Corbett won and was left unharmed.

It was at Premierland that a young Jack Spot first made his mark in the criminal underworld. He earned a reputation for no-nonsense dealing when he worked as a ringside bet collector for the local bookies.

During the twenty years it was licensed to stage boxing, Premierland hosted almost a thousand events. It did occasionally arrange some light-hearted 'Slapstick Boxing' entertainment – the East Enders loved their variety shows. There were several variety and music halls in the area, including the still current and famous Wilton's Music Hall and the prestigious Paragon Theatre just a short walk away.

On some Sunday afternoons, Premierland attracted not only the die-hard boxing fans but a diverse audience including some well-known West End stars of the day. This report of one chaotic Premierland Sunday afternoon event in 1929 is illuminating:

> The Ring announcer called 'Buster' informed all that an additional bout was to be held to settle the ongoing dispute between two Taxi Cab firms in the area over territory poaching and that two representatives from either firm were going to settle matters in the 'Time Old Tradition'. Up stepped two rather tubby cabbies to the jeers of the audience. The great Sam Russell (the country's foremost referee at that time) agreed to referee the fight but on examining the contestants, wisely decided to officiate

from outside the ring. Both boxers were fitted with gloves which looked too large, deliberately I suspect. Off they went. With neither of them landing any meaningful blows the round finished with both hanging onto each other while the crowd heartily sang 'Dear old Pals, Jolly old pals'. The second round did produce a little more aggression from one of them but Sam Russell was forever pulling them over to either warn them or give them some tips on how to actually box. At the beginning of the third round one of the boxers rushed the other who was still rising from his stool and sank his fist into his 'Spare Tyre'. Foul! ... Foul!, yelled the regulars and as Sam waved the offending cabbie to his corner it seemed a signal for both sets of the cabbies supporters to rush the ring. It was everyman for himself and people either ducked under their seats or rushed for the exit as fists and boots began to fly. From the safety of the underneath of my seat a cockney next to me asked, who won?

I was on the brink of suggesting Sam had disqualified one man when another Cockney who was vigorously elbowing his way out, overheard the question and with typical self-confidence of his breed, settled the question: 'That ginger-headed bloke in the blue suit won it ... hands down. I see 'im flatten three of 'em in less than a minute an' as each of 'em hit the floor he put 'is boot in their teeth. Stone the crows mate, you ought to see 'im. Best bit of footwork I've seen in that ring.' ... I decided to take his word for it![1]

In October 1930, Premierland was forced to close after its promoters, Victor Berliner and Manny Lyttlestone, lost the lease. In the early sixties, the New Premierland boxing arena was opened at Poplar Baths but it was short lived.

*

The **Devonshire Sporting Club** was opened in a converted church in Devonshire Road (now called Brenthouse Road) off Mare

Street in Hackney on 21 October 1934, and the hall held 1,500 spectators. The idea for the club came from Joe Morris, a leading boxing manager of the time. Joe got together a syndicate of four businessmen who were interested in turning the old church into a sports arena and dance hall. One of the four was Jack Solomons, who took over the promotions at the hall before going on to become one of Britain's leading boxing promoters and matchmakers.

After a slow start, the hall became one of the most popular boxing venues in London, running decent boxing evenings two or three times a week. Like the Wonderland Arena, hundreds of up-and-coming boxers started their fledgling careers there. Many great boxers like the original 'Fen Tiger', Eric Boon, cut their teeth there and the British lightweight champ Dave Crowley fought at the venue on his way to the top. Some of the evergreen East London boxers at the time were regulars at the club. Harry Lazar, the elder brother of Lew Lazar, fought twenty-three times there in eighteen months, losing twice.

By 1936, larger and more prestigious venues were opening their doors to major fights. The Royal Albert Hall, Earl's Court, Harringay and Olympia could all hold larger audiences. However, in March 1936 a packed Devonshire Club witnessed the match between Harry Mizler and Alby Day for the Southern Area lightweight championship. Mizler won on points over fifteen rounds of pulsating boxing. Reporters ringside regarded the fight as the greatest boxing contest seen in East London for years. The fight was believed to have been aired on the BBC radio service that covered the occasional fight night at the club, with BBC stalwarts Raymond Glendenning and Barrington Dalby on the mikes ringside. Unfortunately, the property was destroyed by bombing in 1940. Jack Solomons de-camped to Soho, where he had his offices and gym in Windmill Street. He moved most of his promotions over to the Harringay Arena.

*

By far and away the top venue for boxing, not only for the East End of London but Great Britain generally, was built in Bethnal Green in 1929 and is now known as **York Hall**. The neo-Gothic structure was first opened as Turkish baths by the Duke of York – hence the name – to serve the local eastern European Jews who made up a significant percentage of the local population.

After the war it was redeveloped slightly. The baths were moved to the basement and the main hall was then used as a venue for boxing and wrestling. It can hold up to 1,200 spectators. Over the past fifty years it has established itself as Britain's premier boxing venue and is rightly called 'the Home of British Boxing'. The hall has a long history of hosting London and national schoolboy and boys' club championships. There is a packed house each February to witness the annual North-East London Divisions.

The London ABA semis and finals are also held there. To this day, top professional fights are still held at this venue. The hall has witnessed some memorable bouts over the years. In the late eighties, Rod Douglas and Nigel Benn fought out two great matches there, winning one each. In April 1999, little-known Jim Twite from Coventry put future professional world heavyweight champion David Haye on the York Hall canvas! A young Ricky Hatton retained assorted intercontinental titles there in 2005, while Carl Froch's first four professional bouts all took place in the York Hall ring. He later returned to defend both his Commonwealth and British titles there.

York Hall was recently voted one of the world's six best boxing venues. High praise indeed when it ranks alongside other legendary venues such as Caesar's Palace, Madison Square Gardens and the Blue Horizon in the States as well as the Kelvin Hall in Glasgow. I think that this ranking is based more on the atmosphere that York Hall generates than on its overall facilities, although they are noticeably better than many previous venues in the area.

On 30 September 2011, dedicated boxing television channel BoxNation broadcast its first live fight from York Hall. In sweltering conditions, Liam Walsh and Paul Appleby had a real battle before the former retained his Commonwealth super-featherweight crown by a tenth-round stoppage in what many considered the fight of the year.

Today, York Hall shares its boxing pedigree with other activities and events such as weddings, conferences and fashion shows. It has become a focal point for the local community. One day you can see ugly, sweaty and bloodied men slugging it out in the ring, and the next day you can be watching elegant and beautiful models parading on the catwalk. Such is life.

*

Boxing venues come in all shapes and sizes. Over the years, town halls, ice rinks, music halls and boarded-over swimming baths have been used to host boxing matches. Baths were particularly popular. Leyton Baths first staged boxing in 1947 and held regular events there until 1961. Some top boxers, including many British and a couple of world champions, fought at Leyton Baths, including Lew Lazar, Albert Finch, Terry Downes, Ron Barton and Randy Turpin's brother Jackie. Terry Spinks fought there six times on his way to the British title.

Although it was reported that the Kray boys followed each other into the ring at the baths in November 1951, I have been reliably informed that they did not. They were apparently scheduled to fight, and posters and programs were produced for the event, but the twins did not show. It is a little-known fact that the twins' elder brother Charlie boxed as well. He fought professionally eighteen times and made his debut at Leyton Baths in November 1948. He was an average boxer and won eleven of his fights before being well beaten by the excellent Lew Lazar in December 1951.

West Ham, Poplar and Hoxton swimming baths were also used. Shoreditch and Bow Town Hall held decent fights after the war. Clapton and Hackney dog tracks were occasionally used as was Ilford Ice Rink. West Ham and Leyton baths in particular staged some very good fights and some top boxers performed there. Five-times British Commonwealth champion Johnny Van Rensburg fought at both venues.

I doubt fans of any era saw bouts of boxing in a quirkier setting than the Londoners of the 1930s, 1940s and 1950s, who watched fights at the Mile End Arena. Situated behind Mile End tube station in the heart of East London, the Arena was very basic to say the least. Really, it was just a piece of waste ground. Its walls were a mix of crumbling brickwork and rickety corrugated iron, and its tiny ring was covered with a canopy that often required holding up with a broom when it rained. The crowd got wet. The changing room was an old shed in the corner. It must have been very uncomfortable to box there, but it was an extremely popular venue. British boxing stars of the day such as Sammy McCarthy, Eric Boon, Harry Mason, Al Phillips, Arthur and Alf Danahar and Harry and Lew Lazar all boxed at the arena. Len Wickwar, who holds the record for the most professional fights in British boxing history with a mind-bending 465 bouts, also fought there in 1933.

The Kray twins made their debuts on the same night in July 1951, and the world-renowned Mickey Duff boxed and then learnt his trade as a matchmaker there around the same time. Because of its open-air structure, Mile End Arena only held boxing shows during the summer, and in the winter the site became a fairground. It first opened for boxing in April 1933 and held its last show in September 1953. Sammy McCarthy recalls fighting there a few times in the early 1950s. According to him, the changing facilities were very primitive. Certainly, there was no bath or shower although he vaguely remembers a sink. All the boxers used the one hut to change, so it was very cramped. The ring was surrounded by rows of basic wooden chairs that were not fixed in place, so they would often tip over. Nevertheless, Sammy says that it had a great atmosphere when it was full and the crowd was in full voice. The great Welsh boxer Tommy Farr echoed his sentiments and offered some thoughts on East End boxing:

The Arena isn't the most comfortable place in the world, but I had a great time because I saw boxing that cracked with all

The Mile End Arena, East London's version of a Roman gladiatorial arena.

the lusty vigour and spirit of the boxing booths as I used to know them ... The place was filled with people who wanted to see fighting – and did. How East Enders know their boxing. They don't want to see anyone who should have ribbons in his hair. It's two-fisted gladiators with guts they demand. When a fight is finished, there's no polite, meaningless applause. That has to be earned. The old booth rule of 'Get the next two on quick' applies. With places like this, boxing won't die.

*

By the mid-1800s, the popularity of boxing was spreading all over the country. London and some of the larger provincial towns and cities were opening up plenty of venues to satisfy the demand. However, for the public in many of the smaller towns and rural locations, getting to see boxing could be difficult. This gap in the market was quickly filled by the travelling fairs and circuses that, by way of the boxing booth, were bringing the noble art to all the corners of the country. Boxing booths were unlicensed affairs where members of the public were encouraged to square-up against supposedly pro or semi-pro boxers for money. In fact, some very good, even great boxers plied their trade in the booths between professional fights. Mostly boxers from outside the capital fought at these shows; great boxers like Jem Mace, Tommy Farr, Jimmy Wilde, Freddie Mills and Randolph Turpin could all be seen working the booths.

The first boxing booths started to appear around 1830, and their popularity can be traced back to the time of a top East End bare-knuckle fighter called **Tom 'the Gasman Champion' Hickman** (*c.* 1795–?). The 'Gasman' nickname was reputedly derived from his nights fighting in the gaslit backstreets of the East End when the speed of his punches would often extinguish the lamps under which he fought! Hickman was involved in one of the most famous fights of the nineteenth century, with wagers laid on the outcome reputedly in the region of £150,000. In 1821, Hickman fought Bill Neat on Hungerfound Downs near Newbury in front of 25,000 spectators. After a long battle, he was eventually urged by the crowd to admit defeat. Soon after this fight he was run down by a horse and carriage and crushed to death – surprisingly, a fairly common occurrence in those days. He was just twenty-seven.

After his death, friends and fellow boxers collected money for his widow and children in order to purchase a boxing booth show as a source of income for them. Boxers also volunteered to fight free of charge for the first year to guarantee them a good start. From this tragic beginning, the Hickman Boxing Show went from strength to strength and travelled until the mid-twentieth century. Many famous boxers were associated with the family, not least Charlie Hickman, great-grandson of Tom, who won the Lonsdale Championship at Crystal Palace in 1931, a feat his illustrious ancestor never achieved.

The showman who really bridged the gap between the freeform bare-knuckle days and the introduction of the Queensberry Rules was Jem Mace. Mace is the man boxing historians see as the pioneer of the modern travelling boxing booth, with its exhibition fights, stage shows and the practice of inviting challengers into the ring. Several boxers from East London found work on the booths, including Pedlar Palmer, George Merritt and Alf Baldock (Teddy Baldock's father).

Although the Hughes and Balls Boxing Booths regularly rolled up in Canning Town, they tended to set up on the fringes of the East End. They were particularly popular around the county fairs of the Midlands and northern England during the nineteenth and early twentieth centuries. London had a rich profusion of boxing venues, so the majority of East End professional fighters found work there rather than on the booths.

One East End boxer who fought around the London venues, including four fights at the Mile End Arena in 1948, also worked the booths. This was **Ted Lewis**. Ted was one of the fighting Lewis family which was covered earlier. Ted's eye injury curtailed his mainstream boxing, but Ted made a living working the booths. He toured with the Tommy Woods Travelling Booth. He was a great East End character, working as a Billingsgate Fish Market porter and boxing at the same time. After he gave up the booths, he carried on working at Billingsgate. Ted lived to the ripe old age of eighty-eight. Before his death in 2016, he reminisced about his fighting days on the booths in an interview with the website *Our Bow*:

The Fairgrounds had boxing booths where members of the public were enticed to have a go by the promoter shouting, '£1 if you can last 3 rounds, £5 if you can knock him out'. You had to be careful with the amateurs and street fighters (gangsters) not to knock them out immediately. The audience had paid 2 shillings each to see a fight. I would keep the fight going for a few rounds. Sometimes nobody from the public would come forwards so a disguised professional would come forward to fight. In this case the action was staged.

Ted gives the example that his opponent would say 'Hit me on the jaw,' so he would hit him on the shoulder with the flat of his hand, making a big 'whack' sound, and his opponent would throw his head back.

Ted fought regularly under the assumed name of Teddy Bartlett. He fought many unofficial fights at racetracks all around the country, including the Epsom Derby. He was earning a lot of money and he and his girlfriend Betty, later his wife, would go to all the West End shows, dining out and dressing well. Ted said, 'I suppose you would call me a wide-boy.'

Ted has always been a stalwart of the local community in Bow, and apart from boxing professionally and working for almost fifty years at Billingsgate Fish Market he was an accomplished photographer, poet and in later years one of the great storytellers in the area – a skill he used on a regular basis with visiting schoolchildren at the Ragged School Museum.

15

EAST END CONNECTIONS

Hopefully you all know now that Bombardier Billy Wells banged the big brass gong preceding J. Arthur Rank films (apparently the gong was actually made of papier-mâché). East End boxing is full of these sorts of anecdotes, side stories, and odd connections. They help to embellish the sport and the characters involved in it.

People of a certain age will remember Kenny Lynch as an all-round entertainer who was very popular in the sixties and seventies. He had a couple of hit singles, and appeared on stage as well as on both big and small screens. **Kenneth Lynch** (1938–) was born in the Custom House area of Stepney, one of thirteen children. His elder sister Maxine was a decent singer, and by the late 1940s she was earning a living around the London clubs. In his teens, Kenny sometimes joined her on stage.

When Kenny reached eighteen, he did his national service in the Royal Army Service Corps. He had done a little bit of boxing as a lad and he carried it on in the Army. One of the trainers there saw something in him and he was singled out for some contests. He became a reasonable boxer and went on to become the regimental featherweight boxing champion. After he left the army, he kept up the boxing for a little while and had some thoughts about earning a living from it. He was also doing a bit of singing around the clubs and pubs as well. Despite the boxing, he had retained his youthful good looks and his singing wasn't bad either. He was spotted by EMI Records, and they signed him up. He released his first single in 1960, and several more followed.

Kenny was another big Hammers fan, and he and Bobby Moore became very good friends and were often seen together at boxing events. Kenny was seldom off our screens in the mid-sixties and is still active to this day. Oh, and one more thing – not content with boxing, acting, dancing, comedy and singing, Kenny also has one more claim to fame with an East End connection. He wrote the first big hit single for five crafty cockney boys, the Small Faces. It was a number-three hit: 'Sha-La-La-La-Lee'. He probably earned some decent money from the royalties! Kenny has more recently

Kenny Lynch, an all-round entertainer who opted for showbiz instead of the ring, seen here with Miss New Zealand ahead of the Miss World competition in 1963. (© Alamy Images)

worked in management and production, helping many newcomers into the business. This black cockney kid has come a long way since first singing with his big sister Maxine in the 1950s. Kenny was awarded an OBE in 2015.

*

Now, how could it be possible that an East End boxer was directly linked to a Wild West gunfighter and lawman as well as an American president? Well, **Billy Madden** was. It is unlikely anyone would recall anything of young Billy in London or on this side of the pond, but he was more widely known in America.

Billy's parents arrived from Ireland in the Shoreditch area of East London in the late 1840s, like many fleeing from the Irish Potato Famine. Billy was born in 1852 and had several brothers and sisters. Family history shows he was the only (living) child in the family while they were resident in London; it is possible that his siblings starved to death in Ireland. From an early age, Billy was taught boxing as a defence against aggressive local youths. With the large increase in the Irish Catholic community, tensions between Catholics, Jews and the local Anglo-Saxon Protestants were never far below the surface. By his early teens Billy had become a useful boxer, but his family found it very difficult to settle in the area. When young Billy reached his teenage years, he and his parents emigrated to America, the Promised Land.

Like many other Irish families leaving these shores at the time, the Maddens settled in the New York area. Billy kept up his boxing there, contesting several amateur fights while working in construction. He started work as a hod carrier but also worked as a plasterer and later a longshoreman. He started to box professionally around 1870. Meanwhile, 1,500 miles away in America's Midwest, legendary lawmen Wyatt Earp and Bat Masterson, alongside keeping the peace in frontier towns like Dodge City and Tombstone, acted as referees in local bare-knuckle prize fights. (Kevin Costner's turn as Wyatt Earp in the film of the same name showcased this part of his career.)¹ Masterson, who took a keen interest in boxing, was known to prefer to use his fists rather than his six-shooter when dealing with aggressive cowboys. However, he was rather handy with both and used them to great effect.

Back East, Billy Madden's boxing career was not overly successful. However, he did produce the odd decent result, and went on to box in several countries. He built up a reputation as a good honest pro, and this allowed him to move into management and promotion.

In the late 1880s, Bat Masterson had left the gunfighting to his friend Wyatt Earp. He moved back to New York and started on a career in freelance journalism, specialising in sports reporting. One night, Masterson found himself ringside at a John L. Sullivan fight. Sullivan was an American boxing legend, and Billy Madden was his manager. There was a crowd disturbance that evening involving Masterson which Madden witnessed. Later, Madden and Sullivan introduced themselves to the ex-gunslinger. Madden and Masterson became great friends as Masterson got more involved in the fight game. Madden also went on to manage Jack Dempsey and Jack McAuliffe, both great future world champions. Madden also started to get involved in politics, and in 1906 was a nominated candidate for state legislature for Brooklyn.

Masterson was appointed as a sports journalist for the *New York Morning Telegraph*, and his newly found profession brought with it some useful contacts. He became good friends with Alfred Lewis, who was editor of the influential *Chicago Times Herald*. This paper and its editor were supporters of American president Theodore Roosevelt, and both Madden and Masterson were introduced to Roosevelt through Lewis. Roosevelt was a keen sportsman and took a liking to the amiable Madden. Both Masterson and the Cockney Irish kid from the London slums moved into elevated political company, becoming regular visitors to the Whitehouse.

Madden later became a very successful real estate dealer and property developer, acquiring a large amount of property. The long

It's a long way from Whitechapel to the White House. The Cockney Kid Billy Madden and the gunfighter Bat Masterson. (Wikicommons)

road from his impoverished birth in the Victorian slums of London through the elevated circles of American politics to his death in 1918 as a wealthy and highly respected American citizen is the very epitome of the American dream. For Madden, the Promised Land certainly delivered.

*

The George Medal, presented for great bravery shown by a civilian, is not commonly awarded. In 1944, it was awarded to **Archibald Ernest 'Archie' Sexton** and it remains the highest non-military award to be bestowed upon a boxer.

Archie Sexton was born in Bethnal Green in 1908. The son of a bare-knuckle boxer, he started his professional boxing in 1925 and fought well over two hundred bouts. He was another of East

London's granite-hard journeyman professionals. Archie boxed a couple title eliminator fights and a British title fight but always just missed out. He was eventually forced to retire after suffering a serious eye injury during a match at the West Ham Baths in 1936.

Although the complete loss of sight in one eye stopped his boxing, he did manage to carry on in the sport as a British Boxing Board referee. Nor did his injury stop him joining the Police War Reserve and Constabulary (Metropolitan Police) at the outbreak of war. In 1944, he was on duty during an air raid when an air-raid shelter was badly hit. He entered the burning structure and helped rescue three people who were trapped. His brave actions were recognized by the award of the George Medal. This story does have a slight twist to it – the shelter was below the Moorfield Eye Hospital! Archie was the father of Dave Sexton, who played for West Ham and Leyton Orient and went on to manage Chelsea and Manchester United. Dave Sexton was regarded as one of the best football coaches of his generation and managed the England under twenty-one squad.

*

Now, here is a straightforward connection question: what is the direct link between Daniel Mendoza, Bethnal Green's legendary bare-knuckle champion, and possibly the world's greatest comedy actor, Peter Sellers? It is not boxing, unless Peter went ten rounds with Henry Cooper and I do not remember that! It is a more direct link. Peter Sellers is in fact the great-great-grandson of Mendoza. Those of you Sellers fans with eagle eyes may have just noticed odd pictures of Mendoza in the background of some of Sellers' film sets. This book is filled with examples of boxing families, sometimes three generations of top boxers from the same family. Not so with Mendoza's lineage. Clearly Peter Sellers did not have the boxing gene; his genius lay elsewhere. However, he did inherit another somewhat unwanted tendency: depression. Seller's depression was well documented, along with his personality disorder. Given the times in which he lived, Mendoza's condition is not so clear but it is evident from his later life that his character changed after leaving boxing. His unsuccessful attempts at business greatly affected him. He died depressed as well as penniless.

*

Britain has produced three, possibly four, truly outstanding world-class professional fighters whose status nobody disputes. Two of them actually fought around the same time, either side of the First World War. One was the Welsh Wizard, Jimmy Wilde, and the other was Aldgate's finest, Ted 'Kid' Lewis. For would-be boxers growing up in the twenties and thirties, these two great boxers were their idols. **Albert Carroll** was born in Mile End in 1934, and by the time he was evacuated during the war, around 1942, he would have known all about the exploits of Wilde and Lewis. Young Albert and his sister were evacuated to Wales and were boarded with a Mrs King, who lived in Derrick Street in Tylorstown, literally within a few yards of Jimmy Wilde's boyhood home! When Carroll got back to London, he started boxing. In 1950, he reached the finals of the East London Schoolboy Boxing Championship. Two years later, he turned professional. His first pro fight was a two-minute six-rounder that he won.

It is not known if young Albert ever met the Tylorstown Terror, as Wilde was known, but he was about to meet his other idol. After that first match, he was astonished to see his manager, Curly Carr, approach him with none other than Ted 'Kid' Lewis. Lewis congratulated Albert, and is said to have signed the £5 note which young Albert got for winning the fight, although it was apparently spent by mistake later. It looks like some shopkeeper ended up with a sporting great's autograph in his till![2]

*

Here is a cracking East End connection: what links an East End boxer of the early twentieth century to an award-winning BBC TV series from the 1980s and a modern classic of literature?

Harry Isaacs (1893–1958) was born on the Stepney/Wapping border and learned to box at the Judean Club. Like many young Jewish men following in the footsteps of Daniel Mendoza, he started at an early age. He turned professional at seventeen and used the ring name **Harry Reeve**, going unbeaten in his first eighteen fights. He had a few mixed results between 1912 and 1913, but his form came good in 1914 and he fought for the British middleweight title, narrowly losing after twenty rounds. He moved up to light-heavyweight and had a crack at that title in 1916; this time, he won.

Harry Reeve relinquished the title later in 1916 and enlisted in the Army. He joined the Military Police, and in 1917 he was posted to the giant military base at Étaples on the northern French coast. The base was supposed to be a holding and clearing area for returning troops and raw recruits moving up the line to the front. In reality, it was a type of boot camp for toughening men up before battle. It gained a notorious reputation for its brutal regime. During the summer of 1917, relationships between the NCOs and the troops in training deteriorated. In September, a number of troops were upset at the arrest of one of their number and about a hundred men gathered to protest. The arrival of military police only made matters worse, and scuffles broke out. Suddenly, the sound of shooting was heard.

A French woman standing nearby was shot and injured, and a Corporal W. B. Wood of the 4th Battalion, Gordon Highlanders, was shot in the head and killed instantly. Word soon got around the camp, and over a thousand men confronted the MPs, who ran off to the nearby town. Harry Reeve was identified as the shooter. The ill feeling that had been bubbling for months now surfaced in what became known as the Étaples Mutiny. The mutiny was eventually put down, and Private Harry Reeve was absolved of any blame for the shooting.

Details and events leading up to the mutiny form a large part of Vera Brittain's literary masterpiece *Testament of Youth*. Brittain, who was politician Shirley Williams' mother, was a VAD

(Voluntary Aid Detachment) nurse attached to the medical unit of the camp. The Étaples Mutiny was also the central event around which the BBC TV series *The Monocle Mutineer* was set.

*

One last interesting story worth telling is that of **Albert Foreman** (1904–1954). Albert was born in Whitechapel, and his name cropped up earlier in this book in his title fight against Fred Webster at Premierland in 1930. Albert was orphaned before his sixth birthday and went to live in an orphanage in North West London until he was fourteen. Towards the end of the First World War, he was allowed to join the Black Watch Regiment as a drummer boy. Being underage, he did not see active service. He stayed with the regiment for a couple of years after the end of the war, and it is thought that it was during his time in the regiment – which had a reputation for developing good boxers – that he learnt how to box.

After leaving the Army, Foreman moved back to East London. He started boxing professionally at seventeen, and in August 1920 he travelled to Sunderland for his debut fight against the vastly experienced Tyne and Wear fighter Joe Durham. He gained a very good draw, setting him on his career path. Foreman fought his next forty-odd fights in and around East London, including several at Premierland. His record over these first few years was rather mixed. It looked like he was going to be another 'also-ran' in boxing circles. After four straight losses in 1923, Foreman called time on his fighting around the capital, emigrated to Canada and settled in Montreal. He picked up boxing again over there, and after a few fights in Montreal travelled across the border to the States and boxed there for a few years. Little is known about his life at this point, although it appears that he joined the US military for a short stint. Whether or not he received further coaching during his service is not known, but his boxing most certainly improved.

Foreman occasionally boxed for the US Army as well as professionally, reeling off twenty-five wins and one draw over the next four years. His early fights were recorded as taking place at Fort Myer in Virginia, which was a large military base. Future general George Patton, who would achieve fame in the Second World War, was the base commander there at the time. By the end of 1926, Foreman had left the military and was living in Washington, D.C., fighting up and down the eastern side of the States with considerable success.

In 1928, brimming with confidence, Foreman headed back over the border to fight for the Canadian lightweight title and knocked out Leo 'Kid' Roy in the second round. It was a big shock at the time, as most Canadian boxing fans had probably never heard of him as a Canadian boxer. The boxing authorities were asked to look more closely into the match and Foreman's legitimacy to hold the title. The Canadian Boxing Federation required a boxer to be a Canadian citizen and have resided in the country for at least six months prior to a title bout. Foreman was English-born, and a former United States serviceman, so it was thought that he might be a US citizen. Furthermore, there was doubt he had resided in Canada for six months, although he had lived in Montreal off-and-on for four years. Most of his bouts, the papers reported, had taken place in the United States.

The long and the short of it was that Foreman kept the title on his residency basis and defended it once before returning to England to fight for the British and Empire title in that fight with Webster at Premierland in 1930. Foreman was a late starter as it took well over ten years to reach the pinnacle of his career. He boxed another three times for the title before retiring as holder of both the Canadian and British Empire lightweight titles in 1933.

Foreman's adventures did not stop after he left the ring. He joined the *Montreal Standard* as a photojournalist in 1934, and was highly acclaimed for his work in that field. Just after the outbreak of war, in 1940, he joined the Royal Air Force. Many Canadians joined the RAF, and with his extensive military background Foreman was trained as a gunner. By late 1942, he was operationally active with 207 Bomber Squadron. After the introduction of the Lancaster bomber in early 1943 he flew night missions over Germany, mostly as a rear gunner. During 1943, 207 Squadron became part of the famous Bomber Group 5. This group developed precision aerial bombing and was noted for its use of the 'Tall Boy' bomb. The legendary 617 Squadron, 'The Dambusters', were also part of this group, and in early March 1945 Foreman was posted to the Dambusters and took part in a series of raids on the Wolf's Lair, Hitler's stronghold in Bavaria. Foreman arrived at 617 Squadron too late to participate in the Dambusters raids on the Ruhr dams in 1943 or the attack on the *Tirpitz* in 1944. He did, however, fly almost forty missions and was awarded the Distinguished Flying Cross.

16

LEGACY – THEN AND NOW

My story of boxing in London's East End finishes shortly after the turn of the millennium. Of the many characters that have appeared in these pages, very few are around today. Nonetheless, boxing carries on and the East End is still a focal point for the sport. Although dozens of gyms and clubs that were around half a century ago have now vanished, there is still a strong boxing heartbeat in this part of the capital.

From the 1980s up to the present day, huge changes have been taking place in the area. The massive Dockland developments have swept away huge swaths of Wapping, Stepney, Limehouse, Poplar and Silvertown. Whitechapel, Bethnal Green and Bow have seen less development, but a huge slice of Stratford and parts of Leyton and Hackney, together with their local industries, have given way to the giant Olympic Park complex. The mammoth Temple Mills railway marshalling yards which straddled Stratford and Leyton, once a huge employer in the area, have gone. The famous Boleyn Ground, once home of West Ham Football Club, will soon become flats; the team has moved to the Olympic Park Stadium. The journey from Gardiners Corner at Aldgate east along the highway to Limehouse would be unrecognisable to those boxers who used the route to get to the many clubs and venues that once populated that part of East London.

Billingsgate Fish Market moved out of the City and relocated a couple of miles west in the Isle of Dogs. Modern and state-of-the-art in 1981, it is now dwarfed by the giant Canary Wharf complex that looms up behind it. Spitalfields market moved out of Spitalfields and now resides at Leyton. The shipping which used the huge Royal Docks complex along with places like East and West India Docks and Millwall Docks began to dry up by the late 1970s – containerisation saw to that. Once a huge draw for boxers seeking casual work, and a place where retired fighters could earn a crust later in life, these areas are now part of London's enormous financial hub. All this redevelopment is a legacy for the region. The Afro-Caribbean, Bangladeshi and Indian communities that sprung up here after the war have, by and large, replaced the Jewish and Irish communities, and they may reap the rewards – time will tell.

As for boxing, some of the old gyms have been replaced with new-style gyms catering for the 'city type'. Many boxing clubs fell by the wayside. Eton Manor, my old boys' club, which produced fine amateur boxers like two-time gold medallist Harry Mallins, has gone. Its large ground in Leyton was redeveloped for the 2012 Paralympic Games. However, Repton and West Ham boxing clubs are still very much carrying on the long tradition of the sport.

Most of the old match venues have gone. The need for a multitude of venues to host boxing matches faded in the sixties and seventies as demand dropped and TV started to cover the sport. ExCeL in the Docklands was used as the boxing venue for the Olympics, and boxing still takes place there. As part of the 2012 London Games, the Copper Box arena was built specifically to hold several Olympic activities. As part of the Olympic legacy, this arena is also used for boxing.

Bethnal Green has somewhat escaped large-scale redevelopments, and York Hall is still a major venue for boxing, but the days of using swimming baths, ice rinks, public houses and town halls are long gone. As long as boxing clubs and gyms are still around, young boys and girls interested in the sport will seek them out. There is no doubting that the demographics in the area have changed, but this has been the case since the Huguenots first settled in Spitalfields more than three centuries ago.

Boxing in the East End has changed. The unlicensed fights are still around, but with the dockland developments the various boxing venues in the area have diversified. Events such as 'White Collar Boxing' are catered for. The rise of martial arts means that these events run alongside the traditional sport of boxing. Visit some gyms in the area and you can see young men and women pursuing not only these activities but also weightlifting, arm wrestling and even yoga. One such gym is the Peacock in Caxton Road, Canning Town. It was originally founded by the Bowers Brothers in an empty room at the bottom of a tower block in the mid-1970s. With a long family involvement in boxing, fourth-generation boxers Tony and Martin Bowers, were destined to follow in that tradition. However, it was not their proximity to boxing that first drew them in but rather social troubles in the deprived area.

With vandalism and petty crime rife in the tower blocks throughout Newham, particularly the Barnwood Court area where they lived, the Bowers realised that some form of popular recreation was needed to keep youths off the streets. Still at school but with maturity beyond their years, they decided to try and do something about it. Thus the 'Rumble Room' was created. The Bowers were about the same age as the kids that used it, and they came from the same background. Its popularity increased, and after a few years they were forced to expand the operation. They wound up in Caxton Road, and by then the gym had embraced the wider activities that many modern gyms accommodate.

*

In 2009, the Heritage Lottery Fund made a grant available to ensure the history of East London's boxing tradition will never be forgotten despite the changing environment. A project tracing the history of East End boxing from 1891 to 1990 will develop an archive of photographs, programmes and other boxing memorabilia and make it available to boxing fans and the general public via the project website. It is run by the London Ex-Boxers Association and the story is one of social integration as well as sport. The association will be interviewing a range of local people in what is seen as the first attempt to view East End boxing as a significant part of the cultural heritage of the area.

One legacy of the East End's boxing traditions and the 2012 Olympics is a new boxing club opened in Leyton in 2013, on the edge of the Olympic Park, which highlights the way a lot of new clubs in most sports these days are set up for and by the community. The East London Boxing Academy was set up by local Waltham Forest residents. It is a voluntary, non-profit project. The club has a number of community members from a range of backgrounds who help in the day-to-day running of the academy. They help to keep young people off the streets, away from trouble, and provide an environment where kids can learn a number of skills alongside boxing, such as communication and group development.

Perhaps boxing's greatest achievement in terms of its legacy is not a physical one but a cultural one. The Huguenots, the Irish, the Jews, the Afro-Caribbeans and the Subcontinental immigrants who arrived in East London in huge numbers over the years have lived, worked and boxed side by side with their white Anglo-Saxon Protestant neighbours. By and large they did so peacefully. They became part of the East End fabric but never abandoned their identities.

The story of boxing in London's East End is not one that comes full circle. The progress of the sport, the area and the ever-changing demographics of the place have ensured that very little has been left unaltered in this part of London since Jack Broughton plied his trade at the riverside wharves and pubs in the eighteenth century. What certainly *has* changed is boxing itself. Jack Broughton would not recognise the sport which he took up three centuries ago, nor the topography of the East End in which he lived. He may well be surprised, though, that the area is still very much associated with his noble art.

APPENDICES

Notable London Boxing Clubs Alumni

Repton Boxing Club
Terry Barker
Darren Barker
Frank Buglioni
Michael Carter
Tony Cesay
Johnny Cheshire
Charlie Edwards
Courtney Fry
Danny Happe
Audley Harrison
Roy Hilton
Harvey Horn
Maurice Hope
Danny Hunt
Paul Lawson
Neville Mead

Silvester Mittee
Gary Nichols
Stephen Oates
Moss O'Brian
Dave Odwell
Alan Richardson
John H Stracey
Timothy Taylor
Martin Ward
Kevin Wing
Joe Young

West Ham Boys' Club
Tom Baker (also Repton)
Nigel Benn
Ralph Charles
Ron Cooper

Ron Hinson
Mark Kaylor
Kevin Lear
Matthew Marsh
Kevin Mitchell
Ron Redrup
Dudley O'Shaughnessy
Lucian Reid
Terry Spinks
Billy Walker
Paul Warwick

Clapton Young Men's Boxing Club
F. Hobsday
A. Curnick
E. Swash

Oxford and St George's and St George's and Stepney
Johnny Brown
Young Johnny Brown
Benny Caplan
Rod Douglas
Terry Marsh
Sammy McCarthy
Harry Mizler

Judean Club
Jack Kid Berg

Phil Hickman (aka J Brown)
Young Josephs
Harry Reeves
Ted Kid Lewis
Ted Lewis

Broad Street
Rod Douglas
Billy Wells
Michael Lomax

Fairburn
Adrian Elliot
John Beckles

Limehouse & Poplar
Teddy White
Albert Smith
Johnny Waples

Eton Manor
Billy Davis
Fred Grace
Harry Mallin
Fred Mallin
Nicky Gargano

Crown & Manor
Jason Matthews
Ian Nappa

The Venues

There have been well over a hundred venues used for official boxing in the East London area. Most have since been pulled down or converted, but in their heyday virtually every area of this part of London had at least one arena for boxing. Here is a list of some of the popular official boxing venues:

Bethnal Green Drill Hall
Bethnal Green Excelsior Baths and Hall
Bethnal Green Town Hall
Bethnal Green York Hall
Bow Baths
Bow Drill Hall Tredegar Road
Bow Town Hall
Canning Town Public Hall
Clapton Greyhound Track
East Ham Swimming Baths
Forest Gate Ice Rink
Hackney Devonshire Club
Hackney Greyhound Track
Hackney Manor Hall
Haggerston Baths
Hoxton Hall
Hoxton Pitfield Street Baths
Ilford Ice Skating Rink
Leyton Swimming Baths
Mile End Arena
Mile End Baths
Mile End Paragon Theatre
Poplar Hippodrome
Shoreditch Town Hall
Stepney Judeans Club
Stepney Osbourn Social Club
Stepney Palladium
Stratford Palladium
Stratford Town Hall
West Ham Swimming Baths
Whitechapel Pavilion Arena
Whitechapel Pavilion Theatre
Whitechapel Premierland
Whitechapel Wonderland

The very early bare-knuckle fights often took place in open spaces on common land. In the East End of London, given the density of the housing that existed then, only a couple of areas were used for this. Hackney Marshes and London Fields in Hackney were popular areas that hosted the odd match. Mainly, though, it was the docks, wharves and public houses that were the scene for this activity. Occasionally a match could take place in a backstreet cul-de-sac in view of residents. During the mid- and late Victorian periods, the authorities began to clamp down on these unofficial bouts in residential areas and most matches moved from outdoor spaces into the many inns and pubs that were everywhere to be seen around East London.

Given the clamour to fight 'off-street', pubs hastily converted back rooms or backyard areas to accommodate the demand. Some pubs have gone down in East End folklore as fighting pubs.

We know about the two famous Wapping pubs, the Prospect of Whitby and the Town of Ramsgate. In this later period, two of the most famous pubs to host such events were the Blue Anchor in Church Street, just off Shoreditch High Street, and the Five Inkhorns quite close by. These staged hundreds of unofficial fights, as well as some official boxing events, in the years between 1865 and 1900. Two local boxing entrepreneurs, Bill Richardson and John Flemming, ran the pubs and organised the events. They also helped in the training of boxers. There were dozens of other pubs in the area that featured gloved and ungloved fights. Unfortunately, the demise of pubs nationwide means that only the odd few remain today.

Fighting Pubs of the Old East End

Anchor & Hope, Ratcliffe
 Highway
Bakers Arms, Hackney
Bakers Arms, Haggerston
Beavers Arms, Whitechapel
Blade Bone, Bethnal Green
Blue Angel, Spitalfields
Blue Coat Boy, Spitalfields
The Britannia, Shadwell
Builders Arms, Poplar
The Cedars, West Ham
Coach & Horses, Homerton
Five Inkhorns, Shoreditch
Gardener's Arms, Old Ford
Gate Tavern, Mile End

George & Dragon, Hoxton
The Griffin, Shoreditch
Halfway House, Hackney
Hope Tavern, Bethnal Green
Middleton Arms, Bow
Nursery Arms, Bow
Plough & Harrow, Leytonstone
Queen Victoria, Bethnal Green
Royal Duke, Stepney
Royal Standard, Bethnal
 Green
Spread Eagle, Shoreditch
Star of the East, Whitechapel
The Steamship, Poplar
The Victory, Stepney

List of East London Professional World, European, English, British and Commonwealth (Empire) Champions, 1730–2016

Barney Aaron
Joseph Anderson
Vic Andreetti
Tom Baker
Teddy Baldock
Ron Barton
Jimmy Batten
Nigel Benn
Jack Kid Berg
Tom Berry
Jack Broughton
Johnny Brown
Ralph Charles
Nicky Cook
Dick Corbett
Harry Corbett
Walter Croot
Samuel Elias
(Young) Dutch Sam
  Elias
Al Foreman
John L Gardener
Arthur Hayes (Seaman)
Mike Honeyman
Tom Ireland
Fred Johnson
Aschel (Young) Joseph
Mark Kaylor
Sam Kellar
Tom King
Kevin Lear

Lennox Lewis
Ted 'Kid' Lewis
Joe Lucy
Colin Lynes
Charlie Magri
Matthew Marsh
Terry Marsh
Billy Matthews
Harry Mason
Sammy McCarthy
Daniel Mendoza
Kevin Mitchell
Harry Mizler
Ted Moore
Bill Mortimer
Pat O'Keeffe
Alf Pattenden
Pedlar Palmer
Al Phillips
Eddie Phillips
Mark Reefer
Harry Reeve
Jack Scales
Jem Smith
Terry Spinks
John H. Stracey
James (Jem) Ward
Nick Ward
Harry Ware
Peter Waterman
Bombardier Billy Wells

NOTES

1. *The Early Years: The Gloves Are Off*

1. 'When the two contestants were ready, they stepped to the centre of the arena, and raising their mighty arms, set to. Each landed heavy blows with their fists, and they ground their teeth, as the sweat poured over their limbs. Euryalus sought an opening, but noble Epeius swung and struck his jaw, and he went straight down, his legs collapsing under him. Like a fish that leaps in the weed-strewn shallows, under a ripple stirred by the north wind, then falls back into the dark wave, so Euryalus leapt when he was struck, but the big-hearted Epeius, lifted him and set him on his feet, and all his friends crowded round, and supported him from the ring, his feet trailing, his head lolling, as he spat out clots of blood. He was still confused when they sat him down in his corner.' Translated from Homer's *Iliad*, Book 23, 763–769, p. 503 (*c.* 2nd century BC).

2. The Town of Ramsgate pub is situated immediately beside the historic Wapping Old Steps, a fairly steep stairway that runs from the road down to the river. At low tide a ring was pegged out on the sand-and-shingle river foreshore for the fighters. The steps and the pub's backyard area, which overlooked the fight area, were a perfect vantage point.

3. The very early prize fights very rarely took place in roped-off rings. An area of open ground was found, and the two pugilists would 'come up to scratch', which was a line scratched on the bare ground marking roughly the centre of the fight area and would then be asked to 'toe the line', when each boxer put their front foot on the line prior to the start of the contest. Many modern-day phrases originated in the vocabulary of early boxing: toe the line; come up to scratch; saved by the bell; below the belt; punching above his/her weight; on the ropes; out for the count; glutton for punishment; throwing in the towel; throwing your hat into the ring; blow by blow account; leading with your chin; beating someone to the punch; getting out of a tight corner; the gloves are off; having someone in your corner; ringside view; in-fighting.

2. *The Early Years: The Gloves Are On*

1. Spitalfields Rookery was one of two rookeries in close proximity to each other. The other was the truly horrific Old Nichols Rookery. The poverty, crime and infant death rate was unimaginable there. Eventually the authorities acted, and the area was cleared in 1891.

3. *Twentieth-century Boys*

1. The first black boxer to contest a British title was Dick Turpin against Vince Hawkins in June 1948. It was felt to be significant enough to warrant coverage on BBC Radio. Dick Turpin comprehensively won the fight before a crowd of 40,000 at Villa Park to become the first black boxer of the modern era to hold a British title. His more illustrious younger brother Randolph, went on to become Britain's first black world champion in 1951 after beating the legendary Sugar Ray Robinson.

2. Ted Lewis's final pro record was: 299 bouts, 233 won, 41 lost, 25 draws, 65 no decisions, 80 knockouts. Over that period he fought competitively at six different weight levels.

3. The Irish stood side by side with their Jewish neighbours to fight the fascists. During the bleak days of the 1912 London Docks Strike, which greatly affected the large Irish labour force, the Jewish community greatly supported the Irish families.

4. *Charge of the Light Brigade*

1. The official death toll given for the Bethnal Green tube disaster was 173. This was the Second World War's largest single civilian loss of life not directly involving enemy action. A bomb that hit South Hallsville School in Canning Town on 10 September 1940 when the large basement was being used as a temporary shelter was officially given as claiming seventy-seven lives. Subsequent post-war examinations of National Archive reports of the deaths that occurred that night indicate that almost 600 died, included another young East London boxer, lightweight hopeful Michael Williams. It was the largest mass death of civilians in this country during the war.

2. Frankie Carbo was a New York Mafia soldier from the Lucchese crime family who operated as a boxing promoter and a gunman with Murder Inc. He became highly skilled at fixing high-profile bouts and became known as 'The Czar of Boxing'. He is also credited with the murder of fellow gangster Bugsy Siegel in 1947.

3. Marion 'Kiki' Roberts, the popular New York dancer and showgirl, was thought to be Diamond's moll who caught Berg's roaming eye.

5. *The Golden Years*

1. British professional champions Henry Cooper (Army), Ron Barton (Air Force), Brian Curvis (Army), Randolph Turpin (Royal Navy), Joe Erskine (Army) and Jack Gardner (Army) all won senior ABA titles boxing for their respective services.

2. Until the arrival of Anthony Joshua, no British Olympic champion had ever gone on to win an outright world professional title. Remember outright world heavyweight champion Lennox Lewis won his gold medal boxing for Canada.

3. Britain took seven boxers to the 1956 games. The US took a team of ten, including future world champion Jose Torres. They finished with just three medals, Torres being beaten in the final by the brilliant Hungarian amateur Laszlo Papp. Dick McTaggart MBE was amateur Scottish, British, Commonwealth and European Champion. His British record of 634 bouts, winning 610 in twelve years of senior amateur boxing including five ABA titles between 1956 and 1965, will surely go unsurpassed. Fred and Harry Mallin are regarded as two of Britain's greatest amateur boxers.

6. *Changing Times*

1. Several London firemen boxed at a high amateur level. Assistant Chief Officer Alfie Shawyer was the ABA middleweight champion in 1933 and went over to New York to pick up a Golden Gloves title in 1935. Probably the most famous London 'Fighting Fireman' was Anthony Stuart. He joined the Army at eighteen and served in the Royal Signals in the late 1920s. He had done some boxing as a junior but his skills were honed in the Army and he represented the Royal Signals at heavyweight in the ABA championships in 1929 and 1930. Losing in the final of the 1929 championships, he won the title the following year. He joined the London Fire Brigade in 1930 and fought for them in the finals six times up until 1937, winning three times and being runner-up twice. He also won an Empire Games (Commonwealth Games) gold medal in 1930 and was a losing quarter-finalist at the Berlin Games in 1936. A couple of years later he hung up his gloves and prepared for another battle; this time against the firestorms of the London Blitz.

7. The Good, the Bad and the Ugly

1. James Burke was born near deaf so was often referred to as the 'Deaf 'un'. He also found employment as a Thames waterman.

9. Fighting Families of the East End

1. The licence of the Salmon and Ball pub in Shoreditch was in the hands of the Goodson family for many years and several of the family's names appeared over the pub door up until 1927 when it was demolished.

2. Billy Bird from Chelsea is thought to be the second most prolific British boxer ever after Len Wickwar. Bird fought continuously from 1920 to 1948, amassing almost 360 bouts of boxing. He holds the world record for most knockouts with 138 KOs. This is seven more than the American world light-heavyweight champ and knockout specialist Archie Moore.

10. No Guts No Glory

1. **Field Marshal Frederick Sleigh Roberts, 1st Earl Roberts VC** (1832–1914) was one of the most successful British military commanders of his time. From about 1908 he was predicting the rise of Germany as a military power intent on controlling large areas of Europe and Africa. He advocated the introduction of short-term compulsory conscription into the British forces to meet the German threat but was somewhat ridiculed by the political authorities. He was of course proved right, but this type of conscription was not introduced until after the Second World War in 1947. One of the Eton Manor's co-founders, **Gerald Wellesley**, was the grandson of Arthur Wellesley, Duke of Wellington.

2. Eton Manor clubhouse housed a snooker and billiards room, facilities for table tennis, a gym and a boxing ring. In its basement, a rifle range was installed. Their sports ground catered for lawn bowls, tennis, football, rugby and cricket.

It had another gym, squash and badminton courts and a small outdoor pool. It also had one of the country's few floodlit athletic tracks of the day.

11. Movers and Shakers

1. The centre of administration was the Long Room at the London Custom House, where all business connected with entry of ships into the port, assessment of duties, registry of ships and bonds for removal of goods from warehouses was transacted. In 1856 the offices of Collector in the Port of London and Chief Registrar of Shipping were united, and henceforth the Ships Registry Branch of the Long Room dealt with the registry of all ships in the Port of London and also the entry in the chief registrar's books of all returns from outports and colonial registrars of ships registered and subsequent transactions connected with ships.

13. The Journeymen

1. John L. Sullivan, officially the last bare-knuckle world champion and the first gloved world champion. Considered by many to be the first 'superstar' of the ring.
2. Griffo – I believe this was Albert Griffo aka 'Young Griffo', the legendary Australian featherweight and lightweight boxer. Nicknamed the 'Will-O-the Wisp', Griffo was Australian and world featherweight champion, and veteran of over 150 recorded and many more unrecorded fights between 1885 and 1905.

14. Into the Ring

1. *Boxing News* reproduction by J. Jamieson, published 1969.

15. East End Connections

1. After retiring from law enforcement, Wyatt Earp moved to San Francisco to live in peace. The boxing authorities knew that Earp had previous refereeing experience so when in 1896

they decided to hold a world championship match in San Francisco, Earp, as a big local celebrity, was called upon to officiate. Bob Fitzsimmons fought Tom Sharkey. Fitzsimmons was a firm favourite and big money was on him to win. Sharkey worked hard until the seventh but then he started fading. Sharkey had a reputation for sneaking in low blows, and maybe this experience was used to accomplish what happened next because in the eighth round Sharkey, after a mix-up of blows, fell to the canvas claiming a foul. Referee Earp agreed and declared Sharkey the winner. No one in the arena saw the foul, and people started mumbling about a fixed fight. Fitzsimmons' people took it to court. The judge declared that since boxing wasn't strictly legal, the courts were not in a position to make a determination on the outcome of the match. Proof of a fixed fight was never established, but right after the fight Wyatt Earp chose to leave the city.

2. Alex Daley, *Fighting Men of London* (Pitch Publishing, 2014)

ACKNOWLEDGEMENTS

Special thanks go to the following:

West Ham Boxing Club
  (Jason Bull)
West Ham Football Club
Sammy McCarthy
Sammy McCarthy Jnr
Brian Whipp
Jason McKay
Eddie Quill
Jimmy Batten
Terry Marsh

Alan Parsons
Dave Parlour
Dave Porter
Malcolm Field
Tony Debenham and David
  Pracy, Essex County Cricket
  Club
Harold Alderman MBE
Ray Lee, Essex Ex-Boxers
  Association

BIBLIOGRAPHY

Books

Jerry White, *London in the Eighteenth Century* (Vintage Books, 2013)

Liza Picard, *Dr Johnson's London* (Weidenfeld & Nicolson, 2000)

George Rude, *Hanoverian London* (Sutton History Classics, 2003)

Richard Tames, *East End Past* (Historical Publications, 2004)

Alex Daley, *Fighting Men of London* (Pitch Publishing, 2014)

Stephen Hick, *Sparring for Luck* (THAP Publishing, 1982)

Micky Fawcett, *Krayzy Days* (Pen Press Publication, 2014)

Brian Belton, *Days of Iron* (Breedon Books, 2013)

David Lemon and Mike Marshall, *Essex County Cricket Official History* (Kingswood Press, 1987)

David Lemon, *Johnny Won't Hit Today* (Allen & Unwin, 1983)

James Morton, *East End Gangland* (Sphere, 2001)

Gilda O'Neill, *My East End* (Viking, 1999)

V. R. Bennett, *Life and Loves of Lucky Jim* (Createspace Publishing, 2017)

Bettinson & Bennison, *Home of Boxing* (Odhams Press, 1923)

Jack Hare, *Gladiators of the Prize Ring* (Willsons/D. Hare, 1925)

W. Barrington Dalby, *Come in Barry!* (Cassell, 1961)

General Reference Points
Boxing Hall of Fame
Jewish Sports Hall of Fame
British Newspaper Archives
Amateur Boxing Association Records (ABA)
Ancestry UK/Births, Deaths and Marriages
US Ancestry
OurBow.com
BoxRec
Wikipedia
Boxinghistory.com
London Fire Brigade Museum
Imperial War Museum
*Premierland article courtesy Matt Christie of *Boxing News*.

Specific Reference Points
Whipp Family History
Madden family Ancestry (Ancestry US)
Martin Sax (Boxing Links)
Douglas Genealogical Records
Goodson Family History
Anderson Family History
BKB History
Graham Dewsall and Worthing Museum & Art Gallery
Bishopsgate Institute
Royal Albert Hall Archives
The New York Times
Museum of Docklands
British Boxers Web
Independent R's (QPR fanzine)
Spitalfields Life
West Ham Football Club
RAF 617 Squadron – Official Operation Records Book (1943/45)

INDEX

Crawley, Peter 35
Croot, Walter 44
Cruickshank, Isaac 34
Cullen, Maurice 116, 163
Cullis, Stan 118
Curly, Johnny 46
Cuthbert, Johnny 48, 86, 226

Dalby, Barrington 201, 241
Danahar, Arthur 200–201
Dam Busters (617 Squadron) 259
Darrell, Jim 233
Davis, Jimmy 227–228
Davis, Billy 193–194
Davis, George 41
Day, Alby 241
Dempsey, Jack 65, 252
Diamond Jack 'Legs' 83–84
Dickens, Charles (jnr) 183
Dixon, George 69
Doctor Johnson (writer) *see*
  Johnson, Samuel
Doggett Coat and Badge Race 23
Dokes, Michael 221
Douglas, J. W. H. T. 46–51, 73,
  109, 172
Douglas, C. W. 49
Douglas, J. H. (snr) 47, 205
Douglas, Rod 215, 242
Downs, Terry 203
Dowsett, Punch 41
Duff, Micky 197, 208, 244
Duke of Cumberland 23, 27
Dundee, Angelo and Chris 116,
  208
Duran, Roberto 15, 63, 132
Durham, Joe 257

Earp, Wyatt 251–253

Edward VII, King 55, 73
Egan, Pierce 34
Elias, Samuel Dutch 30–31, 34
Elias, Sam Dutch (Young) 34
Elliot, Jack 173
Empire Games/Commonwealth
  Games 113, 117, 121, 180,
  190, 215, 220, 242–244, 269,
  273
England, Bill 176
Essex Regiment 53–54, 60
Étaples Mutiny 256–257
Eton College 191
Essex County Cricket 47–50
Eubank, Chris 145, 215
Felstead Public School 47
Farr, Tommy 217, 244, 246
Fenton, Ted 162
Figg, James 23, 26, 30, 33
Finch, Albert 117, 163, 228, 243
Fitzgerald, Bob 139
Flint, Jimmy 166
Football clubs:
  Arsenal 192
  Brighton 227
  Chelsea 56, 254
  Clapton Orient 70
  Leicester City 53
  Leyton Orient 227, 254
  Manchester United 161
  Millwall 131, 209
  Walthamstow Avenue 227
  West Ham United 161, 187,
  260
Foreman, Al 238, 257–259
Froch, Carl 242

Gans, Joe 148
Gardener, John L. 219–222

King, Johnny   77–78
King, Tom   37–39, 91
Knock, Charlie   237
Kramer, Johnny   144
Kray, Charlie   141, 154, 228
Krays Twins, (Ronnie &
    Reggie)   85, 130, 141,
    143–144, 147, 161, 179, 228
Kirkorov, Kirkor   190

Lake, Harry Bugler   48, 70
Lambert, Alec   63
Lampard family   169
Laing, Kirkland   132
Lawless, Terry   100, 131,
    144–145, 208–210, 212, 220
Lazar, Harry   67, 241
Lazar, Lew   67, 228, 241,
    243–244
Lazarus, Mark   67
Lear, Kevin   187, 190
Lesnevich, Gus   201
Leonard, Benny   63
Lewis, Johnny   170
Lewis, Lennox   136–139
Lewis, Ted 'Kid'   62–66, 69,
    80, 82, 152, 195, 202–203,
    218–219, 223, 230, 238, 255
Lewis, Ted   170–171, 247–248
Levene, Harry   84, 197
Linca, Nicolae   114
London, Brian   219
London Docks (inc.)
    East India Dock   17, 35, 38
    West India Dock   17, 261
    Millwall Docks   75, 178, 187,
    261
    Royal Docks   38, 108, 144, 261

London Ex-Boxers'
    Association   263
London Prize Ring Rules   22, 24,
    175–176
London Stock Exchange   196
Lopez, Ernie   125
Lorenzo, Tommy   73
Loughrey, Jim   110
Lucioni, William   170
Lucy, Joe   104, 118–119, 166, 179
Luxton, Jem   41
Lynch, Kenny   249–250

Maccabiah Games   194
Mace, Jem   38–39, 247
Makepiece, Harry   71
Madden, Billy   251–253
Madigan, Tony   97
Magri, Charlie   152, 209–210,
    223
Maldonado, Mario   132
Mallin, Fred   171
Mallin, Harry   113, 171–173,
    192–193, 261
Manchester Regiment   204
Manley, Joe   134
Mann, Johnny   89, 99–100
Marchant, Tony   166–167
Marconi, Emilio   98
Marsh, Matthew   191
Marsh, Terry   133–136
Martin, Sam   28
Mason, Harry   93, 244
Mason, Ted   216
Masterson, Bat   251–253
May, Mick   149, 191
Mayhew, Henry   18
McAuliffe, Jack   257

Spencer, Thad   121
Spinks, Terry   107–112, 117, 149, 187, 193–194, 229, 243
Spitalfields Wholesale Fruit and Vegetable Market   42 , 100, 115–116, 207, 227, 261
Spot, Jack   66, 80, 82, 85, 164, 239
Stanley, Digger   237
Stracey, John H.   124–128, 185, 208
Stevenson, George   24
Sullivan, Jim   150
Sullivan, John L.   231, 252
Summers, Johnny   148
Surrey Rifles   150
Sutcliffe, Herbert   48
Sykes, Paul   220

Tate & Lyle   207
Theatre Royal (Stratford East)   167
Thomas, Pat   131
Thompson, Carl   207
Thompson, William Bendigo   36
Tibbs, Jimmy   143–147, 208, 212
Tibbs, Mark   147
Til, Paul   63
Todd, Roland   64
Tucker, Ken   161–162
Turpin, Jackie   243
Turpin, Randolph   117, 163, 170, 201, 204, 228, 246
Tyson, Mike   137–139

Upper Cut Club   121

Van Rensburg, Johnny   118, 244
Villiers, Arthur (Major)   114, 192

Wagg, Alfred   192
Walker, Billy   119–124, 162–163, 187, 219
Walker, George   163–164
Ward, James (Jem)   37–38, 158
Warren, Frank   135, 154, 197
Waterman, Dennis   98
Waterman, Peter   97–98
Watney Street Market   100
Watson, Michael   145, 214
Watt, Jim   124, 210
Webster, Fred   238
Wellesley, Gerald   192
Wells, 'Bombardier' Billy   58–62, 64, 150, 166, 177, 249
White, Andy   196
Wicks, Jim   116, 179
Wickwar, Len   244
Wiggs, George   208
Wilde, Jimmy   56–58, 73, 82, 150, 246, 255
Williams, Johnny   205
Wills, Len   192
Wilson, Peter (journalist)   104
Wilton's Music Hall   239
Winston, Ray   160–161
Winstone, Howard   110, 194
Woodcock, Bruce   199
Woollard, Eddie   96–97, 193

Zanon, Lorenzo   220